Barbara Cartland

Barbara Cartland

by Gwen Robyns

DOUBLEDAY & COMPANY, INC.

GARDEN CITY, NEW YORK

1985

*All photographs are reproduced
by kind permission of Barbara Cartland*

First published in 1984 by Sidgwick & Jackson Limited, London

Library of Congress Cataloging in Publication Data
Robyns, Gwen.
Barbara Cartland.
Includes index.
1. Cartland, Barbara, 1902-   —Biography.
2. Novelists, English—20th century—Biography.
I. Title.
PR6005.A765Z87   1985   823'.912 [B]   84-45675
ISBN 0-385-19818-3

To Barbara with love –
for sharing her memories with me, and
those hours awash with laughter

Acknowledgements

Every biography is only as good as its friends. Barbara Cartland brought me many: people whose lives she had changed through coming in contact with them, and who were willing to share their experiences with me.

There were not only her close friends, but unknown people like the company director on the 17.07 from Paddington to Worcester, who saw me reading a Barbara Cartland romantic novel and lent across to whisper, 'She changed my life'. Hearing Barbara speak about vitamins and healthy living, she changed her whole eating pattern and stodgy habits, with the result that she was able to cope with a very exacting job better than she had ever done before.

There was the elderly lady in Denmark who asked as she lay dying, 'I would like to read a Barbara Cartland novel in English'. When I heard of this, I told Barbara and a parcel tied up in pink ribbon went off that day, lovingly inscribed. The old lady had all three books read to her before she finally closed her eyes.

To Barbara's sons I owe a special thank you. Their appreciation of their mother is enormous, and to be with Barbara, Ian and Glen lighting each other up is sheer joy.

To Audrey Elliott, Hazel Clark and Caron Painter, Barbara's secretaries, I am indebted for their hours of patience with me. And to Nigel Gordon, her chef, for all those delicious meals he cooked for me during the months of research I spent at Camfield Place.

INTRODUCTION

*To me the greatest privilege to which we are entitled is
to be alive.*

Barbara Cartland

It is a daunting challenge to be asked to write the biography of a living
legend. And this was my dilemma when I took on the task of discovering
what makes Barbara Cartland different from all other women.

Not only what motivates her to become, according to the *Guinness Book
of Records*, 'the best selling author in the world with 350,000,000 books',
but why at the age of eighty-three she continues to write twenty to thirty
thousand words every week, year in year out.

When clearly money is not the chief incentive why does she strive each
year to better her own record? Is it just ruthless ambition or sheer
professionalism? She has been quoted as saying: 'I write because I really
believe that I can help people and my romantic novels are the platform
with which I can do this.'

Who are these fans of Barbara Cartland . . . these millions of faceless
people scattered round the world? She is read in every language except
Chinese, including Hebrew and Swahili. The Japanese have just discovered
Barbara Cartland and her love stories, so I feel it will only be a matter of
time before Peking gets the message.

The popular conception that it is women who go to bed with Barbara
Cartland Dukes under their pillow is entirely wrong. Research by her
various publishers reveals that, in fact, she is read as much by men as by
women. The late President Sadat regularly borrowed his wife's copies.
Jania Husain, President of India, wrote from New Delhi in 1968, what
must be considered by Indian standards an unusually effusive letter: 'Your
book on "Love" is wonderful, and I at seventy-one read it with absorbing
interest!' The exclamation is his not mine.

In America a survey revealed that she was read as much by the
university faculty of Boston as by housewives in Wichita Falls, and ages
ranged from love-lorn schoolgirls to love-starved great-grandmothers.

Typical of the sackloads of American mail that arrive each week is this
letter from Frances Moody-Newman of Palm Beach, Florida. It empha-

11

sizes the theurgical power of a Barbara Cartland novel and is similar in thought to hundreds of fan letters that I read:

> A dear friend of mine, Ruth Graham, the wife of the famous Rev. Billy Graham, was in the Mayo Clinic this fall having a hip replacement. She suffered severe complications from the operation. When the Grahams were in Monte Carlo this summer I gave them a lot of my great Barbara Cartland books and they fell in love with them. She wrote me that the only thing that relieved her pain and suffering were your books. Your books do so much good, Barbara dear, every time I get depressed I read your books and forget my problems.

Thousands of overworked, lonely housewives will understand the sentiments of Mrs Miner from Michigan who writes: 'While I am reading one of your books, I find myself fantasizing like I am the one who fell in love with the Duke and he fell in love with me. . . . I just wanted you to know how much I love your books. Please keep writing them. I love you for writing them. They help me to get away.'

As the historical backgrounds are always as accurate as Barbara Cartland can research, her books are, in effect, a combination of love story and instant history course, as Marie Hoff of Arizona found out: 'I have 297 of your books, some have been read twice. I never liked history when I went to school, but your books have sure made me realize what I missed by not being made to study it.'

It has been said many times that in the 1920s Barbara Cartland had more proposals than any other débutante in London and that her suitors were among the most eligible in the land. Why then did she choose an unknown Scottish printer called Alexander McCorquodale? 'I had forty-nine proposals before I accepted number fifty, the wrong one', she explains, 'but it all became right when I married his cousin Hugh.'

Barbara Cartland has always been attracted to vital men, ambitious men, larger-than-life men: Sir Winston Churchill, Earl Mountbatten of Burma, Lord Beaverbrook, Lord Birkenhead, the Duke of Sutherland, and, most of all, her brother Ronald Cartland, M.P. for King's Norton.

Whereas all the virgins in her love stories are penniless and innocent, her heroes never are. They are men who have lived and achieved success. If they happen to have a title, imposing estate, untold wealth, dark saturnine looks, a sardonic smile and a chest like Superman, all the better.

There must also be something very special about a woman in her seventies who became the confidante of Lord Mountbatten during the last years of his life. 'Yes, I loved him and I think he loved me', Barbara

Cartland says. 'You see, we had so much in common and had known each other since the early twenties. We never had to go through the rigmarole of explaining about our pasts which is so tiresome. I thought he was the most wonderful, handsome and magnetic man of this century.'

Over two hundred letters written to each other testify to the depth of their devotion. While Barbara Cartland's letters are stored in the archives at Broadlands, Lord Mountbatten's are kept tied up with pink ribbon at Camfield Place, her house in the Hertfordshire countryside.

There was scarcely a night during the last years that they did not telephone each other at 9.00 p.m. to 'talk the day over'. Only the most official engagement or foreign travel prevented this romantic ritual. Yet she did not shed a tear in public when she heard the news of his tragic death. She kept her grief for the hours she spent alone with her memories and the shooting labrador named 'Duke' that he had given her, and which came from the Royal kennels at Sandringham.

In *Who's Who*, it is Barbara Cartland who occupies more space than any other entry - ninety-six lines - which prompted one acid pen to write of 'a self-publicizing juggernaut'.

Though she batters you with her ego, cynicism apart, so much of what she says makes unbelievable sense. She is rarely wrong.

I also knew that beyond the public image there is a private Barbara Cartland, whom only her closest of personal friends is allowed to know: the Barbara who unconsciously changes people's lives in the most unexpected ways; who cares realistically for the under-privileged and down-trodden; who blasts loud and strong whenever she senses injustice. 'I am not a modest little flower doing my little bit in the corner. I am a whirlwind. All my campaigns have been very noisy what with all the helpful publicity. I suppose some people say that I am just a crusading busybody, but it all works. It works.'

Behind the vivid show business personality - Barbara has deliberately made herself into a world celebrity - there is also a sensitive woman who believes passionately in the power of daily prayer, reincarnation, mysticism and the belief that we are all part of a greater life force. 'We are put on this earth to help our fellow human beings in whatever way we can and leave it a better place because we have passed through it.'

There is also the Barbara Cartland who says that there is no problem about health that cannot be relieved by taking vitamins. To prove it she takes seventy-eight (at last count) every morning and looks twenty years younger than her contemporaries. She is a power-house of energy and enthusiasm and because of this she wants to share her own experience of vitamin therapy with the whole world. In her time she has taken on the health of the entire nation with her endorsement of vitamins, elixirs, pure drinking water and lead-free lipsticks.

Barbara Cartland refuses to accept any payment for the regular articles she writes in health magazines, but does allow the publication to pay for the stamps for the replies to the letters that pour in afterwards. Every year she personally answers about 10,000 letters that arrive in sacks and are delivered to Camfield Place twice a day.

'I consider myself an expert on love, sex, and health. Without health you can have very little of the other two', she says. She has campaigned against water fluoridation, pornography, television violence, low pay for midwives, poor conditions for old people, discrimination against gypsies and ugly gym-slips for school girls. More important, she has also had two parliamentary laws changed as a result of her campaigning.

Though she has no financial interest with any health food manufacturers, Barbara Cartland often advises them about new products, testing not only on herself, her family, her staff and her dogs but also her followers all over the world. This book was written on a daily dose of Selenium Ace, Super Oxide Dismatase and beastly tasting cod liver oil.

My first meeting to discuss writing this official biography was a nerve-racking experience. It had been twenty years since we had last met at a newspaper luncheon. I knew that Barbara Cartland preferred little boys to little girls, and men to women. 'Women have such petty minds and clutter them up with personal jealousies. Men are so much more direct and honest.' The only time she enjoyed working with women was during the war when they 'called on a reserve of strength which they had seldom used before'.

I knew, too, that below that halo of spun gold was a mind as crisp and shrewd as Margaret Thatcher's in one of her peak performances during question time in the House of Commons. And, like the Prime Minister, Barbara Cartland does not suffer fools lightly. Her wit can be barb sharp when she is annoyed or bored, and frothily feminine when she is amused. Her laughter is infectious.

It is almost two years since I took the toy train from King's Cross to Hatfield in Hertfordshire on a dreary autumn day. It was late afternoon, the train was dirty, the sky leaden with rain, and I was cold and frightened. Waiting at the station was a white Rolls Royce, and as the chauffeur tucked me into a pink mohair rug I felt the first brush with Cartland magic. By the time we drove through the Nile blue wrought iron gates down the long winding drive I was less apprehensive. Would she permit the book? Could we get along together? Were the stories of her intolerance all too true?

In my research over the next year I was to visit Barbara Cartland hundreds of times. I saw the four hundred acres change through the seasons from crisp white winter, with the oak trees clothed in delicate tracery of snow and hoar frost, to springtime drifts of daffodils and playful squirrels. In June the eiderdown of dark green rhododendrons that stretches round the lake became a dazzling patchwork of pink, purple and cerise. And finally, in the muted golden sunshine of autumn, I saw the landscape that had been planned by that imaginative gardener, 'Capability' Brown, and which stretches endlessly over the Lea Valley, become an English pastoral tapestry.

On this my first day we drove up to the imposing red-brick Victorian mansion, whose wheel windows are edged with the same blue paint as the gates. At the left of the massive door a giant magnolia, weary from the summer months, was dropping its leathery leaves like soup plates.

In the entrance hall lay a voluptuous white fox coat nonchalantly flung across the armchair. It remains there all the year round for use when its owner takes her twice daily walks with her dogs. Huge Chinese *jardinières* filled with shocking pink rhododendrons stood round the hall. I gasped with delight and said 'How fantastic . . . and at this time of year!' 'They are wax madam', the chauffeur replied, without a smile.

I was swept into a large bright pink, scarab blue and gilt drawing room. It was blinding in its exuberance on that dull autumn day. As one waspish wag commented: 'Barbara has cornered the market in gold leaf.' There were gilt urns and gold cupids holding huge flower displays - some fake, some real, but never mixed; swags of glorious coloured fabrics; abundant opulence. So this was Barbara Cartland land - a bower fit for the Queen of Romance.

I sat waiting nervously. With a whoosh, and sizzling with zest, Barbara Cartland almost danced into the room, followed by a cross-looking white Pekingese. 'He's Twi-Twi', she announced. 'He doesn't like strangers and is always like this until he gets to know you. Here take that', as she threw him her fine lawn handkerchief to play with.

She was wearing coral pink chiffon, five rows of pearls and her favourite set of turquoise and ruby bracelet, bird brooch, and four rings. After the first shock of confrontation my eyes began to take in her features, detail by detail. She was even more imposing than her television performances would suggest and infinitely prettier. It was Randolph Churchill who said, 'Barbara was the prettiest girl in the twenties I'd ever seen.'

As an enthusiastic interviewer Paula Baldwin wrote: 'As a young woman she must have been one of the most beautiful women in the world. As an old woman she must be the most beautiful old woman in the world.'

Her skin is opal white with skilfully blushed cheeks. The hair shines like golden floss. Her pink-tipped hands are those of a woman far younger in years and her legs, that used to dance the nights away when London was young and gay, are in fine shape still.

Barbara Cartland's outrageously false eye lashes, which grow longer with the passing years, are as indispensable to her as Carol Channing's wigs or Danny La Rue's *décolletage*. She wears them with aplomb and only lost her temper once when, in a bout of churlish manners, Liberal leader David Steel recounted on television that they had fallen off during a literary luncheon in Birmingham. He claimed that the offending eye lashes had been knocked off site by Magnus Pyke in one of his extravagant gestures. 'All lies. All lies. All lies. I am shocked and appalled that the leader of a once great political party should so demean himself as to tell a complete and absolute lie to get a cheap laugh. I'm always the first person to laugh at myself but this incident never happened.'

Today I cannot imagine her without that sooty fringe of black and swag of turquoise blue eye shadow which she wears even when she is receiving in her boudoir in the mornings. 'I have told everyone', she says, 'that I am to wear them when I am buried.'

We drifted in to tea in the elegant dining room dotted with handsome family portraits. It was just what you would have wished for . . . lace table cloth, stamp-sized cucumber sandwiches, gooey meringues - 'the Chef made them especially for you' - home-made brandy snaps, buttery tea biscuits and a menacingly rich chocolate cake, made with natural fruit sugar from health stores.

The conversation flitted frothily from subject to subject. All the time Barbara Cartland talked in that girlish voice that remains as breathless and beguiling as when she was first kissed. With infinite manners she ping-ponged the conversation into alleys that might amuse me. I hardly spoke a word, nor was I expected to. Rising eighty-two, her personality punched its way through on that dreary autumn day. Her charm and humour were irresistible.

The reason for my visit was scarcely mentioned as she bubbled on. There was no possible clue as to whether she had changed her mind, whether or not I should write her memoirs since her first refusal by letter some weeks previously.

'Now come along darling, and have some champagne before you go,' she said and then, looking directly into my eyes, suddenly became more serious. 'Tell me when you want to begin and how you like to work. You can come whenever you like and all my papers and letters will be at your disposal. But I must warn you that I have lunch alone, as if I don't I would put on a show for you and not be able to get on with the Duke.'

She was referring to the two-and-a-half hour dictation she does between the hours of 1.00 and 3.30, every afternoon four or five days a week. I was later to learn that her accountant had discovered that if she breaks this rule and lunches with someone it costs £5,000!

I will always remember Barbara Cartland: the months I spent in her company; the lessons about life that I learned from her; the doors that she opened which lead to 'the development of spiritual awareness and the enlightenment of the Soul'.

Not one minute was ever dull, and it was mostly hilarious. I have never met a woman as frank and honest about herself nor with a more far-seeing eye. Even her theory that she has been reincarnated several times becomes plausible when she explains the natural phenomena and spiritual experiences she has known.

Generous, flamboyant, ebullient, witty, intelligent, indiscreet, intolerant, indefatigable. Unique.

One thing I know, life can never die,
Translucent, splendid, flaming like the sun,
Only our bodies wither and deny
The life force when our strength is done.

Barbara Cartland

Though she does have some Scottish blood Barbara Cartland's roots on her mother's side are as English as the oaks that surround her home, Camfield Place. Firstly, she is a direct descendant of the oldest Saxon family in existence, a maternal forbear being Thomas de Scobenhull, High Sheriff of Devonshire in 1032, thirty-four years before the Norman Conquest. Then, through her second husband Hugh McCorquodale's mother, who was a Granville, Barbara's sons are associated with Princess Diana's family, the Spencers, distant though this may be. Duke Rollo, great-grandfather of William the Conqueror, is the catalyst. Three of Rollo's grandsons were Kings of England - Ethelred the Unready, Edward the Confessor and King Canute - while his granddaughter married the Earl of Corbeil, whose family were Granville. All the Earl Spencers down to the present eighth Earl are related to the Earl Granville of 1762, and thus the Princess of Wales comes into the story, as Barbara Cartland's fascination for genealogy and passion for research revealed. She noticed the connection when looking at the family tree which hangs in the hall at Camfield Place, soon after the marriage of her daughter Raine, formerly the Countess of Dartmouth, to the present eighth Earl Spencer in 1976. She wrote to her new son-in-law telling him about it, a fact of which he had not been aware.

In more recent years Barbara Cartland's grandfather, Colonel Scobell, a handsome eccentric whose passion for climbing gained him a medal as one of the first to conquer Mont Blanc, epitomized all the gaiety and romanticism of the late-Victorian period. With his Saxon blue eyes, fine crop of blond curly hair, and dashing side whiskers he was a perfect blue-print for a Barbara Cartland hero, even if she does prefer her heroes to be dark. The attractive Colonel Scobell once said: 'I've slept with women of every nationality in the world, and the Japanese are much the best.' A marble bust of the Colonel stands in the entrance hall at Camfield Place, and it is easy to see his attraction to women. Besides his virility he was also an outstanding dancer, having been taught dancing, among other things, by some of the most attractive ballet dancers of the day.

Son of a rector and a product of Winchester and Trinity College, Oxford, Colonel Scobell inherited a fortune from an uncle Captain Treweeke who had served at the Battle of Trafalgar, 'invented' the Victoria Cross for bravery and became a Liberal Member of Parliament. During the Crimean War Captain Treweeke tabled a motion that a medal which could be worn by all serving men, irrespective of rank, should be struck to commemorate acts of outstanding gallantry. The Government of the day became interested and the suggestion was put into effect in consultation with Queen Victoria. The Queen had been captivated when it was suggested that her name should be associated with this unique medal, with the result that the Captain's motion was withdrawn and the idea was brought forward instead by the Crown. Thus in 1856 the Victoria Cross was instituted by Royal Warrant and has existed ever since.

Though he was a man with an irascible disposition Colonel Scobell was also a romanticist. Barbara tells the story how in 1870, during the Franco-Prussian War, he visited the battlefield just after the battle of Sedan had finished and was distraught to find that he had arrived too late. The ground was covered with bodies of the wounded and dying, and fluttering scraps of white paper. On picking up some of the paper scraps he discovered that the pages were letters that had been written by the soldiers and which had been thrown away when their bodies had been rifled by the human vultures who scoured the battlefields. There is no record, alas, as to whether he was able to return the letters to their rightful owners.

Another bust in the hall at Camfield Place is of Barbara's grandmother Edith Scobell, a very handsome woman who before her marriage was a Palairet. The Palairets were descended from a Frenchman - Antoine Palayret, who was born in 1470 and who became a Huguenot. Edith's mother was Mary Anne Hamilton, the daughter of Andrew Hamilton, a member of the Duke of Hamilton's family, who with William Penn developed the settlement of Pennsylvania in America. A lawyer of considerable talent, he became a local hero when he was able to prove that the State of Pennsylvania owed no allegiance to the British Crown. Mary Anne Hamilton, whose feet were so small that she could only wear shoes that had been made in Paris and whose hands were like a child's so that her wedding ring would not go on Barbara's little finger, inherited a large slice of Philadelphia when still a child, as her parents both died young. She was then brought up in England by a Colonel Johnson and spent her childhood at Upton-on-Severn. It was here that this desirable heiress fell in love with Septimus Henry Palairet, a well bred, impecunious young Captain in the Worcestershire Regiment. Her guardians insisted that, as an heiress, she wait until she was twenty-one years of age before she married. Alas her dreams of married bliss were short-lived, and she died when she was twenty-eight, having given birth to seven children. The last was buried with her in Philadelphia.

After the American fashion Mary Anne's considerable fortune was divided in equal portions amounting to about £2,000 a year for each of her daughters. The sixth daughter was named Edith, and though she had none of her mother's delicacy she had charm and wit, was well informed, and had lots of common sense. One of her *bon mots* was 'All men are polygamists at heart', which could have been said by Barbara Cartland today. Though quite a strongly built girl she had inherited her mother's American bones and exquisite feet and ankles. She also had that indefinable quality called 'style', and as George Scobell, who became her husband, remarked when they met, 'She is not the sort of girl to be kissed under the stairs.' In talking to me about George Scobell Barbara Cartland told how he was strolling up Piccadilly one day from his club when he saw in front of him a perfect pair of ankles. Mesmerized, he followed them as far as the Berkeley Hotel then, on looking up to accost the owner, found himself gazing into the eyes of his wife. She laughed and said, 'So that's how you behave when I am not with you.' Barbara Cartland inherited not only George Scobell's expertise in dancing but also her great-grandmother's legs and ankles.

It was at a ball in Henley that Edith first met George Scobell, who was standing in for his brother Barton. By now George was thirty years of age and ready to settle down, and when his eyes alighted on Edith he knew that his quest was over. He asked for her hand in marriage. Edith was not impressed when George proposed to her at the ball but she did ask him to join the household for luncheon next day. It would not have surprised her at all if he had not turned up as she is noted for having remarked, 'Men who propose at dances are usually drunk and forget all about it when they are sober.' But George had not forgotten and proposed again.

Like her mother Edith had to wait until she was twenty-one before she was allowed to marry, but this was the accepted custom in those days and it gave her plenty of time to prepare her extensive trousseau, which cost £643. 2s. 5d and included the latest craze, a railway basket tarpaulin (a piece of Victorian luggage) costing £2.18s. On their return from honeymoon in Paris George Scobell bought a large Georgian mansion, the Down House, Redmarley, in Gloucestershire and Edith turned all her energy to making it charming. They both enjoyed the life of well-off gentry, entertaining a great deal, hunting, and spending the Season in London. Soon after their wedding they set off on a spectacular trip around the world visiting India, Singapore, China, and Japan, where they stayed for two months travelling decorously from Nagasaki to Yokohama by rickshaw as there were no trains. There were no European hotels in those days, and while George did not mind the rigours of sleeping on the floor Japanese style, Edith sighed for the comfort of a bed and was relieved when they set off for Canada and left the Japanese style behind them.

Though Barbara is the first to admit that tolerance is not one of her strongest points, she does not have George Scobell's chronic bad temper which led him into tyrannical rages. Poor Edith suffered greatly under these outbursts, and the marriage, especially in the beginning, was often stormy. Larger than life in every way, George Scobell found it impossible to accept the restrictions of Victorian family life. Being a man of strong character he rebelled in the only way he knew, much to Edith's distress. Her own brothers were so different - charming, well mannered and considerate to women. George Scobell's thunderous moods, which ricocheted round the house like a tempest, were, according to Barbara, merely an outlet for something far deeper. She wrote of him:

> He wanted beauty - the beauty he sought among Old Masters and young mistresses. He enjoyed physical danger and mental achievement. Trivialities put him into a rage against the conventional security of the English landscape. Only the broad horizons, the snow-capped mountains against a foreign sky, tempestuous seas and strange unknown nationalities could assuage some aching need within himself.

When Edith Scobell was first married, entranced by her handsome husband, she accepted her lot like many Victorian women and took refuge only in tears and mild remonstrations - 'Oh Georgie'. It was only later in life, after she had produced the required number of children, that she challenged her husband with bitter battles of words that took place late in the night within the security of their capacious mahogany bed.

One year after their marriage the child that had been conceived somewhere in the East was born: a daughter whom they called by the family name, Melloney. George was barely able to contain his wrath that the first-born should be a girl and not the son and heir he wanted. The second child, a son, was born in Florence but he does not seem to have survived. The next year another girl arrived whom they called Emily, and though sickly at the beginning she began to improve when it was found that she thrived on the milk of one of the famous Parisian donkeys. A year and seventeen days later there was a third daughter. When the Colonel was told the news by the doctor he exclaimed 'Damnation' and stamped into his study to prepare the birth notice for *The Times*. His bitternes at the arrival of yet another daughter was deep-seated as he wrote: 'On September 5th, 1877, at the Down House, Redmarley, the wife of Sanford G. T. Scobell a daughter.'

The new born was a tiny elfin child with a heart-shaped face, velvet brown eyes and hands and feet like pink shells. So exquisite - a gift to Edith straight from heaven. Her doting mother chose the names Mary Hamilton, probably wishing to perpetuate her own family name since her husband took no notice whatsoever of the new baby daughter. It soon became apparent that Mary, though small, had the gift for life. By the time she was talking her gaiety was such that she was nicknamed Polly, simply because she could not stop chattering.

It was not until two years after Polly that the long-awaited son was born. He was christened John Sanford Scobell, and no one who saw this beautiful child with a head ringed in golden curls and blue eyes could have foreseen that he would grow up to become Major General Sir John Scobell and make a distinguished career in the army.

Polly grew up into a strong character and became Barbara Cartland's 'wonderful Mother Polly', the woman who helped fashion her into what she is today. Although Barbara insists that it was her brother Ronald who was, and still is, the greatest influence in her life (even though he died in France over forty years ago) friends from her childhood have told me that a great deal of the Barbara Cartland we know today was created by Polly.

Polly's own background sets the tone for the way in which she brought up her three children - Barbara, Ronald and Anthony - and gave them an ingrained set of standards in service to their fellow human beings that was to influence their whole lives. For had Ronald Cartland lived it is believed by many people that his outstanding visionary mind and brilliant oratory would have allowed him to fulfil his ambition of becoming Prime Minister. Though only twenty-seven years old when he won the Tory seat of King's Norton in Birmingham, his stirring speeches already had a Churchillian ring about them. It was Polly's son who said:

My philosophy as a Christian rests on the belief that a man's life in this world is a preparation for the next. The fundamentals of Christianity do not change. They are the rule by which one can measure the achievements or failures of the age . . . no Government can change a man's soul, the souls of men change Governments . . .

And it was Polly's influence that inspired her only daughter Barbara to write:

> I have been searching for rainbows all my life. However black, however frightening, however miserable events have been, there has always been something inside me: the knowledge that I was not alone. There has always been hope and faith.

This firm belief that anything was possible, as long as you worked for it, also tinged the thinking of Anthony, Polly's younger son, who claimed as a small boy that he intended to be C.I.G.S. (Chief Imperial General Staff). There is every evidence that had he not been killed as a young man in France during the last war he might well have attained this top military position.

As it happened, Barbara was the only one of Polly's children who lived to be able to fulfil her true potential.

To win you no armour can repel me.
My arrows are the brightness of your eyes.
Your trust's a shining silver shield to guard me,
Your magic - no magician could devise.

Barbara Cartland

As Polly was to influence so deeply her daughter Barbara's life it is interesting to examine her own family background, even though, years later, when tragedy clouded her life and she was left a war widow with three children, she rejected the way in which she herself had been brought up. Polly broke all the traditional Victorian rules and pioneered her own - with magnificent results. She didn't simply shower her children with verbal endearments ('Darling' was the most frequently used word in the Cartland household and still is) - she also fortified their characters with caring concern. Most important of all she inspired them to believe in themselves.

During the first years of Polly's young life Edith and George Scobell were clearly bored with the daily details of their children's upbringing, and like other well-off parents they relegated their children's daily life to nursery maids and governesses. They only saw their young when it was convenient. In later life none of the Scobell children was ever to remember their mother holding them in her arms. It simply was not done, and any servant who felt disposed to show affection to her charges had to do so in secret. As Polly's sister Florence said once, 'Mother is a rock when one is in trouble but a rock is a cold, hard thing to cuddle.' For these were the days before Dr Spock and his disciples, and displays of physical love were considered rather vulgar. Any maternal feelings that Edith might have felt were stifled by convention, with the result that all the children lived in apprehension of the 6.00 p.m. rendezvous in the drawing room with their parents, and especially of their father. While Edith remained discreetly in the background George put the trembling children, who had been all dressed up in their best frocks, through the gruelling ritual of demanding to know what they had learned that day from their governess. One day when Colonel Scobell asked about their lessons little Polly, braver than the others, piped up:

'We learnt about Vortimer and Wortigern.'

'My God', boomed the Colonel, 'the sooner the governess goes the better.' And like her predecessors she did. As every governess began teaching history from the Saxon days there was never time to progress further than the Saxon kings Vortimer and Wortigern. Before Polly reached thirteen years of age, and was ready to go to school, the turn-over of governesses also tallied thirteen as they never stayed longer than a year.

In his perverse way Colonel Scobell did try to involve himself with his children, going as far as cropping the girls' hair short in order to save the expense of an extra maid, who would have been required for brushing their shining heads several times during the day. In Polly's case this enhanced her gamin qualities and she retained a fringe for a great part of her life. Colonel Scobell was frequently heard to say, 'Why I should be blessed with such damned ugly daughters the Lord only knows.' Yet right from the beginning little Polly was undoubtedly his favourite child. She had vivacity and vitality and no one could resist her defiant *joie de vivre* and independent mind. She was also very brave about physical pain. When she was taught to ride a bicycle and broke her arm, she was so afraid she would be stopped in future that she went all through the day doing her lessons without telling anyone what had happened to her.

25

By the time she made her début at a ball in August 1895, Polly had grown into a bewitching young woman. She was not beautiful in the conventional sense, but with her merry face and handspan waist hers was the kind of prettiness that turned men's heads. To her continual delight she was the centre of male attention, though Mrs Scobell admonished all her daughters to 'marry park gates', and 'Do not marry for money but love where money is', was a favourite saying of hers. Polly's diary in her 'coming out' year shows that her life was not very different from the lives of other girls with the same social background. It was filled with halcyon days and nights: '. . . got up at eleven o'clock . . . played golf with Mr H and Captain F . . . I sat at a most amusing table with the Prince (Prince Victor Duleep Singh) . . . in the garden Horace and I got separated and *he proposed to me* . . . Cousin George and I went off to Huntingdon to the Regimental Sports.' In contrast to the 'thrilling and awful fun' days there are glimpses of behind scenes in her own home life at Down House: 'Father's toothache bad again . . . he was in a vile temper. Talked all night . . . Emily, Father, Mother and I played Whist until 11.30 p.m. Father made a terrible row over the marking. Went to bed in tears . . . did the flowers in the church.'

In today's climate of live-in companions, who stay together for years before committing themselves to marriage, it is amusing to note that at the turn of the century men appeared to fall in love and propose marriage on sight. Stirring quadrilles, the sight of a pretty ankle or a glimpse of peach-skin shoulders was heady stuff indeed and simply went to their hearts. Many a man must have been relieved when reason took over the next morning and his beguiling dancing partner of the night before, or in many cases her mother, delivered a polite note by hand declining his proposal.

Polly received a number of proposals during that first year. She became an artist at saying 'No' with a blush and a smile and clearly passed on this feminine art to her daughter Barbara who rejected forty-nine proposals of marriage as a young woman. There was red-haired Arthur, attractive but penniless, the young Scot 'Dondy' also with empty pockets, and even a married man who fell head over heels in love with her at a house party and begged her to run away with him. Polly was terrified that his wife would find out but such were the deceptive dalliances of the time that the wife was blissfully enjoying an affair with another member of the house party - a fact which had totally escaped Polly's innocent eyes.

Barbara also inherited from her mother the ability to attract influential and rich older people who would help her on in life simply because she amused them, was undemanding and decorative, and helped make their

parties go with a swing. In Polly's case it was Mr and Mrs Greswolde
Williams, who not only took her to the Grand National at Aintree, where
they had a box and private luncheon room, but also whisked her off to stay
in London at their permanent suite at the then fashionable Brown's Hotel
in Dover Street. That winter Polly also went with them to the High
Sheriff's Ball at Worcester, where history repeated itself. A handsome
young man walked in, saw Polly waltzing and, just like George Scobell,
said to himself, 'That is the girl I am going to marry.'

Bertram Cartland was good looking, six feet tall with captivating blue
eyes and the ingrained grooming which comes from generations of
self-assurance. The family came to England from Ireland in the twelfth
century. During the Industrial Revolution Bertram's grandfather, who
lived in Worcestershire and was Sheriff of the county, decided to move
into Birmingham, where he amassed a considerable fortune by opening a
brass factory. His son, Barbara's grandfather, James Cartland, an ex-
ceedingly clever man, became a financier who helped build up the city and
was for his services twice offered a baronetcy. This he refused, saying that
he preferred the more uncommon title of 'Esquire', though the real reason
was that in those days, on accepting a baronetcy, the recipient had to put
down £50,000 for his son who would inherit the title. James Cartland
preferred to keep his money fluid. Bertie, however, scorned the world of
commerce and joined the Worcestershire Militia.

Bertram Cartland was more cautious than Polly's previous suitors had
been, and it was not until the third meeting, after a big party hosted by the
Greswolde Williams at the Adelphi in London, that he proposed. At the
end of the party he offered to escort Polly upstairs, and sitting on a sofa in
the corridor outside her bedroom he solemnly 'asked for her hand'. Polly
was not impressed. As she wrote in her diary: 'Absolutely could not say
yes. He was awfully sweet and I do like him - but nothing more. I felt a
brute, of course. Talked until four o'clock. Then went to bed.' For Bertie it
was a searing experience. Not only was he upset at being refused by her
but it was the first set-back that this assured young man had ever received.
In a letter to Polly next morning, slipped under her door, he wrote:

Just a line in case you might think we might have an awkward meeting
this morning. That I was an ass enough to hope that you might be
something to me is entirely my own fault. But I do believe all I told you
because, before God, it is true and I meant every word. You said that
you were not in love with anyone else, so I suppose I can go on hoping. I
have been in love with you since you were at Strensham Court [the
Worcestershire home of the Greswolde Williams] in the summer.

What Bertie did not know was that Polly's eye had been attracted by another young man in the party, Pat Cunningham, to whom next morning she promptly confided the previous night's romantic disaster. Pat, possibly with his own interest at heart, jealously advised Polly not to marry Bertie as he 'was not good enough'. He was too poor to marry her himself but he loved her all his life. Polly sounds flippant when after walking with Bertie next day at Strensham Court, where everyone had been whisked after the races at Liverpool, she writes in her diary: 'The poor dear is very sad, but *que voulez-vous?* I can't marry him.'

A whole year to the day went by before Polly and Bertie were again brought together by the match-making Greswolde Williams: a dazzling year of parties, sister Emily's wedding and flirtations in abundance. She was now even more the adored protégé of the Greswolde Williams and again accepted an invitation to stay with them at Brown's in London for a few days. She was slightly mystified when Bertie met her at the station and the next day took her for a walk in nearby Green Park. The following day he invited her to lunch at Prince's, a fashionable restaurant, after which they went to the Aquarium at Westminster which had been opened in 1876. Back at Brown's, Frank Greswolde Williams excused himself to go to see his sick wife, leaving the young couple alone. And this is how Bertie, complete with stiff white dinner shirt and winged collar, and Polly in her rustling pink silk dress became engaged. When Bertie looked down into Polly's brown eyes and said, 'Oh darling, please change your mind. Say you will marry me - I can't live without you,' Polly answered without hesitation, 'Yes.'

'Darling, how marvellous!' Bertie gasped.

With these words and a chaste kiss Barbara Cartland's parents vowed eternal love.

When Polly broke the news to her family, the Scobells were not at all pleased. As far as Edith was concerned Bertie was a pleasant young man, but his parents were not what she considered 'county'. Polly's visit to Bertie's parents at their pseudo-Gothic Vectis Lodge, Edgbaston, might have been a nerve-racking experience. While a less spirited girl would have paled at meeting the expensively dressed, beautiful but haughty Mrs Cartland, Polly took it in her stride. Polly thought Mrs Cartland was an over-possessive mother to her only child and would very likely be extremely jealous, and in this she proved to be right.

Flora Cartland, who had been born a Falkner, a descendant of Robert the Bruce, gave herself great airs and would not call on any of the people in Birmingham, including Joseph Chamberlain and his wife. She had been practically engaged to a peer, but love for James Cartland had swept her into his arms, just like a Barbara Cartland heroine. James Cartland, Polly knew, was extremely successful as a businessman and, although she did not realize it, he had exceptionally good taste. He collected sporting pictures by Alkin, Herring and Stubbs which were later sold at Christies, and the antique furniture he gave Bertie and Polly as a wedding present has been loved by Barbara all her life and helped to form her own passion for antiques.

When Polly met him, James Cartland was already occupied with the marriage settlement he would have to negotiate with the autocratic Colonel Scobell. When one thinks of the strict financial contracts in marriages in the Muslim world today it is amusing to remember that just one hundred years ago a not so dissimilar situation existed in England. The dowry was an acknowledged accoutrement to every respectable marriage. While James Cartland was prepared to put down a large sum of money for his son, he also wanted the assurance that Colonel Scobell would guarantee the capital of the money from which he allowed Polly an allowance to be secured on the children of the marriage. It was a case of a member of the eccentric Gloucestershire gentry facing a stubborn Midlands businessman. Finally a settlement was drawn up between the two fathers over a series of rows in the next two weeks, when tempers became more and more inflamed. It ended with the settlement being torn up and thrown into the fire. Two men, consumed by their bigotry, were thus to deny Polly an inheritance that would have changed her life in later years and perhaps her daughter Barbara's too.

Polly was married in July 1900 in St Bartholomew's Church, Redmarley, the church where she had been christened. It was a typical fashionable county wedding of the time with the bride in white crêpe de chine, a three-yard long satin train, and a Brussels lace family veil, attended by seven bridesmaids and a page. All the way to the church her father repeated over and over again, 'You are selling yourself on the altar for 7s. 6d.' - which was not calculated to enhance the bride's composure!

Polly passed the next few months in a dream of contentment, setting up the house given by her father-in-law and engaging two grooms, a cook, two housemaids and a personal maid. She was even happier as she flitted from ball to ball, and was able to write in her diary on 31 December, 'A ripping year. The greatest change in my life has come. I am awfully happy, hope to remain always so. Bertie is the best of husbands and I only hope that next year will be as jolly.'

In July the following year Polly gave birth to a baby daughter. There were difficulties with the confinement, and when the doctor asked Bertie which he wanted saved, the mother or the child, he replied: 'Damn the bloody child. Save my wife.' When the baby was born the doctor said to the nurse, 'It's dead.' Yet as a precaution, he began slapping the 8lb girl, and miraculously she began to breathe. Bertie, indoctrinated by the male chauvinism of the period, was disappointed that the baby was a girl, but Polly cradled her daughter with delight. All that mattered to her was that she had her own child whom she would coax back to health.

The baby had a round little face with large emerald green eyes, rosebud mouth, and dimpled hands and feet. She was adorable and was duly christened Mary Barbara Hamilton.

—— 3 ——

Poor I might be but common I am not.

Mary Hamilton (Polly) Cartland

Polly's idyllic, comfortable and amusing life with her handsome Bertie came abruptly to an end which nobody could have foreseen. With the adoration of her new friends who found her such fun, the household running smoothly and a prettily pink and white baby it had been 'two wonderful years'.

The coronation of Edward VII in 1902 had evoked an air of festivity that spanned over many months and the annual social events such as Ascot took on a special splendour that year. In contrast to the last sombre years of Queen Victoria's reign everything was now touched with lightness and brightness. With her new-found maturity Polly was even more attractive than she had been as a young girl, and the Cartlands were much in demand, for hostesses could always rely on Polly to 'sing for her supper'. Mr and Mrs Cartland invited them to join them in their box at Ascot where the Royal procession was taking place for the first time since the Prince Consort had last attended over forty years earlier. In her white pleated crêpe de chine dress trimmed with ecru lace and her daffodil yellow alpaca dust coat with black velvet collar, Polly cut an elegant little figure. Queen Alexandra (King Edward VII was unfortunately ill), still at the height of her beauty, rode down the course in an open landau and the crowds went wild with delight.

In these days of swift communication, when good or bad news is relayed across the world via satellite in a matter of seconds, it is incomprehensible that Polly and Bertie were to hear of events that would change their lives by ordinary letter, though Vectis Lodge was less than twenty-five miles away. When a maid brought in the morning mail and set it on the breakfast table it contained, apart from a batch of the usual invitations, a letter from Mr Cartland asking them to come to the family home as soon as possible. On Friday morning they took the train to Birmingham and arrived to find Mr and Mrs Cartland in mental chaos.

Mrs Cartland was dissolved in tears amid wails of 'Oh Jim! I cannot be poor!' and all the *bonhomie* that a moneyed ambiance had provided had been drained from James Cartland. He was deflated. Due to the economic slump the overanxious bank had called in the loan of £250,000 which it had made to James Cartland in order to finance the Fishguard Railway. The bank demanded its money in cash - immediately. To gauge the enormity of this loan one has to multiply by twenty to relate to today's value.

Deeply shocked, and she was astute enough to know that her own life style would change dramatically, Polly's one concern was for her distraught parents-in-law. She begged them to return with her and Bertie to their home, Bowbrook in Worcestershire. Here at least, from a distance, they could perhaps have been able to think more positively and courageously, but they refused to leave Vectis Lodge; Mrs Cartland on the grounds that she was not well enough to travel and James simply because he felt his place was in his own home. The Cartland seniors' marriage had for many years been a social façade as so many were in those morally deceptive days. While Flora Cartland always worried about her health and her eighteen-inch waist, and preferred to take tea with her women friends, like many other Edwardian husbands, James found his pleasure elsewhere.

His last words to Polly were that he would come and see them on Monday. On the Sunday Polly and Bertie tried to behave as normally as possible in front of the servants, and Polly went to the nursery as usual to play with Barbara who was fast growing into a lively little girl. They even invited some friends to a luncheon party and with her impeccable manners Polly was her usual effervescent self, delighting her friends with her bright chatter. Then in the middle of the meal a parlourmaid called Bertie from the table to inform him that a neighbour of his parents would like to speak to him. The Cartlands' friend had driven over from Birmingham at a top speed of thirty miles an hour. His message was devastating. James Cartland had shot himself that morning.

The financial effect on Polly and Bertie was disastrous. Though their home Bowbrook had been verbally given to them by James Cartland, the lawyers informed them that as they did not possess the title deeds, the house would have to be surrendered in order to pay Mr Cartland's debts. Furthermore, due to their frivolous living in the first years of their married life, combined with the fact that Bertie did not work, they had amassed their own personal debt of £800. It was not at all uncommon for young people with their background to live above their incomes simply because they were willingly given credit by tradesmen as long as there was 'money in the family', but this debt would now have to be met.

When Polly, with her practical mind, suggested that if the debts could not be paid the most sensible thing was to declare bankruptcy she was promptly stifled. James Cartland's brother George and his fashionable wife who lived in Worcester insisted that the name had to be protected at all costs. Not only was the house put up for sale but most of the household treasures which Polly had so lovingly arranged were immediately put under the auctioneer's hammer. The only china left were some chipped blue and white pieces which the auctioneer thought would not fetch anything. Fortunately the furniture was safe as it was entailed to the children of the marriage. But if she was inwardly aching, Polly showed no signs visibly. Her courage was immense. While her mother-in-law crumpled into floods of tears Polly got on with the task of finding her family a new home. She simply refused to allow herself any self pity or morbid thoughts. Life was for living and somehow she would work it out.

I am remembering, as I write this, Barbara Cartland's words when I asked her one day how she had coped with the adversities in her own life. Quite apart from her personal life, she is exposed to disappointments and acid criticism from time to time as the inspiration and fount-head of the huge Barbara Cartland world-wide industry. Does it hurt? How does she cope?

> If I am hurt I pretend that it has never happened. When I receive an offensive or an anonymous letter I tear it up. When someone is rude to me I never speak about it. If a journalist writes something untrue about me I forget it. Of course I have had a lot of knocks in my life that I have put behind me. As Asquith said 'What say they? Let them say!' What is more I have no regrets. I will not look back into the past.
>
> Two wars shattered my life and so many people I loved have been killed but I will not let myself think of my loss, but as Napoleon did I

shut the cupboards of my mind. When I find it difficult to sleep, because emotionally or mentally I am upset, I read one of my own books. I find the last pages of love and happiness take away the pain.

It was Polly's voice stretching down through the years. Of all the splendidly shining characteristics that she gave her daughter, self-survival was among the most important.

The young couple's total income would now be £300 a year. Bertie had never worked for his living, as befitted a gentleman at that time, so their only money came from £200 a year which Mrs Cartland allowed them from her own little private income and the £100 a year which Colonel Scobell had given Polly on her marriage. But while Bertie hovered between bewilderment and despair, Polly refused to be depressed. One of the hundreds of Pollyisms that have come down through the years are her words, 'Poor I may be but common I am not!' Even though she hated losing her elegant home there were no bitter words and she held her head high. As there was no money to buy she immediately set about finding an alternative house they could rent. In the small market town of Pershore, about eight miles south-east of Worcester, on the Earl of Coventry's estate, she found an old farm house with the ostentatious name of Amerie Court. It had pleasant living rooms, six bedrooms, a tennis court, stables and four acres of garden that had become a wilderness. Polly immediately saw its potential as a suitable and elegant background for herself and Bertie and as a home in which to bring up a family. Also the price was right - £40 a year.

Polly, who had been brought up with twelve indoor servants in the Scobell household, and had four herself when she first married, was now faced with the necessity of running her household with just two - a nurse for Barbara and a maid-of-all-work. Though she knew a great deal about the preparation and serving of food, just as Barbara Cartland does today, she had never before had actually to cook or clean. Undaunted by her smaller *ménage* Polly insisted on keeping up the standards, and she herself polished the Georgian silver - candlesticks, tankards, salvers and entrée dishes - wedding presents she had managed to save from being sold. She soon transformed the old farmhouse into an elegant place in which to entertain, and even though they were now poor compared to their friends this did not deter Polly from packing the house with guests whenever there was a ball or social event. The loyalty that she had always showered on her own friends now multiplied back. Besides there was only one Polly! So their aristocratic friends, the Cavendish-Bentincks, the Beauchamps and Coventrys, continued to enjoy her dinner parties, modest as they now were.

Polly and Bertie quickly became involved with the local hunt crowd and as they had only been able to keep one horse called Sir Lydston, the Masters of the Croome Hunt, first Lord Charles Cavendish-Bentinck and then Mr Dudley Smith, not only came to the rescue and mounted Polly but kept Bertie's horse at the kennels along with the other hunt horses.

My Mother, who was a brilliant rider, looked her best on a horse. She of course rode side saddle - no lady in those days rode any other way. Her habit had been made by Busvine when she was at Bowbrook and despite having had a baby it fitted her waist which was still only twenty inches. The coat had a velvet collar and she always wore a bunch of violets. A white stock, starched until it cut her neck, a gold pin, a yellow waistcoat, a top hat and veil completed her outfit. She was always exquisitely neat and no matter how fast she galloped, however much she jumped, and was always in front of the field, she never had a hair out of place at the end of the day.

When Polly took the field the men's eyes were only for her. It was not that she was a flirt by nature - she made it quite clear that Bertie and Barbara were her life - but just that men found her irresistible. This was not without incidence, as on the occasion when Polly went off with friends to a party without Bertie, who was still suffering from a regimental dinner he had attended the night before. She returned home to find that in a fit of pique he had burnt a brand new black and white dress which she had saved up for and never worn. Only then did Polly sit down and cry. Nothing that Bertie did to comfort her could compensate for losing her dress through his stupid act of jealousy. Polly knew that it would be a long, long time before she could afford another.

Normally Polly's patience with Bertie was infinite. Whereas his mother was considerably annoyed by his indolence and was constantly chiding him, 'Bertie you must get some proper work', Polly encouraged him to lead the life that befits the English country gentleman - even if it had to be tailored to suit their new situation. As part of this new life Polly and Bertie bicycled everywhere - Bertie even went off to shoots on his bicycle with his gun case attached by a special strap. They cycled to tennis parties, and, always immaculate in her social behaviour, Polly formally called on her neighbours but instead of being conveyed by motor, carriage or even dog cart, she set off on her bicycle and prayed that the rain would keep off.

With her extraordinary energy Polly persuaded Bertie to help her transform the weed-filled garden into a brilliant seed catalogue display. While Bertie set about taming the lawns Polly flanked the drive with herbaceous borders filled with colour - peonies, delphiniums, scarlet poppies and an edging of yards and yards of powdery sweet Mrs Sinpkins pinks. Her vitality was extraordinary and her mental strength flowed out in all directions.

The four acres of Amerie Court were in reality one large orchard planted with the unique Pershore plums for which the district was famous. These plums are quite different from any others grown in England and are bright red or deep golden in colour. In the spring the garden was veiled with blossom, and in the golden autumn sunlight the trees looked as if they were festooned with rubies and topazes.

Mummy made enough jam that first year to keep us going for three years. We ate plums in every guise . . . plum tarts, plum pies, plum 'fools' and stewed plums, with the result that today I loathe plums and never eat them.

The beauty of the orchard inspired the young Barbara's imagination and took her into a fairyland which has influenced her whole life. Because she was then an only child, and she had a lot of time to wander about the garden alone, she peopled it with fairies, sprites and goblins that became to her more real than human beings. She can remember to this day listening at the trees to hear the movements of the Little People who lived inside them, and she was sure she saw fairy wings among the flowers. As she stood under trees, pink and white with blossom, she felt a kind of strange spiritual ecstacy which later she tried to express in her novels.

I never drive through Worcestershire in the spring without the memory of our garden like a pink and white fairyland and filled with the sweet scent of wallflowers.

All through her life Polly believed that with the help of God through prayer there was nothing that she could not accomplish. Once when she was staying with the Greswolde Williams in Liverpool for the Grand National, she was up before the household was astir and went to early Holy Communion simply because it was the Feast of the Annunciation. Her prayers were a necessary part of her daily life and remained so until she died, just as they are for Barbara.

Keeping Daddy from being bored all the time was one of Mummy's very real problems. He no longer had the money to indulge in the hobbies of his rich friends and like any other gentleman at that time he was apt to become tiresome and even bad tempered when he had nothing to do.

With or without the Lord's help, by now Polly had made a comfortable life for Barbara and Bertie who she was determined should not feel deprived through the Cartland family misfortune. Whenever her husband was restless or bored she unobtrusively organized him into doing something that would amuse him. It is quite probable that he was never aware of how much he depended on his wife during this shifting period of his life. Nor was Barbara neglected. A round, peachy child, she did not have her mother's petite bones but the face was lively and pretty and her green eyes were already her most striking feature. Self-contained, she was happy to be alone living in her own fantasy world of make believe.

Though 'park gates' were in the far distance Polly was determined that Barbara should make the right friends, and even if money was short she always had a pretty party dress. Appearances had to be kept up so when Barbara went to a party her mother hired an ancient cab, mildewed with age, from the local hotel. Together, wrapped in rugs with their feet on foot warmers, they would set out for the party. Barbara recalls these outings well: 'My hair was straight and lank, and so it had to be done up in innumerable rags until we turned into the lodge gates of our destination, when my Mother would pull out all the rags and comb my hair into sausage curls over her finger.'

On the surface life was 'wonderful' but beneath it there was the constant worry about money, and, plan as Polly and Bertie might, there was an endless struggle to keep their heads above water. Purely because of Polly's popularity the local tradespeople were thoughtful and patient in collecting their accounts. Much of the £800 they had owed on James Cartland's death was still unpaid, a constant anguish to Polly's pride. In addition, Bertie was not well and his sparks of jealousy became more frequent. By now Polly was pregnant again and in desperation about how they were going to manage financially Bertie went to the Birmingham races and splurged £300 on a horse in a reckless bet. It lost! To meet what she felt was a debt of honour Polly sold her precious set of turquoise and diamond jewellery and Bertie sold his expensive Purdie guns.

The reaction of the Scobell family when they heard the news was understandable. Colonel Scobell's fury was like a tornado. He raged and raved until Polly could stand it no longer, and for the first time her strength deserted her. She went to her room, flung herself on her bed and wept. And wept. There were even grave worries that she might have a miscarriage.

It was a miserable Christmas with Polly ill and Bertie frantic at the bills which continued to pour relentlessly in. Even the patient tradespeople were restive. Polly had never felt so miserable during her whole life - even the thought of her baby, now due, could not console her. On 3 January 1907, three weeks early, Polly gave birth to a whopping big son. Bertie was so elated that he took to his bed with a heart attack, and it was left to Polly to keep the household together.

Through all her prayers Polly had hoped for a miracle, and now it came in the shape of Uncle George Cartland, a younger brother of James, who had been called to the Bar in 1879 and practised on the Midland circuit. Hearing of their plight he visited them and immediately took charge of their finances. He not only settled all the outstanding bills and writs but also put their personal expenses in order by strictly supervising their allowance. He was just, but firm, and there was not a penny over for frivolities. To be able to hold her head proudly again was the best tonic Polly could have and in her beguiling way she wrote in her diary three weeks after the birth of her son: 'Went to the Ball in the evening and enjoyed it awfully. Wore my blue dress. Everyone seemed pleased to see me. Danced quite a lot until 2 a.m. Bertie very sweet.'

Among the hundreds of letters and years of diaries that Mrs Polly Cartland left to Barbara is this tender letter from Bertie who loved her with all his heart. Polly had gone to stay with her parents a few days after the ball to recover from all the stress she had undergone over the last few weeks.

My own Wife,

Just back and so pleased to find your sweet note waiting for me. Darling whatever I do, or don't do, remember that you are and always have been the only thing in the world I love.

. . . Everyone says there was no one to touch you at the Hunt Ball. Lady Dudley picked you out as being the smartest and prettiest woman in the room. Charlie Coventry [The Hon. Charles Coventry] amongst others came and told me there was no one to touch you and that everyone said so.

Yours Bertie

4

My Mother's pride and high standards kept her going,
and the invincible courage she showed all through her
difficult and tragic life.

Barbara Cartland

'Mummy, do let's send back the new baby. Everyone asks after him and no one after me', was Barbara's reaction to the arrival of her brother Ronald. It was natural enough when one considers that until then she had been the centre of attention and now everyone, and especially Bertie, was elated with the birth of a much wanted heir. Bertie's health, exacerbated by money worries, had not been good in the previous year and the arrival of a son, whom they called John Ronald Hamilton Cartland, not only boosted his ego but gave him the impetus to do something worthwhile with his life, something that would please not only Colonel Scobell and his own mother, but, most of all, Polly.

Through all their married years Bertie, despite his oftimes selfish ways, was devoted to Polly. Her patience had endured throughout his frailties and now with a second child to support he was inspired to try and find some useful and profitable occupation. The first step he took towards getting himself together was to promise Polly that he would give up all alcohol, as his doctors had been advising for some time, because it was bad for his heart. He was not an alcoholic but, like many gentlemen of the period, he drank too much, and what was considered quite normal for other men to drink was sheer poison for Bertie. Barbara points out that 'It was very unusual and almost unheard of at that time for gentlemen to be teetotal. With whisky at 3s 6d a bottle, gin 3s and champagne 5s 6d drink flowed at every party and in every household.' However, Bertie took to drinking gallons of tea, and thoughtfully wherever he went Polly saw to it that his friends automatically served him tea instead of alcohol. No-one but Polly knew what an effort of will this entailed or how much self-control.

That Bertie was able to achieve this was made possible by the intangible strength that his wife gave him. It was her constant and tender concern that steered this marriage through a difficult period. When I asked Barbara if her mother was bossy in the way she handled Bertie she replied:

Oh, no, no, no. She was terribly feminine but she was an example of the power women can have in their family life without all that nonsense of Women's Lib. Mummy was such fun that we all wanted to be with her. Her energy was astounding and even when she came to stay here at Camfield Place well into her eighties and something was needed from upstairs she would say 'I'll do it . . . I'll do it.' It became a by-word in the family and the boys still jokingly say 'I'll do it . . . I'll do it', just like Mummy did.

There was never a more contented or happier baby than Ronald. Polly attributed much of the change in Bertie as due to his new son and thus Ronald became her unending delight. It was as if he for whom she had been waiting had come to her at last. This special bond between Polly and her son was to last until his death in France in the last war.

I think the real reason I resented Ronald was that my Mother looked at him in a different way from how she looked at me. Her eyes seemed to have a light behind them and her voice was full of love.

I knew then I was not a part of her as I was before, but complete in myself, and I felt alone. Even when people were all round me I felt lonely and it was a strange and rather frightening feeling.

Like many plump little girls Barbara was now losing her front teeth and going through a decidedly plain period. That she was acutely aware of this did not make it any easier to bear. She used to pray every night to God that he would make her prettier. 'I must be pretty. I must be pretty', she constantly pleaded. She still remembers the pain she felt when as a child she overheard one of her mother's friend's cruel remark: 'Poor Mrs Cartland, what will she do when that plain daughter "comes out"? She has good legs so she can always make her walk on her head!' Her hair was lank and hung like two horse's tails down either side of her round serious face. It was not until she began taking vitamins in the 1950s that Barbara Cartland's hair became naturally curly as it is today.

A precocious child, Barbara was fastidious about her clothes and delighted in dressing up. Polly had difficulty in making her wear certain dresses which she hated, but there was no money available to buy different ones. To allay her jealousy Polly did her utmost to make Barbara feel involved with Ronald. Cocktail parties were not yet invented and in upper-class families the hours between tea and dinner were kept sacred for the children.

At 5.00 p.m. to the minute Barbara and Ronald, now changed into a pretty frilly dress and a sailor suit, were brought down by their Nanny to the drawing room, just as Polly and Bertie had been in their childhood. Polly saw no reason why, because they now lived in reduced circumstances, standards should be lowered. But whereas the Scobell children lived in fear of their nightly interrogation Polly arranged all kinds of games for hers. They played tiddly winks, spillikins, snakes and ladders, old maid and some of Polly's own invention. Even Bertie took part, and at the slightest sign of boredom he whisked them off to the piano and in her clear voice Polly led them into singing such favourites as 'You are my honeysuckle, I am the bee'. In his romantic moments Bertie used to call Polly 'Sue' so the current rage, 'Sue, Sue, Sue, I'm very much in love with you', was always a favourite. Bertie, who was intrigued by the new 'motors' that his friends were now buying, although he could not afford one himself, would join in the chorus of the music hall hit 'He would have to get under, get out and get under, to start up his little machine'.

Barbara was a self-possessed child and mature for her years. Though Polly was not much of a reader, being too active to sit for long periods, Bertie had a lot of books in his smoking room. Naturally it contained few novels but there were Dickens, Scott, and stacks of *Punch* magazines which Barbara devoured from the moment she could read. Though these formed a strange choice for a little girl her delight in words and her joy in reading was formed in these early days. Polly encouraged her daughter by reading her fairy stories, and her secret world was peopled with princesses, goblins, fairies and dragons.

Polly Cartland was a veritable squirrel, keeping all her letters, the scrapbooks she made through the years, and personal titbits. Among her memorabilia, which came into Barbara's hands after her mother died, was a book written in astonishingly grown-up handwriting. It was Barbara's very first story, written at the age of five and a half years.

Several universities, including Boston, have approached her with requests to leave her manuscripts to their libraries but as yet she has only parted with a few. I feel it would be a great pity if her most important papers, and especially this first work, should ever leave England. There is something so essentially English about Barbara Cartland, and though her sales in America, where she is a cult figure, are even larger than in England, her virgins and Dukes should remain in the country which bred them.

For a child of five years the story shows maturity and discipline in the use of apt words and crisp sentences, which are among the most noticeable features of her writing today. Here is the story just as it was written seventy-six years ago:

The Little Slide Maker
by Barbara Cartland

Once upon a time there was a little girl and her name was Mary. Now this little girl was very fond of making slides. Her father was the village doctor. One evening he came home late. Mr Joe Carter stepped into the slide. Poor old man. He said I hope no slide will be made down Winter Hill or it will be a bad look out for old Betsy Gray.

Then Mary felt very unhappy for it was just down Winter Hill that she had made all her slides. That evening when she had been put to bed she got up and got a spade. When she got to the hill she found that the dirt at the side of the road was quite hard but she found some in the garden at the top of the hill.

The End

When I commented on the maturity of the story Barbara replied: 'Don't you see, it all proves reincarnation. I was being guided in what I was writing and it comes out even in a very young child.'

If Barbara showed signs of naughtiness, it was really her sense of play acting and search for adventure. Polly had always forbidden her children to go outside the gate and walk up the road. One day Barbara not only defied her mother's rule but went out wearing Polly's five diamond engagement ring on her finger. Luckily no one noticed! Though never a tom-boy in the strict sense of the word Barbara courted adventure, any new experience, just as she does today. This often brought her into disrepute with Polly who used to punish her by sending her to bed for the afternoon.

Only once was Bertie driven to spanking both Barbara and Ronald. It was Ronald's birthday and Barbara had been forbidden to go into his room and talk to him before they were called. She not only disobeyed but together they tried to light the gas and in doing so Ronald fell into the round tin bath which had not yet been emptied. After the beating Polly was so furious that she threw Ronald's birthday present, a copy of the Bible, on his bed saying, 'Here is your present', and slammed the door. Barbara was packed off to bed 'until you learn how to behave'.

In 1911 Bertie was made Provisional Secretary of the Primrose League for five counties. (The League was a Conservative political club founded in the nineteenth century adopting the name of Disraeli's favourite flower.) The prestige was enormous and though the salary was only £100 a year there were expenses. For Polly, who had been so patient, it meant the vindication of the years of trust that she had invested in her husband, and

41

for Bertie it meant a new lease of life.

On his bicycle he visited the surrounding villages, organized and attended meetings and to everyone's surprise, including his own, he turned out to be an extremely competent, hard-working organizer and an eloquent public speaker. Politics seemed to fill the home from morning until evening and the young Ronald was soon obsessed with his ambition to be a Member of Parliament.

The first school that Barbara went to was the Worcester High School. Every morning a dog-cart arrived at Amerie Court containing Betty and Alice, the daughters of Lord and Lady Cavendish-Bentinck. He was the brother of the Duke of Portland and lived at Burlington House nearby. From there the three little girls went with their governess by train to Snow Hill Station. Barbara does not remember what the governess did all day but she was there to pick up her three charges when school was over. They went back by train to Defford Station and after that to Burlington House. Later in the evening either Bertie or Cecil Lushington, a charming young man they called Lud who boarded nearby while he was learning fruit farming, picked her up. He, of course, fell madly in love with Polly and would do anything to please her. Barbara would climb on to the back of her father's or Lud's bicycle for the three mile journey home.

> I used to pray for rain which meant I could stay at Burlington which I loved. Lord Charles and his wife were, and still are, my ideal of what real aristocrats should be. Lord Charles was tall, handsome, dashing and a magnificent rider. Lady Charles was beautiful, dignified, gentle and sweet. She is in dozens of my books and I longed to grow up and be just like her.
>
> Burlington is also in my books. Already by then I had a fascination for the large country houses where I went to parties. It was at Burlington that I saw my first ghost. It was in the garden and I watched it from under the table in the schoolroom when playing hide and seek. The ghost was white, ethereal and very lovely. It moved from the darkness of the trees across the lawn. Years later I heard that Burlington House is reputed to be haunted.

This interest in the supernatural has remained with Barbara all her life and began her preoccupation with the whole mystical experience of the life cycle.

Life at Amerie Court was always busy and varied now that Bertie was involved with politics. There was a constant flow of important speakers from London whom Polly invited to stay with them. She insisted on her children meeting all the guests, with the result that they grew up totally at ease in company. Barbara is not a snob in the accepted sense of the word - 'give me an interesting dustman rather than a boring Duke' - but she has absolutely no nerves when meeting people or appearing on television or making a speech. She has a fluency and grace of manner that was nurtured right back in those early days at Pershore.

When Barbara was eleven Lord Charles Cavendish-Bentinck left Burlington House with his family. As there was no way of getting her to school in Worcester without the dog-cart and the governess, Polly decided she should go instead to the Junior House of Malvern College for Girls. Barbara was not happy there: 'I hated it at first', she says. 'The older girls snubbed me because they thought I was "uppish", which was actually because I had always been with grown-ups, or the very sweet, gentle, ladylike Betty and Alice [Cavendish-Bentinck].'

It was in fact the first time in her life that Barbara had come into contact with the world outside her small sheltered one where ladies behaved like ladies, and men were always gentlemen. It was also a sharp awakening from the secret world of fairies and goblins where she felt most at home. She already believed in her thoughts and imagination in what the Greeks called the knowledge of 'I am I', and she was, to begin with, completely baffled by her obstreperous, noisy class-mates.

In April 1914 the Duchess of Abercom, President of the Womens' Unionist Association, asked the head of the Primrose League to find someone who could organize all the arrangements for bringing over the ten thousand women and children who were being evacuated from Ulster because of the civil unrest over the Home Rule Bill. Bertie was invited to London for an interview and secured the job at a princely £40 a month. This meant that together with the £300 income they already had, and the extra £300 a year that had been left them by Mrs Cartland when she died, for the first time in their marriage finances were looking better.

The new job meant a move to London, and as usual it was Polly, filled with excitement, who went up to find a house for the family. She found a flat at Queen's Gate in Kensington, and the whole family moved to London. She was pregnant and expecting her third child in September. For Polly those first few weeks were intoxicating as she took the children to the Zoo, met old friends she had not seen for years, visited Ranelagh to watch the polo and coped with Bertie and his exciting new life. It was a sweltering hot summer but her energy was inexhaustible, until after one desperately tiring day at the Eton and Harrow match at Lord's Cricket Ground when she could not get a taxi home, her baby was born prematurely during the night - a still-born girl.

War with the Kaiser's Germany seemed inevitable. In the words of Britain's Foreign Secretary at the time, Sir Edward Grey, 'The lamps are going out all over Europe. We shall not see them lit again in our lifetime.' Soon, with war imminent, Bertie was called up and he proceeded to Worcester Barracks while Polly immediately volunteered to do war work in various ways. Bertie was transferred from the Worcester Barracks to Plymouth. Close friend Sybil Monsell, wife of the Member of Parliament for South Worcestershire, who was later to play a most important role in Barbara's life, sent a car so that he could rush over to say goodbye to Polly, now back at Amerie Court.

Though Bertie would be just a few hours' distance away, mentally the gap was as wide as if he had been going to the trenches in Flanders. That night he wrote to his wife this tender love letter which I found in a box at Camfield Place, nestling amid all the other Bertie letters now yellowing with time. I quote it as a measure of his evergreen love for Polly.

My Darling,

Just a line before post. I loved seeing you, my dearest. There has never been anyone in the world for me but you and you alone can do everything for me. Sybil is a brick, but I couldn't thank her. I felt so miserable when I left. Take care of yourself. Darling I love you. God bless you.

Your own Bertie

As a special treat in the summer holidays before they left London Bertie took Barbara to see the American actresses Shirley Kellogg and Ethel Levy in *Hello Ragtime* at the Hippodrome. It was the first time Barbara had seen chorus girls in figure-moulding dresses that flared out into frills below the knees. These showtime dresses were in fact to herald the coming of the hobble skirt for ladies of fashion. Barbara sat very quietly throughout the performance as the showgirls kicked their way across the stage, but there was not a detail that escaped her saucer-wide eyes.

Polly found her return to Amerie depressing partly because of her own ill health and because of the void in her life without her husband. A third child called Anthony ('Tony'), born in 1912, now filled the nursery and Polly had to face the crisis that the children's nanny was going to have an illegitimate baby and wanted to leave at once. Though Polly dearly loved her children it was not part of her scheme of living to be involved in the daily bathing and feeding routine. Her quicksilver personality wanted to be free to do whatever new interest attracted that powerhouse of energy within her tiny frame. In this respect Barbara was to become exactly like her mother when she had her own family years later.

Tony's arrival had not been so hurtful to Barbara as when Ronald was born. She had adapted to sharing Polly and had even begun to take an interest in Ronald who was now an active and engaging little boy. She feels she might have felt differently about the baby girl Polly lost in a miscarriage, had she lived - this would have posed a real conflict within Barbara. 'I wouldn't have liked a sister, would I?' Though many of her readers are women Barbara Cartland never has liked, nor ever will like, women in general. She prefers to be in the company of men, though to her special women friends she is caring and considerate and her generosity and loyalty are unquestionable.

Once a new nurse was engaged Polly immediately set off for Plymouth where Bertie was stationed under canvas at Fort Tregantle. It was the first time in their years together that they had been apart for any length of time, and for Polly the ordeal was tormenting. She had lost not only her husband, lover, friend and confidant but her surrogate child, since it was Polly's motivation and protection that had been the resolute influence in Bertie's life since they married. Now she had to share him with the Army.

Polly installed herself in a nearby hotel and sat and waited for the cold light of dawn when Bertie would creep back to her for a few hours together. The excitement of war was intoxicating without, as yet, the horror. Young wives travelled like camp followers to be near their husbands right up to the day of embarkation.

I don't remember any special farewell with my Father, but of course, he was the first man in my life, and even if we were not as close as I was with my Mother, I adored him.

When he came home he wanted to be alone with Mummy and for her to centre her entire attention on him. He used to say to her, 'Forget the children. I want you to myself!' I suppose I instinctively felt this in the way that children do.

Once again Polly's talent for collecting true friends was to bring rewards for the family. This time Wilfred Ashley, the widowed son-in-law of Sir Ernest Cassel, the eminent financier and friend of King Edward VII, suggested that they might like to stay at his Hampshire home, Broadlands, for Bertie's last leave. Wilfred had recently been remarried to another friend, the Hon. Mrs Lionel Forbes Sempill, and they had come to Amerie Court while on their honeymoon. Their transportation, to the delight of Barbara and Ronald, was a large open car. Polly and Bertie naturally accepted their invitation, for what more romantic way to spend these last days before embarkation?

Broadlands had originally belonged to the Prime Minister, Lord Palmerston, before he left it to his secretary, whose descendant was Wilfred Ashley. Today the house is known as the home of the late Earl Mountbatten, for through Wilfred Ashley's daughter Edwina, who became the Earl's wife, it passed to the Mountbatten family. In its magnificent setting at Romsey, Broadlands is one of the most romantic houses in England. Not only did the Queen and Prince Philip begin their honeymoon there but the tradition passed to the Prince and Princess of Wales.

Destiny, luck - call it what you will - has always played a role in Barbara Cartland's life. Like glowing threads of silk in a tapestry, the Ashleys and Cartlands would be woven together for years to come. After one day's shooting, when they bagged eighty-five brace of partridge, Bertie had to go back to camp for a few days. On the Sunday morning Polly took the two young Ashley girls to church - blue-eyed Edwina, already showing promise of the beauty that was to come, and Mary, a shy wistful child with red hair.

Eventually Mr and Mrs Ashley were called to London leaving Bertie and Polly to spend the remainder of his leave alone together. By day they wandered in the beautiful grounds with their massive trees and elegant lawns. They talked and caressed the nights away in the capacious bed that was later used by the Royal honeymooners.

There was so much to say and so little time. Not even Barbara, still away at school, or the boys with their Nanny, could intrude in these last poignant days. Days to fill Polly's whole heart in the bleak years ahead.

5

We are created with eyes to see and ears to hear, but we limit our vision and dull our hearing because we forget we were also given a sixth sense. It is called intuition and it is that which transforms the commonplace and the mundane into the esoteric.

Barbara Cartland

After she left Malvern College Barbara began to show signs of blooming into an exceptionally pretty young woman. The legs were stretching out, hair tamed and the puppy fat had melted from her face. Her green eyes, which were later described as 'Barbara's headlights', dominated her face.

It was not uncommon in those days for genteel families who could not afford a governess exclusively for their own children to invite the children of their friends to share the governess and apportion expenses. Polly now arranged that Barbara would stay with a family in Bath. This proved to be a failure. Barbara at that delicate age of thirteen - part child, part woman - may have been over-sensitive or perhaps her ego was misunderstood. She felt a misfit, and the girl she companioned was a year older than she was and something of a bully.

> The truth is that I simply hated going away from home. It is always the children who are unhappy in their family life who go back to school without any fuss. Children who adore their parents are the ones who shed floods of tears at the thought of being separated. I adored my home and couldn't bear the thought of leaving Mummy.

Polly was an 'Anglo-Catholic' and brought up her children to share her High Church beliefs. Barbara was deeply concerned with her faith at this time, and when she said her prayers she placed a crucifix in front of her between two tiny candles. One has a curious picture of this serious young girl in her nightgown bothering to set up her own altar all alone in her bedroom. On such an occasion one night she had her first really spiritual experience when she received a visitation from an angel. As she wrote at the time:

> I have seen an angel! I was in my bedroom thinking of my mother and praying, when on the wall in front of me I saw the huge outline of an angel. His head nearly touched the ceiling and his feet were only a few inches off the floor. He was outlined in light like a line drawing and only his wings had any substance. He did not move and his face which was very beautiful was turned sideways. I knelt looking at him in amazement for perhaps sixty seconds then slowly he faded.

The experience was so vivid that it has always remained with her. Barbara told me:

> I can see the angel just as clearly today. He was a very masculine looking angel and it wasn't until many years later that I realised when I visited the Sistine Chapel in Rome that my angel was like a drawing by Michelangelo. I had never heard of Michelangelo at that time, as I was

so badly educated, but it was exactly like one of his angels. I have never seen an angel since but I don't really need to as that angel will always be with me.

Barbara did not tell the family she was living with about her vision. She was astute enough to know that it would have sounded all too strange related over the roast beef and Yorkshire pudding at Sunday lunch. But she did tell Polly, to whom she confided everything. Polly accepted the account as a proof of her own religious beliefs and she was not surprised.

Barbara had been prepared for confirmation by a saintly young parson with whom Polly had been friendly when he was at Tewkesbury Abbey. Barbara went to stay with his family in Winchester for three weeks and her lessons took place in the beautiful ancient cathedral. The Reverend Allan awoke in Barbara spiritual feelings and high ideals she had never known before. When she was confirmed she dedicated her life to helping people to find God.

It was when Barbara went to Somerset to stay with another family at Nailsea Court that she had further esoteric experiences which she accepted perfectly calmly as they only confirmed in her mind that she was part of a whole mystical life force.

With Bertie away at the Front, Polly had given up Amerie Court and was living with her mother and knew that there was no convenient way for Barbara to be educated. Polly had heard of a widower, Commander Evans, who had retired from the Navy, and who had three daughters, the youngest called Primrose. She was the same age as Barbara and lonely, living at home with only a governess.

Nailsea Court was a lovely, large sixteenth-century house, creepy with ghosts. The house has been used with different backgrounds in dozens of Barbara Cartland novels including *No Heart is Free* and several other of her earlier ones and two of her more recent - *A Gentleman in Love* and *Shaft of Sunlight*. The house was filled with oak panelling and furniture that had belonged in the seventeenth century to Judge Jeffreys, 'the hanging Judge', as he was called. All the serenity and mellowness that one associates with old houses was shattered by his cruel presence. Several of the lavatories were the old-fashioned sandpit variety which were emptied by the gardeners. They were a favourite place for the cats to have their kittens, and before use the girls always had to check to see that a small family was not ensconced down below.

Early on Sunday mornings Barbara used to bicycle about a mile and a half to the very ancient church to take Holy Communion. Having just been confirmed she was swept into a religious ecstacy by the mysticism of this holy ritual. It was as if she became part of all those of the past who had worshipped in the church. As she was to write at the time:

> When I kneel in an ancient pew I know that all round me there is the living, breathing faith of those who have prayed as I am praying. I can feel the vibrations they have left behind and which live on even as they are still part of life which cannot die.
>
> It is strange, eerie yet fascinating, and although there are other churches I could attend, I go back Sunday after Sunday to the one where those who lived in the haunted house worshipped for centuries.

Next door to the church was a beautiful manor house built in the time of Charles II but which now stood empty with its windows boarded up because it was haunted. Barbara had a compelling desire to get into the house but was never able to. However, it featured in *Cupid Rides Pillion*, a dramatic story of the Restoration. At Nailsea Court, though she loved being there, she was constantly aware of other spirits who inhabited the house. 'I always felt', she says, 'that there was someone going upstairs ahead of me or behind me.'

> One night as I lay in bed I heard footsteps dragging their way upstairs and my heart began thumping with terror. After some time I heard a strange tick-tick like that of a clock.
>
> Instinctively I began to say a prayer that Mummy had taught us and to this day whenever I am in a house haunted by some tormented soul I always repeat it. 'Lighten our darkness we beseech Thee O Lord, and by thy great mercy defend us from all perils and dangers of the night. . . .'
>
> As I lay there terrified with my head under the sheet I heard the footsteps outside my door. It was not until some time later that I was told that a Cavalier who had been wounded by the Roundheads in the Civil War had come back to the house and crawled upstairs to die in the room where I was sleeping. I had slipped back in time and picked up the vibrations of over three hundred years ago. When the tick-tick stopped suddenly the Cavalier must have died and his heart was silent.

It was years later that Barbara, remembering her esoteric experiences at Nailsea Court, wrote this poem:

Ghosts

I heard your footsteps coming up the stairs,
Or were you moving just ahead?

I keep wondering who you are and where
You lie unknown.

I hear you move across the room and sigh,
I hear you close the door and wonder why.
What do you regret? I half suspect
You hate to be alone.

Whisper your secret, let me share your crime,
Or are you seeking someone all the time
You love, and whom you cannot find
In body, soul or mind?

Can empty arms, an aching heart,
Survive the grave, and must we part
With flesh, to suffer still more pain
'Til we return and live again?

While staying at Nailsea Court Barbara was nearly killed by a bullet from a revolver. A jolly Major came to stay while on leave, and taken, one suspects, by her pretty vivacity, he invited her to go to his bedroom, which was next to the Billiard Room. He told her he would show her how his revolver worked. The Major demonstrated how a soldier releases the chamber which contains five bullets, and after remarking 'Now it is empty', he jokingly pointed it at Barbara and pulled the trigger. Out shot a sixth bullet which whizzed a fraction of an inch past her temple, so close that it actually scorched her hair which she wore puffed out at the sides and tied back with a bow. Here are Barbara's own words:

I went when he invited me because I was so innocent and he seemed very old. Had he asked me to his bedroom upstairs naturally I wouldn't have gone but the Billiard Room seemed perfectly acceptable to me. I have never seen a man go so green when he saw what a close shave it had been and he begged me not to tell anybody.

He then tipped the estate carpenter to patch up the wall where the bullet had lodged. Just a fraction more and I would have been dead. As it was I was deaf in one ear for forty-eight hours.

At Nailsea Court Barbara began riding, hoping to be as good as Polly. But as all the good horses in the area had been commandeered for the war the girls were left with old nags. The horse Barbara rode was inclined to rush at a brick wall, then stop dead so she fell over its head, and there was another horse which always tried to bite the leg of anyone who rode it.

Once or twice a week Barbara wrote to Polly and to Bertie in France. They were letters filled with chat and illustrated with her own amusing drawings. To Polly she wrote:

> You can't think how I miss you dear one, especially our lovely, lovely talks in the evening when I had you all to myself. I loved those talks, they helped me more than you can imagine. I long for someone to run to here. And I know it's very selfish but I do love to have you all to myself without any of the family wanting you too . . . I would give the world to be with you - the best of love to the sweetest, dearest, prettiest, angelist, rippingist, adorable Mother anyone ever had.

After two years at Nailsea Court Barbara's friend Primrose went to a boarding school, and Polly sent Barbara to a finishing school, Netley Abbey on Southampton Water. She seemed very happy and able to adjust as she wrote to Polly:

> I am happy here and like it as much as I could like any place away from home and you, darling Mummy. We have long talks with Miss Downie [the headmistress] about everything under the sun and she's not a bit like a school-mistress. We even mentioned divorce the other day!!! Fancy any other school mistress doing that. But she is so nice at explaining and telling us what we ought to be like when we grow up that I ought to be quite a 'perfect' woman some day.

The spiritual experiences continued: on one occasion when Barbara had sneaked a look at the headmistress's *Times* to get a glimpse of the list of casualties, which was strictly forbidden to the pupils, she returned to her room in a sad and thoughtful mood. There was not a family in the whole country who had not been touched by death on the battlefield. The whole room smelled of violets - fresh violets. In those days girls did not have toilet water or bath preparations so there was no worldly explanation. It was Barbara's first manifestation of flowers. In later years, when her husband Hugh died, she was to have a similar remarkable experience. It is not surprising that though she was only seventeen she accepted the violet phenomenon as a celestial experience. Even by then she had highly developed psychic powers and was not at all frightened when her own life became entwined with the other world. The spirit world, against a background of religion, had replaced the fantasy world of fairies, nymphs and elves. They were part of the eternal circle of life.

At Netley Abbey a girl called Valerie Taylor, who later became a well known actress, developed a crush on Barbara. Spy scares were in the news and Valerie used to pretend to be a man in disguise and to have got into the school by climbing through the lavatory window as she announced, 'I have arrived.' Remembering back, Barbara thinks that the most extraordinary thing was that 'I half believed she was a man and she was a spy, simply because I wanted to believe it. It was all part of the craving I had for adventure.'

Barbara was also in the school play which was taken to entertain the wounded soldiers at nearby Netley Hospital. The play was set in Japan, and she was given the role of a Prince. She infuriated her teacher by refusing to hold the flag stiffly, as a real Japanese would, and insisted on waving it madly. They call this kind of exhibitionism 'scene stealing' in the legitimate theatre but to Barbara it was just having a good time. Much of Barbara Cartland's exuberance today is misunderstood, for in fact she is behaving exactly as she has always done in the past. She is merely getting the most out of a given situation, being entertaining and having lots of fun.

Despite his age Bertie was a fine soldier, and he distinguished himself as an infantry officer in France. All those frustrated years when he and Polly had been deprived of money, and he was without any real interests to occupy his mind, were now behind him. He had found his *métier* and self-esteem. Despite the discomfort of the mud and rain in the front line at Flanders this was still very much a gentleman's war. Bertie not only wrote every day to Polly, but, as he found it impossible to get his linen washed according to his own fastidious standards, he used to send his laundry home. Polly had it washed and ironed and posted it back to Flanders. Surprisingly the parcels all arrived and nothing was lost in the post.

Bertie, after a month's sick leave, was offered a safe post as Garrison Adjutant at Folkestone, a post many men would have envied, but he preferred to return to France and be with his men. Personal valour, and of course its subsequent reward of medals, was the ambition of every front-line officer and Bertie was no different. He desperately wanted to win a medal to make Polly proud of him and vindicate all those wasted years. If Polly harboured a secret desire that her Bertie would win a V.C. for gallantry she was no different from thousands of other young war wives. The Union Jack stood for honour, justice and glory.

Bertie never won his medal and wrote to Polly somewhat disillusioned, 'One is too old really to be ambitious for mere gauds and baubles, especially when you see how these are dished out.' His finest hour was in May 1917 at the Battle of Messines. As Basil Niblett, the vicar's son at Redmarley, was to write to Polly after Bertie had been killed:

. . . I remember so well when I rejoined the 10th after being away on a course, several officers coming up to me and saying, 'Do you know our new Major? He's simply splendid', and then they told me stories of what he had done in the Battle of Messines.

Many a time his Company and mine held the front line side by side and that's the time when one finds out a man's real worth. Always bright, always brave, he filled us with strength to carry on.

Polly was staying at Walton with Mrs Scobell. It had been a hot, trying day as she had taken Tony into Cheltenham to see a doctor who advised that the child's tonsils must be taken out at once. The two women were having tea when the butler came into the room and handed Polly a telegram. In all wars the telegram is the symbol of bad news. It is the dread of every woman with a man at the Front. Even as she opened it Polly knew what to expect.

WAR OFFICE
DEEPLY REGRET MAJOR J. B. F. CARTLAND WORCESTER REGT., KILLED IN ACTION MAY TWENTY SEVENTH, 1917. ARMY COUNCIL EXPRESS SYMPATHY.
SECRETARY WAR OFFICE

Polly was stunned. She could not believe that her Bertie, the other half of her life, had been extinguished. All the penny-pinching years they had spent together were now forgotten. All Polly could think of were the glorious plans they had made for Bertie to stand as a Member of Parliament. She could already feel the aching loneliness without him in the years that stretched ahead.

Her sadness was punctuated by the reality that alone she was responsible for three children and their future. And now there was no Bertie to turn to when her own unquenchable energy needed support. Ronald and Barbara were away at school and must be told, and Tony was due to be operated on the next day in a nursing home in Cheltenham. Alone in her room Polly wrote to both her children. When Barbara received her letter she did not cry, she showed no sign of grief outwardly but went to her room. Her first thought was to write to Polly to comfort her.

My Ownest Darling,
I can't tell you how I loved your letter. I think you are simply too wonderful . . . No wonder Daddy loved you as he did - and does.
I suppose you couldn't have me home for a few days? But don't bother about me, really it is only that I should so love to see you if it is only for a

moment. If I could only tell you how much I love you, my Darling, it might help a wee bit. You are such a brave Mother that you will make up for all.

You and Daddy were an absolute ideal Mother and Father and you, my angel, were a perfect Wife and a perfect Mother. I feel so awfully proud of him and in a way its lovely to remember him so young and cheery. Do take care of yourself. All my love, my wonderful brave Mummy.

Babs

PS I have had my coat and skirt dyed black. Would you like me to have my coat-frock done?

— 6 —

Love is next to Godliness with certain safeguards.

Barbara Cartland

Ronald, though only eleven years old, wrote his mother this mature letter:

I know I am the eldest son, I must be everything to you, and Pray God I shall never offend he who is dead or you, my darling. I shall soon be with you Angel, and then I hope I shall be able to cheer you up . . . I wish I was at home to help you answer your two hundred letters. Darling, where shall we live now? I being the son who should and will look after you, must know, for you, darling are alone. There is no Daddy to keep us alive. But God will keep us . . . I will be your right hand, my dearest one. All my love, Angel,

I am ever,
Your very loving son,
Ronald

Love to Tony

While Barbara fretted to return home Polly kept her at school until the arrangements for a memorial service at Tewkesbury Abbey on 17 June had been completed. Barbara was to come home from school the day before to be with her mother and two brothers. Just as Polly was getting dressed and preparing herself to go to early Communion before the service a telegram boy arrived at the door. She opened it away from the children so that she could read it in private as telegrams were still regarded as omens of ill will. She read: 'MAJOR J.B.F. CARTLAND, WORCESTER REGIMENT PREVIOUSLY REPORTED KILLED IN ACTION NOW REPORTED MISSING MAY 27TH AND NOT KILLED FURTHER NEWS WHEN RECEIVED.'

Polly's joy was immeasurable. After the children had been told, friends were contacted immediately and the memorial service put off. Like a miniature whirlwind Polly rushed about organizing the family. Her courage never wavered. It was as if the whole household had been recharged with vitality. Hope had replaced despair. Now it was a question of just waiting until the prisoners' reports came through the International Red Cross. Of course Bertie was safe!

It was not in Polly's character to seek the help of professional clairvoyants. She had her own direct line to the Lord and her faith was strong enough to sustain her most of the time. But this was different, and influenced by the thousands of war wives who sought comfort from the thriving fortune-telling industry, she succumbed at a garden fete which was being held at Budleigh Salterton in Devon in aid of the Red Cross. Dressed as a gypsy the fortune teller looked at Polly's palm and murmured: 'I see you are a widow. . .' Only then did Polly's courage waver. She burst into tears and rushed out of the tent and back to where she was staying, where she sobbed her heart out. Nor did it help when General Sir Francis Davies, Military Secretary to the War Office, wrote to her that, as there was no further news, she must prepare herself for the worst.

As if in defiance, with her practical mind she took the children to Exeter and had a family portrait taken so that it would be ready to send to Bertie as soon as she received some news of him. She knew what joy it would give him to see how the children had developed over the last few months.

Of course Ronald, Tony and I were all caught up in Mummy's agony but remember four years is a long time, when you are young, for a father to be away from his children. We had seen very little of him since 1914 except for a few months when we had all been at Seaford together. However dark life had become for Mummy it was filled with the promise of adventure for me. I was young and I wanted to live and dance.

There was also the salient fact that Barbara had been brought up almost entirely by women during this period. The only men she ever met were the husbands of her mother's friends.

On 23 September Polly received a letter from the War Office confirming that Bertie had been killed in the trenches with his men on 27 May, the day on which he had first been reported missing. The enemy assault had been so devastating and concentrated that there were few identifiable bodies and no personal belongings left to send back to relatives. The uncertainty of the last four months began to show on Polly's brave little face as she went about in her 'widow's weeds', wearing a small hat edged with white and a long black widow's veil over her brown hair. The unshed tears of the last months now flowed, and it was only the children that kept her going.

During these tragic weeks Barbara had a vivid dream of her father riding a bicycle down a road and laughing and joking as he always had. He rode off, although she wanted him to stop, but when she woke up she felt sure he was not dead. It was not until Polly visited a well-known clairvoyant some months afterwards that Bertie came through to the medium with this message: 'I went to Babs because I couldn't make Sue understand.' The use of the two pet names convinced Polly of the veracity of the message and even though the content was slender enough, at the time it gave her great comfort.

Polly decided to have a memorial, a Calvary, erected inside the gates of Tewkesbury Abbey. In addition to Bertie's name and regiment was the inscription 'Love's strength standest in love's sacrifice'. After the last war the names of her two sons Ronald and Anthony, both killed in action, were added.

The last years with Bertie had become Polly's inspiration. Now as a one-parent family she was determined to temper her boundless love for her children with the discipline they would need to face the new world that was emerging from the chaos of war. Normal standards had to be kept up, and Polly became more insistent than ever. Despite the fact that dinner might consist of little more than Polly's home-grown vegetables, eggs, or sardines, the children were all made to change for dinner.

Today at weekends, which are kept strictly for her children, grandchildren and friends, everyone at Barbara's home, Camfield Place, is expected to change for dinner. Barbara invariably wears one of her floaty chiffon gowns with elegant jewellery and the men wear dinner jackets. The habit goes right back to Polly's determination to maintain traditional standards right through her life and, still more important, pass them on to her own children.

Even more than monitoring her children's manners Polly took on the immense task of forming their characters for the years ahead. There would be no wasted years as Bertie had had before he showed his full worth. No untrained, unskilled minds. With love and determination she fired her children with ambition. With the will to succeed. Polly believed in the power of goodness and love. This applied especially to her own children, to whom she gave complete devotion and loyalty. She drilled into them that whatever happened to them in life they could always come to her and their home. Whatever the world had to say about her family Polly was behind them like a tigress and her cubs. 'If I had committed a murder I knew Mummy would somehow have got me out of it', says Barbara.

This did not, however, deter Polly from demanding obedience, and if she erred on the side of severity, in such matters as manners and social graces, she carried the responsibility of being both father and mother to her children. Despite her boundless love Polly could bring her children to heel with a sharp retort. To the family's favourite Pollyism, 'Poor I may be, but common I'm not', was now added, 'I work my fingers to the bone - and not a word of thanks.' Both sayings have been handed down through the years in the Cartland family and always bring laughter.

One strict family rule which Barbara Cartland was to apply when bringing up her own children was that all family tiffs had to be sorted out and made up before bedtime. 'Never let the sun go down on your wrath!' was a Polly saying, and the making-up was impulsive, warm and loving. 'I'm sorry darling, terribly sorry! You do love me don't you?'

Even though my sons are nearly middle-aged men now, we never part at night without patching up a quarrel. All families have disagreements, it is only natural, but they should never be allowed to fester into something lasting and ugly.

Mummy lit a flame in all three of us that was to burn brighter year by year. She made us believe in ourselves and our capabilities. She made us see that anything was possible if we really wanted it and worked hard enough. To Mummy there were no heights that her children could not attain.

The worst thing she could say to us was 'You spoil yourself!'

In return Polly's children gave her overwhelming devotion. As Barbara wrote in her last term at school: 'I don't think I shall live three months until the end of term. Its such a waste of time not being with you, darling. Why, why do the holidays have to rush by like an express train?'

When she was eighteen Barbara left school, and Polly took rooms at Bembridge in the Isle of Wight where she had some friends.

It was while previously staying at Exmouth that Barbara had discovered the delights of the public lending library and, ever since, her head had been deep in the novels of Ethel M. Dell, Berta Ruck, C. and M. Williamson and Elinor Glyn, who was considered 'wildly improper'. Ethel M. Dell's influence was to colour Barbara's thoughts for years. She really believed all heroes should be tall silent men, seething with burning passions, but passions so controlled that one was not aware of them until they broke down under an overwhelming love. Good women were soft, sweet, easily frightened yet longing to be dominated by a strong masculine man. Now her own world of romance began to unfold before her eyes! It seemed that God had indeed been listening to her prayers, for she had grown into an extremely pretty young woman with porcelain pink-and-white complexion, compelling green eyes and wonderful gaiety. She was a hit wherever she went.

While Ronald and Tony were perfectly happy to build sandcastles on the beach with a small boy called David Niven, Barbara bathed and sailed, and danced the evenings away. Just nine days after her arrival she had her first proposal. The daring man in question was over forty, which to Barbara's eyes was positively ancient. He was a Colonel with a red handlebar moustache. Barbara was frightened by his approach and rushed to tell her mother all about it and ask for her help. 'You must learn to look after yourself', Polly said.

Another suitor, Sir Hercules Languishe, an elderly married man, was confronted by a furious Polly who told him in no uncertain terms to leave her daughter alone. He was not in the least perturbed by Polly's attack but told her that she was prettier than her daughter anyway and asked her out to dinner! Polly made a rule which Barbara was obliged to keep. She was *never* to go out with a married man. This was because at the back of her astute mind was the Edwardian adage, 'an unmarried man could be made to marry the girl - a married man could hide behind his wife.'

When I asked Barbara if her Army suitor had been bold enough to attempt a kiss she replied: 'Certainly not. We were not mauled in those days. Our innocence protected us. I was quite determined that the only man who would ever be allowed to kiss me on the lips was the one I would marry.'

At Bembridge Barbara had another brush with death. She went out in one of the red winged sailing boats with three young men. One was in love with her but still at Eton. He afterwards became the first English bull-fighter; another was Max Niven whose younger brother David was on the beach with Ronald and Tony; the third was Hugo Baxendale, who had been courting the Nivens' sister Joyce until he met Barbara. He was later to play an important and enduring part in Barbara's life. On this particular day a storm blew up unexpectedly, and the three young men had the greatest difficulty in bringing the yacht into the harbour. At one moment it seemed impossible - but Barbara prayed frantically and her prayers were answered.

Sir Hercules Languishe, despite Polly's instructions, continued to hover in the background at Bembridge. He owned a thirteenth-century castle in County Kilkenny in Ireland and was Commodore of the Royal Yacht Club. Fate was playing its cards again, for eighteen months later Barbara was to become engaged to his son Terence ('Pingo') who had served in France with the Irish Guards.

Now that Barbara was grown up Polly had to find a way to give her new clothes, as everything she owned was outdated. Barbara had inherited her mother's stylish eye for fashion and together they collected a small 'coming out' wardrobe. Polly gave Barbara an allowance of £50 a year to dress herself. Though it was exactly the same amount that Polly herself had been given she felt it was not really sufficient, but it was all that she could allow from her meagre widow's income. Barbara was very fastidious about her clothes and was always careful with her black silk stockings. There were only two colours in those days - black or white. As dresses came to the ankle the part above the calf was made of cotton for the sake of economy.

In 1918 there was still a strong feeling of patriotism in the air and many public schools were giving scholarships to the sons of men killed in action. Polly put both the boys' names down for Charterhouse, Bertie's old school. If, as had been intended, he had gone to Eton Polly would have been able to educate the boys without paying fees. But, unfortunately, Mrs Cartland had thought her precious only son was delicate and sent him instead to Charterhouse. Ronald was accepted when he passed the entrance examination. Tony was still a little too young and continued at his preparatory school at Seaford. Polly had to pay £150 a year each for them, which left her only £300 for everything else. No matter the sacrifice, she was determined that her sons were to be well educated.

Polly was well aware that her small family had now reached a crisis point, and, as Bertie would not be returning, alone she had to face up to a whole new way of living. She was prepared to go anywhere that the children wanted but they had to decide. In her usual practical way she called the children together and asked where they would like to live.

Barbara was the first to answer . . . 'London . . . oh, Mummy, London please.' And when they left Bembridge they moved straight to London into a house Polly had rented furnished in Neville Street, in a part of South Kensington that had seen better days. It was not Mayfair. It was not Belgravia. But it was London and that was all that mattered to Barbara.

The house was a typical three-storied London terraced one, with a dingy basement and high, narrow rooms. After the charm of Amerie Court it took all Polly's ingenuity to make it look like a home, but once again with that special touch of magic she managed to achieve just that. Polly was amazingly skilful in turning any house she occupied into *her* home. She changed the cheap furniture round in rented houses, added some personal bits of her own, filled the vases with flowers and suddenly it all looked right.

While the packing cases still stood around in their first London home, Polly shooed Barbara and Ronald out for a walk after supper in the early evening. Tony had been put to bed and she felt that she could cope with the unpacking better on her own. Brother and sister clasped each other's hands as they wandered round a maze of streets until they saw in the darkness South Kensington Underground Station. Barbara was almost in a trance. This was London. This was her new world. This was the beginning of a great adventure!

Suddenly they stopped short and turning to her brother she asked, 'What do you want to do most of all?'

'I shall be Prime Minister', Ronald replied quietly.

'I shall get to know everybody - everybody in London', Barbara cried excitedly.

7

*Every woman dreams of love. When she is young she
prays she will find it. When she is middle aged she
hopes for it and when she is old she remembers it.*

Barbara Cartland

Through London friends of Polly and Bertie - the Kerr Smileys and the
Eyres Monsells - invitations addressed to 'Miss Cartland and Partner'
began to arrive through the letter box. The only problem was that Barbara
did not know any 'partners' in London. The war casualties had left two
million surplus women, and eligible, virile young men were courted and
cajoled by scheming mamas. London was a female predatory jungle.

Barbara's success at Bembridge had proved to her that men were
attracted by her scrumptious looks, but the difficulty was, how was she
going to get to know any men in London? The dancing fever had hit the
town and Barbara wanted desperately to be part of it. There were *thés
dansants*, dinner-*dansants*, supper-*dansants*, and at country-house
weekends there was dancing round the clock. Dancing schools
mushroomed overnight and new dances like the Charleston, Black Bottom
and Tango were all the rage. It was natural for Barbara to dance well
because, even though she was tall and completely unlike her petite mother,
she was extremely graceful, as she still is. She was also fun, and her face
was always rippling with laughter. In fact she was typical of the
pink-and-white English rose soldiers had dreamed about in the four long
years of war. On their return to England all the young men wanted was to
find a job and settle down. They wanted to sleep in a bed with clean sheets
after the mud and dirt of the trenches. They also wanted to love - to be
loved and married.

Though Polly had strict ideas about Sunday, and the children were
never allowed to play cards on the Sabbath, she struck a bargain with
Barbara. If she would agree to teach in the children's Sunday School at St
Paul's Church in Knightsbridge Polly would allow her to go to the smart
thés dansants that American-born Mrs Maud Kerr Smiley gave every
Sunday afternoon in her large house in Belgrave Square. Four years later
Barbara was to use this house in her first novel, *Jigsaw*.

As a Sunday School teacher Barbara was a huge success. She not only had the biggest class but held them spellbound. The secret was simple - her story-telling. Once she had read the children a set Bible story and answered their questions she quickly switched to her own ideas of 'getting over' what they should know. The conventional creeds were left behind as she continued her own Sunday serial that included good knights on white chargers, maidens in distress, treacherous enemies on black beautiful steeds and wicked fire-eating dragons. Good always prevailed over evil but, with consummate skill, she knew how to crescendo to a 'cliff hanger' that left her pupils agog until the following Sunday. There were no absentees in Barbara's class.

Before the advent of the motor car, when people whooshed off to the country for weekends, it had been the fashion for London Society to gather in Hyde Park at Stanhope Gate and parade there every Sunday morning. This was called the 'Church Parade', and after the war the custom still lingered on. After Sunday School Barbara used to rush off to join her girl friends there and hope that she would meet somebody's brother. With her own brothers still schoolboys, Barbara had to rely on her girl friends for introductions. 'I used to pray and pray', she says, 'that I would see someone who would ask me to lunch at Claridges afterwards, which was the smart thing to do. When they did I would sweep proudly into the restaurant feeling that with my frock-coated escort I was really creating a sensation!'

Although make-up, as we know it today, was still waiting for the magic of Helena Rubinstein and Elizabeth Arden, Barbara began to experiment with her face. From the three shades of rice powder available, chalk white, sulphur yellow, and *café au lait*, she chose the white which made her petal-fine skin almost translucent. There was no eye make-up except for actresses, but with her large, almost iridescent green eyes, Barbara did not need it. Lipstick in bright red was now acceptable, and for the first time all women were able to wear what had in the past been a trade-mark of the harlot. With her fluffed out spun gold hair and striking colouring Barbara had a romantic aura. She was a combination of innocence and desirability. Men were still an unknown and fascinating species to her. She was the prototype of the three-hundred-odd virgins she was to create in her novels during the years to come.

Actually she resembled Edwina Ashley. Many years later Lord Mountbatten was to confirm that Barbara looked like Edwina when he married her in 1922, even if her colouring was different. Though her wardrobe was modest, assisted by Polly, she had chosen well. Her navy-blue serge suit, which came just above her ankles, was trimmed with silk braid and worn with a pretty white blouse and perky hat. For the afternoon she had a loose-waisted black dress which showed off her fair colouring and was worn with a large picture hat. From the best shop in Cheltenham, Mrs Scobell gave Barbara an evening gown which was white trimmed with silver tassels and with silver on the belt. Barbara thought it was absolutely beautiful and it cost the enormous sum of fifteen pounds. Both Polly and Barbara had an eye for bargains and for a few shillings they picked up deliciously pretty hats, for no 'lady' could then be seen anywhere public in London without one.

Barbara was an instant success at the *thés dansants* and quite soon after arriving was introduced to Mrs Kerr Smiley's brother, Ernest Simpson. They made an arresting couple dancing together - she with her pretty fluffiness and he with his Guards Officer finesse, black, patent leather-smooth hair, and square jutting chin. They were both good dancers and experts at twirling round and round the room. Once after Ernest Simpson had escorted her home in a taxi she wrote to Polly, 'Ernest took me home and tried to kiss me. Such cheek!' His sister, however, made sure he was out of bounds, and she told everybody, 'It's no use you girls losing your heart to Ernest - he's got to marry money.'

Ernest Simpson did not marry money, but seventeen years later he was mesmerized by Mrs Wallis Spencer, a divorced siren from Baltimore, Pennsylvania. Some years later, in 1936, she was to pressure him into allowing her a second divorce as she was in love with the King, Edward VIII, and hoped to marry him. This romance was not only to rock the British Constitution but cost a King his crown, the respect of his family and his Empire.

Barbara's path in the coming years was to cross that of Wallis and Ernest Simpson countless times as they threaded their way through the London social scene. Their last meeting was many years later, when Barbara dined with Ernest and a very close friend, the former Princess George Imeretinsky, who had become his fourth wife, at their elegant London house in Phillimore Gardens. Now a successful businessman, the memories of those years of humiliation were behind Ernest. He looked more mature and immensely happy with his new adoring wife. As she left the house that night Barbara whispered in his ear, 'I am so very glad you are happy Ernest, no one deserves it more, no one could have behaved better in the Hell you passed through.' He squeezed her fingers with intensity. 'Thank you Barbara. I suppose in time one will forget.'

In the evenings of the twenties it was only the well-off young men, or those who had returned to their jobs, who could afford to take a girl to dinner and then a night of dancing. Because a girl was not allowed to dine alone with a man it was economically convenient that she should dine at home and then be collected afterwards by her beau for a night's dancing.

The men dined at their clubs, which were at that time the cheapest places to eat in London. All prices were, however, astonishingly low by today's standards - a five-course meal at the *Jardin des Gourmets* for five shillings, five courses at the Trocadero for seven shillings and sixpence, and dancing after dinner at the Berkeley plus a jug of beer or fruit juice was only ten shillings per person. Nevertheless, it was still a strain for many unemployed young ex-soldiers desperately trying to rehabilitate themselves into civilian life.

After an evening of dancing the smart thing to do was to call at the green-painted coffee stand at Hyde Park Corner. There the taxis would pull up like bees round a honey-pot, and the driver would then fetch his fare cups of coffee. The taxi driver would eat and play cards at the stand while his young people sat in the back of his cab whispering 'sweet nothings'. This land-mark of London disappeared during the last war but returned and remained at Hyde Park Corner until well into the 1950s. One wonders how many proposals of marriage were made within its precincts.

I can recall so vividly the musty, leathery smell of the high-roofed taxis; the fragrance of the milky coffee in the thick white cups; the sense of being isolated in a tiny world which contained only a man and me. It was warm, cosy and intimate, and aroused a delicious feeling of anticipation. Would he try to kiss me? Would he propose?

We would talk until the stars went out, the darkness faded. Then regretfully I'd say, 'I must go home', and my young man would fetch the cabman from the green wooden shelter known as the 'Junior Turf Club' where he had been sitting waiting with his colleagues.

It was at this same green coffee stall that Barbara experienced one of the most dramatic moments of her life. She was secretly engaged to Dick Usher, a young officer in the Life Guards. He had declared his love for her in poems and daily love letters to be left on her breakfast tray. With one special delivery of red roses he wrote: 'Good morning darling, I want these roses to see you.'

Dick was no different from thousands of other young men who were all caught up in the romanticism of the early 1920s. Though immaculately mannered, he belonged to that lost generation of young officers who had returned from the war with their nerves frayed and raw. Emotionally they had been completely unprepared for the war in France, where at one period, when the fighting was at its worst, a subaltern's life was rated at twenty minutes, and the ones lucky enough to return were still dazed with horror.

(Above left) *Barbara's enchanting mother, Mary Hamilton (Polly) Scobell, at the time of her engagement in 1899.* (Above right) *Barbara's father, Bertram Cartland. A dashing young man, he first saw Polly at a Hunt Ball and said, 'That's the girl I'm going to marry'.* (Below) *The Down House, Redmarley, the home of Barbara's grandparents. She has used this house in many of her novels*

DOWN HOUSE, REDMARLEY.

(Above) *Amerie Court, Pershore, where Barbara's parents moved after the family's financial crisis. She will always remember the pink and white plum blossom in the orchard in the spring and the scent of wall-flowers.* (Below) *The world's top-selling author, aged eleven months. Even then she loved hats!*

Polly had her family photographed every
year. This striking portrait of her with
Barbara was taken on a visit to Eastbourne

Although she was jealous of her brother
Ronald when he was born, Barbara soon
grew to love him and insisted on taking him
for rides in her make-believe pony chaise

(Above left) *Ronald, aged four, on his pony with Barbara leading him. Perhaps even then he saw himself as a future Prime Minister.* (Above right) *Barbara, Ronald and Anthony pose with Polly in 1916. Barbara, at fifteen, is a typical young 'flapper'.* (Below) *Barbara, front left, surrounded by friends at her third birthday party on 9 July 1904. Hats were all the rage for fashionable little girls that year*

(Above left) *Always quick to snap up a bargain, Barbara bought this hat for two shillings and sixpence and trimmed it with a bunch of provocative red cherries.* (Above right) *Sweet nineteen with four proposals of marriage behind her, Barbara already has that air of innocence that men found irresistible*

Dec 21st 1925.

Fashionably attired, though money was short, Polly and Barbara were pictured in the Tatler *at the stylish London wedding of the Hon. Peggy Coventry to E.B. Hoare, of banking fame*

(Above) *Barbara chose 23 April, St George's Day, for her wedding in 1927. In attendance were three pageboys and eleven bridesmaids. The bridesmaids all wore pink.* (Below) *Barbara and Alexander (Sachie) McCorquodale are piped by the Argyll and Sutherland Highlanders as they leave St Margaret's, Westminster, after their wedding*

(Above) 'The best dressed baby in the park' is how Raine McCorquodale (Countess Spencer) was described in the press. Barbara and her dog, Wogs, share the picture. (Below) Dogs have always been a feature of Barbara's home life. This family snapshot shows Barbara and Sachie in the Orkney Islands where they rented a house soon after their marriage

(Above) *Barbara, second from right, in the White Star liner dress that she designed for the pageant in aid of British industries in 1930. (Below left) As 'champagne' Barbara was a sensation at the Christmas Dinner pageant held at the Kit Kat Club. Her dress was made from a new material called Cellophane. (Below right) Barbara thought this photograph so shocking that for years she dared not show it to anyone*

Barbara had entered into this romance in her usual light-hearted way and wisely Polly had begged her to wait a month until the engagement was announced in *The Times*. She knew that a month was a long time and anything could happen. Barbara had fully intended to take Dick's proposal seriously but she asked Polly something she had never asked before, 'How does one have a baby?' It was a subject that had never been discussed at any of the schools she had attended and she vaguely thought it had something to do with a man kissing a girl's neck. This was because in one novel Barbara had borrowed for twopence from the lending library she had read: 'He kissed her neck passionately and she knew what he meant!' Completely innocent, Barbara was horrified at the truth. When Polly told her, she broke off her engagement and walked about looking at married couples thinking, 'How *could* they do *that!*'

Two nights after she had told Dick she would not marry him, Barbara found herself at the same party with him. Although she would have preferred not to dance with him he insisted and begged her to allow him to take her home. She was quite certain that nothing would make her change her mind, but Barbara felt sorry for Dick and agreed. They took a taxi to the coffee stall at Hyde Park, and the driver brought back two cups of coffee. Just as Barbara was beginning to sip her coffee Dick whipped out his revolver and declared dramatically: 'Unless you marry me I will shoot myself.' Remembering the Major at Nailsea Court, who had fired a bullet through her hair not long before, Barbara tried to keep calm and play for time. They talked until dawn when Dick's nervous tension began to flag, and, showing obvious signs of tiredness, he agreed to take Barbara home. She had promised to give him her answer when she got there.

Although she tried to explain in the taxi that she did not love him, in his desperate state he refused to accept it. It was not until they arrived at Polly's house that Barbara jumped out, opened the front door and said to Dick, 'No I can't marry you', and shut it again quickly. Just as she always did Barbara rushed upstairs to her mother's bedroom and told her all about it. 'You've got to get me out of it, Mummy', were words that Polly had heard before. She soothed Barbara and promised that when Dick called she would see him.

In the sanity of the next morning Dick Usher sat and wrote a long impassioned letter to Mrs Cartland begging her to help him:

You, *even you*, don't know the dull, dull agony, the dark gnawing hopeless life that will be mine if I lose Barbara having once held her love. I've read her letter, I've thought of every word she ever said, and then it all comes back again, the blank soulless life that's before me.

If only I wasn't cursed with such a big, big love it might be easier, but you know that I just worship Barbara with my whole heart and soul and body and that to lose her is worse than a million times the torture of the damned. . . .

However, due to Polly's skilful handling of this love-lorn young man he passed out of Barbara's life.

Thirteen years later Dick Usher did shoot himself. He had been married in Kenya, where he had settled, and was piloting his own aeroplane to South Africa for the honeymoon. The machine got into a bad spin and crashed, killing the bride. Dick was found dead among the wreckage, a revolver in his hand. He left a note saying: 'I have killed my darling and I no longer wish to live.'

As the beaux queued up, and they did, Barbara had her own system of rating them - four-star meant a dinner and dancing, three-star was a luncheon date, two-star tea, preferably at the Ritz, and one-star was delighted to be allowed to drive her in his car to have a meal with someone else! Life was a bubble and she never wanted harsh reality to intrude. She was, and still is, incurably romantic.

In August of 1919 Barbara went back to Bembridge on the Isle of Wight with friends. The London scene had placed its own touch of magic on her. Though still beguilingly innocent she had brushed with sophistication and it had left its mark. She was even more desirable to the young men who flocked there every summer.

Among the most attractive of the young men was the twenty-five-year-old Terence Languishe, who had served in France with the Irish Guards. He was the son of Sir Hercules Languishe, of County Kilkenny, who had pursued Barbara Lolita-fashion the year before until Polly had put her foot down. 'Pingo', as everyone called Terence, was charming, impetuous and penniless. Barbara and Pingo's courtship was fleeting, but she was swept away by his persuasive Irish charm, as she told me:

There was a fancy dress ball, and as I could not afford to spend any money on anything elaborate I obtained some black-out material which had been used in the war to hide the lights, and made myself a short, full dress. With it I had a red sash and wore a red handkerchief on my head so that I looked like a pirate.

Six young men, who were all my admirers, wore black outfits too, which must have been infuriating for all the other girls at the dance. One of the men, a charming, delightful Irishman who was six years older than I was, took me out onto the beach. The moon was rising over the sea and the waves were lapping on the shore. The band behind us was playing 'Everything is Peaches Down in Georgia'. It was so romantic that it was impossible to say anything but 'yes' when he asked me to marry him.

One of Pingo's daily letters which lies alongside a bunch of others at Camfield Place today just said, 'I LOVE YOU, I LOVE YOU' for five long pages.

When Polly met Pingo, she too was captivated by his charm but she was worried about him having no money. Although there was Knocktopher Abbey, the family castle in Ireland which he would one day inherit with the title, Sir Hercules was very much alive, so what were these two young people going to live on in the meantime? Polly told Pingo that he must get a job, and Lady Languishe too was of the same opinion. As she wrote to her: 'Alas, people cannot live on love, and I am, I admit, frightened for their future.' The only thing Pingo could find to do in a world where a million men were seeking employment was to join the Secret Police Force in Ireland. Very dangerous, and it meant leaving Barbara, but it would bring him in £600 a year. Pingo left for Ireland and the engagement was announced in *The Times*. Barbara wrote to Pingo every day, as he wrote to her.

On 21 November - 'Bloody Sunday' - ten officers and four other ranks serving with the Special Force were murdered in their beds. Among them was Pingo's best friend Peter Ames, a former member of the Brigade of Guards, who had just become engaged to Lady Millicent Orr-Ewing, niece of the Duke of Roxburghe. Millicent was also a very great friend of Barbara. She was very beautiful and had turned many heads during the short time since she had made her début, but she had fallen head-over-heels in love with Peter Ames. Barbara remembered one night in London going home from a dance and seeing them as the dawn broke, sitting on the doorstep of Millicent's house in Hill Street, because they could not bear to leave each other.

On 21 November Barbara received a telegram from Pingo saying 'Peter killed this morning, tell Millicent.' Barbara was shattered: 'I immediately went over to Millicent's house in Hill Street and found her at the top of the house in her own little sitting room. I just walked in, sat down beside her and said, "Darling, it's too awful but Peter is dead." ' The two girls sat stunned. It was their first personal brush with terrorism - so terrible in its ugly, senseless brutality. After a little while Millicent dissolved into tears but Barbara, as always throughout her life when she received a shock, sat tearless. She just felt numb as if the world had receded from her and she was living in a kind of vacuum. On these occasions, and there were many of them to come, she carried on exactly as usual until finally, sometimes a long time after it had happened, the tears came and she felt the whole agony of what had occurred.

Peter Ames' body was brought back to England and a requiem was sung for him in Westminster Cathedral. Polly and Barbara went to the service and saw the unusually long coffin - 'he was one of the tall Ames' - draped with a Union Jack and flanked with soldiers with inverted arms. The impression on Barbara was traumatic and she became unusually silent as she left the Cathedral and walked with Polly through the damp London streets to catch a bus.

At last she spoke: 'I can't marry Pingo Mummy - I hate violence! I hate Ireland! Get me out of it. Get me out of it - please.'

Once more Polly was left to cope. Because of her own ability to win men's hearts, she understood more than some mothers would have. She promised to sort it out with Pingo. When Pingo received Barbara's letter saying she could not marry him he wired her dramatically: 'Retract your decision immediately or I will go out and get shot.' He asked for compassionate leave and rushed to London but Barbara refused to see him.

It was not that she was heartless in breaking off the engagement and refusing to talk to Pingo about it - it was just the horror of what had happened, which seemed to express all she had felt during the war. It must have been the same for many girls of her age in their sensitive, tender years, knowing that they were losing every man they knew. The reports from Flanders had been horrifying when they spoke of the slaughter and the agonizing condition of the wounded. Barbara had lost not only her father in the war, but her two uncles - the Hon. Alfred Maitland, son of the Earl of Lauderdale, and Captain Fritz Nixon-Echersall. Also Lud (Cecil Lushington), whom she had known and loved as a child, had been killed, and so had the first young man, a midshipman who died in the Battle of Zetland, who, when she was at Nailsea Court, asked to kiss her. On top of all this, every house in Worcestershire, where she had been taken to parties by Polly ever since she could walk, had a son who had never returned from Flanders.

This all culminated in her feeling that to have a husband in danger from the violence in Ireland was something she could not face. She might be left, as Polly was, crushed, broken and alone. 'I can't see Pingo, Mummy', she said over and over again. 'I cannot speak to him.' What she was really frightened of was that he would persuade her to marry him whatever the consequences.

Dear, patient, sympathetic Polly by now had plenty of experience in handling Barbara's distraught 'fiancés' but Pingo was different. Perhaps because he was older, and with his romantic Irish background, he took the breaking of the engagement worse than any of the previous men. In desperation he asked if he could write to Mrs Cartland to which she agreed. It was the only link he had to Barbara and he was terrified of losing it. 'She loves me really, I know she does; and I'll make her happy. I promise you I will Mrs Cartland, if only you'll persuade her to marry me', he pleaded in a letter. But Polly could not do this. Secretly she was relieved for she had nurtured doubts all along about this engagement.

The wedding presents, and there were quite a lot of them, were all returned but even Polly's patience was giving out, and after Pingo had left again for Ireland she said firmly to Barbara, 'No more engagements until you are absolutely sure of your own mind and then you must marry him.'

'At that moment', Barbara says, 'I had no wish to be married to anyone. I did not want to love anybody and be hurt as Millicent had been. I just wanted, like the rest of England, to dance, to forget wars, death and tears and misery. I wanted to make my marriage, when it did happen, a success, but I was frightened now of any deep emotion. The war had left scars that would never heal!'

Even today she finds it impossible to read books on the war or to watch the films on television. It actually still hurts her to think of what she felt all those years ago which she hid under a façade of 'it doesn't matter' and about which she would not let anyone talk to her.

8

Love is tempestuous, unpredictable and inescapable.
Who can resist love?

Barbara Cartland

Because Polly was worried, not only about Pingo but also money, she suggested that Barbara might find something 'to do'. It was an optimistic daydream, because a Society girl in those days did nothing but hope that she would be asked to parties, which meant the opportunity to dance. To dance in the arms of a good-looking young man was tantamount to being in heaven!

An artist who had come to Nailsea Court had told Barbara that she had a capacity for art and ought to take lessons, but these never materialized. However, the Christmas after she left school Barbara had earned some pocket money by drawing menu cards for her mother's friends. They were pretty dancing ladies cut out in cardboard with real tulle skirts and they were a great success. Barbara made £12 in this her first business enterprise. The menu cards were so good that a superior gift shop in the Burlington Arcade offered to take as many as she could make, and for a short while she decided to be an artist.

In 1980, when she told this story on the Mike Wallace *60-Minute Show* in America, it started her, at the age of seventy-nine, on a career as a designer of wallpapers with Kirk-Brummel, the biggest decorating firm in the country. For these designs, which were called 'Decorating with Love', she received the following year the accolade of 'The Achiever of the Year' from the National Home Fashion Association in the U.S.A. She and her son Ian went out to Colorado Springs to receive it and everyone present wore 'Cartland Pink'.

By 1920 Polly had moved into the very heart of Belgravia and rented a little house in Eaton Terrace, in which the furniture from Amerie Court filled the rooms. But just as she did every year she had also rented a house in the country for the holidays. She felt strongly that London was no place for two energetic boys. Polly always chose to be as near as possible to Tewkesbury so that she could see her own mother and this year she found a pretty house with a garden at three and a quarter guineas a week at Bredon in Gloucestershire. Barbara was not pleased at this. It meant being away from London, and although there were many of her childhood friends in the vicinity there was not much dancing - only a few paper chases, tennis parties and gymkhanas.

Although he was still at Charterhouse Ronald had matured into a brilliant, interesting boy and considered himself 'head of the family'. All the persuasive and dynamic energy that he was to project as an out-standing young politician in the years to come was already fermenting in him. One morning at Bredon he announced to the family over breakfast that he wanted absolute quiet that day as he was preparing an important essay to take back to school. Bored, and with perhaps a little sisterly aggression, Barbara picked up an exercise book and said to the family that she was going to write a novel. 'You will never finish it', they all laughed.

In the many facets of Barbara Cartland's character today, determination and self-discipline rate high. Her professionalism at the age of over eighty is almost frightening. Publishers who commission a non-fiction book, as opposed to her novels, 'to be delivered in a month' need have no fear. Three weeks to the day a perfectly typed and bound manuscript will be placed on their desk.

All the past years of heady reading of Ethel M. Dell and Elinor Glyn had not been wasted. To this day she has not fully recovered from the effect of E. M. Dell's *The Sheik*. Instinctively she had absorbed the format for the romantic novel. She went to her room and began writing. Words, feelings, fantasy all poured out as she scribbled away. When a few chapters had been completed she showed them to Polly who criticized and complimented just as she had done with Bertie when he read his speeches to her. Though not a reader of any substance herself she recognized that Barbara's novel had pace, glamour, excitement and style. The stuff that dreams are made of - especially for lonely women.

Practical as always Polly asked to luncheon Dick Coventry, a cousin of Lord Coventry, who was a writer himself and whose poems were published in *Country Life*. Afterwards Barbara was asked to read aloud the chapters she had finished. Most authors would shrivel up with embarrassment if asked to read their own work aloud. Only extrovert giants like Hans Christian Andersen, Charles Dickens and, of course, Elinor Glyn had the audacity actually to enjoy hearing their own voices. Young Barbara Cartland's reading was like music as in her clear, girlish voice she enacted each page. There was no question of being shy, for she was transported into another world - a world peopled by her own creation.

At the end of the reading Dick Coventry told her: 'It's very good - finish it.' And this she did in three months, writing on scraps of paper during the day and at odd moments lying on her bed while waiting for some young man to pick her up to take her out dancing. These are the last few lines from that first Barbara Cartland novel:

Their eyes met. Each was conscious of the flame of love and desire within the other; explanations, words were unnecessary. They knew . . . the moment was so poignant, so holy . . . this was life . . . this was happiness . . . at last they realised the immortal divinity of unity . . . 'one flesh'.

The Heavens were open, they could hardly breathe, there seemed as if there could be no climax to this but death. Then humanity broke under the strain. With a sound which was the speech of gods, knowing no language or nationality, Peter took his wife into his arms. . . .

Sixty years later I pick up *Fire in the Blood*, published in 1983, and read:

All she knew was that she was close against him and he was kissing her wildly, passionately, demandingly and the world stood still.

He kissed her until he carried her as he had before up to the peak of Olympus, and they were no longer human but one with the gods.

Barbara Cartland has never had to change her style, simply because this is what her readers wanted then and still want now. Three hundred and seventy million readers cannot be wrong!

Barbara dedicated the book to Polly who had encouraged her so much and sent the manuscript off to the publisher Gerald Duckworth. The novel was called *Jigsaw*, cost seven shillings and sixpence and, to everyone's surprise, was not only accepted but caused a minor sensation. Not only because the author was only twenty-three years old but because as Barbara says, 'It was so unusual for a lady to soil her lily-white hands with work.'

Widely publicized as 'Mayfair with the lid off' and 'Mayfair from within', *Jigsaw* is the story of a beguiling heroine called Mona who threads her way innocently through the depravity of Mayfair only to end up in the arms of the heir to a Dukedom. Before the last page she had been tempted by a handsome stranger 'with dark hair brushed from a broad brow, under which glinted two dark eyes mocking and laughing intermittently'. Though sorely tempted as they drive away into the dawn, reason prevails and she returns to her dullish Lord Peter Leadenhall, son and heir of the Scottish Duke of Glenac. The moral is that goodness prevails over what is wrong, however tempting it may be.

In his illuminating biography *Crusader in Pink*, Henry Cloud draws the perceptive analogy that 'throughout Barbara's life, there would always be two sorts of men - the Alecs and the Peters. And in *Jigsaw*, Mona finally rejects the selfish Alec, cleaves to the sturdy Peter, and finally embarks on motherhood and happiness.'

Any similarity between Mona the heroine and the author was not purely accidental! Mona was Barbara and Barbara was Mona:

There are two me's. One is the impatient rather aggressive Crusader, sometimes over-powering with a tendency to fight violently for what I believe is right. And the other image I have of myself is - sweet, soft, gentle, understanding, perceptive and very feminine - longing to be protected by a strong masculine man. It is a kind of idealistic mental and spiritual virginity which I have given to my heroines, and which I have always had myself.

Mona was, in fact, the prototype of all those spiritual virgins to follow, almost all of whose Christian names end with 'a'. There are Bertilla, Torilla, Dorinda, Benedicta, Angelina, Mariska, Orissa, Paulina, Alida, Anita, Gracilda, Quenella, Salena, Delora, Ivona, Pandita, Matilda and three hundred more. 'Yes', said Barbara, when I mentioned this to her, 'I always try and give my heroine a name ending in "a" simply because *Jigsaw* brought me such luck and started me off on my writing career. I must admit it is getting very difficult now that I am coming up to my three hundred and eightieth virgin!'

The reviews of *Jigsaw* were mainly favourable and provoked passion in the critics' pens. As the *Publisher's Circular and Booksellers' Record* wrote:

A vivid and moving story of the difficulties and temptation which confront a young girl in her first entry into the richest and gayest set in London Society. The intoxication of her new freedom and her love of adventure lead her inevitably to exploit her wit and beauty to her own unhappiness but by good luck and her own native goodness she finds peace and happiness at last. It is a dramatic conflict of emotions, written with zest and freshness which will win the admiration of all readers.

Louis J. McQuilland in *G.K.'s Weekly* was less generous:

Miss Cartland is either a very inexperienced young girl or an extraordinary guileless woman. There is nothing of life even in Mayfair about *Jigsaw*. It is simply a mix of the old fashioned novelette and the modern feverish novel of the amateur.

I have doubted Miss Cartland's familiarity with the wickedness of Michael Arlen's Mayfair but the word 'lousy' seems to reinstate her. Of course Mona goes back to the Duke. She had no need to make apologies.

'I've wanted you so much Mona my darling, can you ever forgive me, my wife . . . mine?'

All the same I prefer an old fashioned novelette, the Duchesses are more ducal in them and their friends are never verminous.

The reviewer in the *News Chronicle* was more succinct, when he wrote: 'If this is Mayfair then let me live in Whitechapel.'

Students of the Barbara Cartland technique are fascinated by this early novel because it is clearly the prototype for the millions of words that she was to write in the next fifty-nine years. *Jigsaw* was to earn Barbara the sum of £250; it went into six editions and was translated into five languages. In England it was published on the same day as *Troy Park*, by another young writer Edith Sitwell.

Polly was inordinately proud of her mini-celebrity daughter, but not all the Cartland family were so enthusiastic. Great Aunt Annie Cartland, who lived at the Priory, in Kings Heath, the family seat, wrote to Polly disapprovingly that a well-brought-up girl should publicly have expressed her thoughts about love - not that they were surprised, as they had already heard rumours that Barbara used lipstick and powder, which in their eyes damned a woman as 'fast'. Nor were the Scobell aunts any better. One wrote to Polly that Barbara had 'tarnished' her good name. Like a tigress Polly fiercely defended her young, and letters flew back and forth.

Quite unperturbed by all this family criticism Barbara was bathing in the balmy sunshine of her success. Invitations poured in, and her dancing diary was fully booked. Gossip columns were just becoming a feature of not only glossy magazines like the *Tatler* but also the national newspapers. Viscount Castlerosse, with his huge stomach and insatiable appetite, was one of the most flamboyant figures in London. He circled social events like a huge house-trained seal, and his column in the *Sunday Express* was the fear and delight of every erring married couple. His wit was caustic and hilarious and immensely amusing as long as you were not on the end of his barbed pen. Lady Eleanor Smith and the Marquess of Donegal were also gossip writers drawn from the aristocratic world.

The *Daily Express* depended for their column on a series of socially conscious young men and women who flitted from party to party picking up snippets of gossip wherever they could. The men were always charming, most had come straight from public school - nowadays they come with university degrees - and were immaculately groomed and mannered. One of the most helpful had been Richard Viner. He met Barbara at a party, and, sometime before *Jigsaw* was published, suggested that she 'feed' the *Express* titbits of gossip for which she would be paid. Barbara was amused and thought five shillings a paragraph was a great deal of money - which it was in those days.

In 1923, after the publication of *Jigsaw*, Polly decided to take Barbara and her friend Freda Parsons to Paris. This was not only because Polly thought Paris would be very educational for Barbara, as it had been impossible to go abroad during the war, but also because she thought it would get her away from Hugo Baxendale with whom she was spending, Polly thought, too much time. Hugo, delightful, good-looking, fair-haired and blue-eyed, whom Barbara had met at Bembridge, had just come out of the Navy. Needless to say he had no money but had been fortunate enough to get a job in a house agents.

Polly was, of course, ambitious for her daughter, and she very much favoured young Viscount Elmley, whom Barbara had known all her life as his father, Earl Beauchamp, lived in Worcestershire. He had been Lord Lieutenant of the county and Barbara had gone to parties with the Lygon girls and their brothers at their home, Madresfield Court, ever since she could remember. Barbara, however, did not find the 'boy next door', by now Member of Parliament for Yarmouth, whom she had known for so long, particularly attractive, although he was one of her beaux during this period. Though they were to remain friends until his death in 1979 Barbara did not love him enough for marriage and told Polly at the time: 'But Mummy I can't marry a house.'

Many years later when he succeeded to the Earldom he took a Danish wife, Mona, who looks remarkably like Barbara. The two women are still close friends. Madresfield, incidentally, was the inspiration for the house in Evelyn Waugh's novel *Brideshead Revisited* though the recent television series was actually shot at Castle Howard in Yorkshire.

Polly thought a change of scene would do Barbara good. Freda Parsons, who was at that moment Barbara's greatest friend, was the daughter of Sir Charles and Lady Parsons, and very attractive, although quite a different type to Barbara - small, dark and with a quiet, sweet manner.

She had, however, been responsible for another shock in Barbara's life when Angus Bowes-Lyon, a cousin of the Earl of Strathmore and in the Brigade of Guards, shot himself because she refused to marry him. When Barbara had been threatened by young men with revolvers, everyone said, 'A man who threatens to take his life never does,' but in the tense aftermath of war it often did happen. Angus Bowes-Lyon, who was highly-strung and sensitive, shot himself outside the New Zealand Golf Course at Wimbledon one morning and Freda had to go to the enquiry. Because Barbara would never let a friend down, she went with her. The whole proceeding was extremely upsetting, added to which Angus Bowes-Lyon's greatest friend, Tim, who had been in love with Barbara for a long time, threatened on their return to London, that if Barbara did not marry him, he would do the same thing.

It was a relief to everyone to get away to Paris, though Barbara received little education there because as soon as they arrived young men appeared from nowhere and took her racing at Longchamps, dancing at Ciros and, of course, to all the nightclubs in Montmartre. Polly perforce went round the museums, the Louvre and the churches by herself, which was rather lonely for her and not at all what she had intended. The two girls became enraptured with the Paris fashions. The first thing they noticed was that smart Parisiennes were wearing short-length jackets and not full length.

They both owned cheap but warm goat-skin coats which were then obtainable in London. They promptly cut them shorter with nail scissors on the floor of their bedrooms in the hotel. 'We were mortified when we went out and saw that all the Paris taxi drivers were wearing short goat-skin coats like ours.'

Paris certainly gave Barbara an interest in and knowledge of clothes she had never had before. Like the Queen Mother, Barbara has developed her own particular style in dressing. She wears her clothes with panache and knows exactly what effect she is creating:

> People expect me to dress in pink and it is my favourite colour. Pink makes me feel happy and also inspired. When I get up in the morning in my Nile blue bedroom with its coral pink curtains I feel everything that happens during the day will be an adventure.
>
> Did you know that in Milford, New Hampshire in America, the cells of the town jail have been painted pink on the orders of the Chief of Police? He did it after he had watched a television documentary on the therapeutic value of colours. He says it 'worked like a treat and all the prisoners were a lot calmer!'

Whatever the sniping television critics say about the way Barbara chooses to appear in public, most women envy her style. She has adoring letters from the men too. As Douglas Byng once wrote to her when he was thanking her for her telegram on his birthday: 'They asked me on television what I missed most these days and I said "elegance". I only see it when you are on television.'

9

Aim for the Stars – they are only just out of reach.

Barbara Cartland

Barbara Cartland's career in gossip journalism extended over many years: she wrote for the *Daily Express, Daily Mail* and *Daily Mirror* - £2 a paragraph - and took over the Eve column in the *Tatler* for three years. The only stipulation she made was that she was not asked to go near the newspaper offices and that she would deal only with the editor. No-one was to know her identity. This was because, 'The one thing I wanted to avoid was being asked to parties or fawned on because I was Press. I wanted only to be myself.'

> The last letter of Eve was written by me because she walked out after fifteen or twenty years. They rang me up hysterically and said 'Can you do her last letter', so I copied her style and then continued for three years. It used to make me laugh when people said 'Oh that terrible *Tatler*, I cannot think where they get such stories - which are quite untrue.' I knew they had sent in a letter saying please mention me doing so and so.

Some years later, when she was social editor for the *Sunday Observer*, no one had any idea who she was, including Lady Astor who was married to the proprietor. She was, however, in the early 1920s, also sending features to the *Daily Express* signed under her own name. Those early articles hit the right note with 'Youth Speaks Out' and 'Flaming Youth' and were all the more acceptable written by a 'social débutante'.

One day in 1921, after she had been telephoning in her gossip pieces to the *Daily Express* for a few months, Barbara received a message that Lord Beaverbrook would like to see her. She was expected at the Hyde Park Hotel, where he kept a permanent suite, at 5.00 p.m. Whatever his original motive in asking Barbara to his suite, Beaverbrook quickly became intrigued and amused by her gaiety and complete lack of self-consciousness. Again this showed Polly's influence, for she had brought up all her children to be self-confident. They did not know the meaning of the

77

word 'shy'. Their over-bearing grandfather, Colonel Scobell, used to say to his children 'Stop being shy! Shyness is just conceit. You are thinking about yourself!'

To editors and reporters who worked on the *Express* Group a summons to see 'the Beaver' was like a direct missive from the Archangel or the Devil. Strong men were known to tremble before entering his presence. He could reduce intelligent editors to blithering idiots with his sadistic humour. In her naivete Barbara was totally unaware of this and effervesced at their first meeting. She found him 'omnipotent, enigmatic, with a strange dynamic vitality'.

Lady Diana Cooper once described Max Beaverbrook as 'a strange attractive gnome with the odour of genius about him'. He had a puckish, bulldog face with a large head on top of a chunky body which in those days was encased in badly fitting navy-blue suits bought for him by his valet from Harrods. As Barbara was shown into the suite her first reaction was to think how old he was. Forty-four was positively ancient to a young girl. Her second thought was that he looked like' Billikins', a lucky charm she had carried in the war.

Beaverbrook is recognized as one of the great Fleet Street personalities of all time, he and Lord Northcliffe ranking second to none. He had a flair for creating newspapers brimming with excitement and sensation that were acceptable to all social classes. Whatever the content, and it was often scandalous, the *Daily Express* could lie in equanimity alongside *The Times* on any breakfast table. He had the art of titillating all his readers from dustmen to dukes. In the social world, too, he had managed to work his way up the ladder, from selling newspapers on the streets of New Brunswick in Canada to being acceptable in aristocratic and, even more important, the political circles of Britain. He was a brilliant example that power, vitality and charm can crash through any social barrier.

'So you want to be a journalist?' he said to young Barbara. 'I like the way you write but you have a lot to learn.'

Barbara replied, 'I had not really thought of journalism. You see I am trying to write a novel. I do the gossip paragraphs in your paper just to earn some money.'

'I will teach you to write', Lord Beaverbrook offered.

A strange friendship thus began between the new Fleet Street giant and the young Society girl. They complemented each other - Barbara was always to be attracted by brains, power and success and Beaverbrook admired her beguiling charm, courage and spirit. It was the Professor Higgins and Eliza Doolittle syndrome of its time on a different social level. Every evening at five o'clock, Barbara would take the paragraphs she had written to the Hyde Park Hotel. Max would edit them, sign them and send them off to his newspapers.

'It was fantastic what he taught me. Far more than I realized at the time', Barbara told me. Whatever she had not learned in the schoolroom during English lessons she was now getting in a crash course in this 'college-for-one' from one of the greatest experts in the world on the techniques of modern journalism. Neither could possibly have foreseen that sixty years later Barbara would be listed in the *Guinness Book of Records* as 'the world's best selling author'. It was inevitable that there would come a day when Max Beaverbrook fell in love with Barbara.

> He had always been very sweet, charming and gentle with me, and then one day he said to me unexpectedly, 'You are very lovely and look like Diana Cooper when she was young.'
> I looked at him in surprise and he said, 'I want to kiss you.'
> I stiffened and said, 'I have made up my mind that from now on I will not kiss anyone except the man I marry.'
> 'I respect you for that', Max replied.'

Although Barbara had been kissed by the young men to whom she had been engaged she did not really like being kissed or touched. It was part of the strange complex which meant she was a virgin not only physically, but also mentally and spiritually. It is this purity of mind as well as body which she still strives to portray in her books. In her three hundredth novel, *Bewitched*, the elfin heroine says to her husband on her wedding night, 'I do not like being touched.' That was an echo of Barbara all down the years: she did not like any physical contact except with someone she really loved. It may seem curious that after this discussion the relationship between her and Max continued to flourish.

Lady Beaverbrook was a charming person who was very kind to Barbara when they met, which was seldom, as she preferred to stay in the country. Looking back Barbara thinks that Beaverbrook's love for her awakened in him an interest in women that he did not have before.

All through her life Barbara has had this strange facility of altering other people's lives. On her eightieth birthday, when she had a party of close friends at Camfield, every one of them said their lives had been changed since they came in contact with her, and she thinks now that Max's life was changed too. He was to become embittered when his great friend, Sir James Dunn, asked her to marry him. Up until then, Max had been extremely possessive in that he seemed to concentrate on her as if nothing else mattered:

It was very flattering to a young girl. He wanted to know where I had been, what I had done, where I had eaten and who took me home. He made me feel that at that moment nothing else mattered, and I have never known anyone like him.

Looking back I am sure I am right in believing I was the first woman Max was in love with after he was married, as there had certainly not been a breath of scandal about him with anyone else, and I can understand now how inexperienced he was at expressing his feelings in love.

Strangely enough, despite the way he dressed, he had very good taste in other ways. He always had new ideas and commissioned craftsmen to make him original furniture instead of buying antiques. This good taste extended to women's dress too. He realized that Barbara had pretty feet as well as pretty ankles. 'Your shoes are wrong!' he said gruffly. 'Buy yourself a decent pair which I will give you.' No lady, according to Polly, accepted any present from a man except scent or gloves. Barbara pacified her conscience by telling herself that because she did not wear gloves in the evening, as no-one did in the twenties, shoes were not very different. She bought herself a pair of shoes, but Max did not like them, and it was not until years later when the first Parisian shoe shop opened in Bond Street that she understood what he had had in mind.

Barbara found herself being asked to Max's special parties. A car would be sent to take her to his small, unimpressive house called the Vineyards, near Hurlingham. Here she met his most intimate circle of friends - Winston Churchill, Lord Birkenhead, Viscount Castlerosse and the millionaire Canadian financier, Sir James Dunn:

> I had never met such alive men before as in that intimate circle. They weren't afraid of any one and they talked more passionately than I had ever heard men talk before. They were always trying to cap each other's stories.
>
> Winston Churchill was the most talkative. He would begin to tell a story when the others would interrupt. 'We've heard that one before, Winston.' 'Well Barbara hasn't,' he would answer and continued to the end.

She never dined alone with Beaverbrook, yet he took her to the country to visit his sons at their preparatory school. They had a spirited argument *en route* as Barbara tried to persuade him to send them afterwards to a famous public school like Eton or Harrow, but Max insisted they should start at the bottom as he had. 'How can they do that', she said, 'when you are such a success, and a Lord?'

When they were alone, she duelled with him with words just as Winston and 'F. E.' (F. E. Smith, Lord Birkenhead) did at dinner parties. Max also told her very movingly of his love and admiration for Bonar Law, the Prime Minister who had died of cancer in his arms. He confided too, and she felt he had never spoken of it before, how hurt he had been in Canada when they ostracized him socially for having sold newspapers in the street. These very intimate confidences were the beginnings in Barbara's life of hearing secrets from all sorts and kinds of people because they thought 'you will understand'.

As well as Barbara and furniture, Max was also interested in music, and various musicians, orchestral groups and choirs were invited to his parties to perform for his friends. As the house was so small, the musicians with large instruments were usually forced to play in the garden. One of these performances was especially memorable, as Barbara recalls:

> I remember a night when a Russian choir had arrived in England to be met at Southampton and rushed by cars to The Vineyards to sing at a dinner at eight. As they stepped into the dining room, Max, in one of his most puckish moods, had a film of Russian life taken immediately after the Revolution projected onto the wall behind his chair.
>
> It was a propaganda film, and there were various horrifying close-up shots of children crawling with lice and dying of starvation. The Russians, who could not speak English, were stunned, as well they might have been, and Lord Birkenhead whispered to me: 'We'll get a knife in our backs at any moment.'

Barbara relished the small dinner parties she attended with the Beaverbrook circle. Lady Beaverbrook was never present but Barbara was chaperoned by Norman Holden, the banker, and his wife who were always there. Barbara was never aware how different she was from the other guests, and she remembers that she was completely at ease, gay and bouncy. 'I used to listen to their stories and ask for more. They all made a great fuss of me. I think they regarded me as something of a mascot. Perhaps it was just being very young and pretty.' Young was the operative word - she must have looked like a spring flower among the sophisticated worldly men all over forty, and in a way she gave them back their youth.

> After some months of this I used to wonder how soon I could get away. Max would always send me back to London in a car and when I

arrived at Eaton Terrace Hugo Baxendale was waiting with his car round the corner. He used to pick me up and away we'd go dancing. Max would have been furious had he known, as he was very jealous of me.

He did so much for me, and years later I told him when we met in Manchester in the 1945 Election immediately after the war: 'Max, I will be eternally grateful to you because it was you who taught me how to write. You who made me a success.'

He was by then a very old man and replied, 'You always had it in you, Barbara, and I am very proud of you.'

The most interesting of all the men Barbara met was his greatest and closest friend, Winston Churchill. She found his magnetism irresistible. In the years to come she was to know at first hand how loyal he could be, when he befriended her brother Ronald at the beginning of his Parliamentary career. But this was a long way off from the day Barbara came across Winston Churchill standing by his easel in the garden at Cherkley, Beaverbrook's large country house near Leatherhead, painting a landscape. In her bright manner she asked him: 'Why are you painting that bush purple?'

'That is how I see it - and that is how it is', he growled.

It was many years before Barbara realized that magnetic people with strong personalities see colour more brilliantly than other, ordinary folk. Barbara, like Winston, finds colour everywhere.

When Ronald was in the House of Commons he told Churchill that Barbara had just finished another novel. 'When I met your sister in the twenties', he said, 'I knew she had great potential - as you have now, my boy.'

Another 'regular' at Hurlingham and Cherkley was the brilliant Lord Birkenhead. He captivated the young Barbara with his worldly charm and sophistication. Tall and elegant with his dark saturnine looks and hooded eye-lids, and his sarcasm and cynical wit, she used him as a model for her *Bucks and Beaux*. Although Lord Birkenhead's sharp tongue made him many enemies, and almost destroyed his early Parliamentary career, to Barbara he was kind, charming and great fun, except on one occasion, when, daringly, Barbara attacked him for making a young, pretty but very stupid girl fall in love with him. In other words, seducing her. F. E. was furious. 'You go to blazes!' he exclaimed. Then, suddenly, he saw the funny side of it and said: 'I shall be very interested, Barbara, to see what you make of your life in future.'

Even though she was still in her early twenties Barbara showed a mental bravery that has been characteristic of her all her life. On one occasion she was invited to a smart dinner party in a night club by the intellectual Wemyss, Charteris and Asquith set. The others were all talking and laughing during the cabaret and a woman singer was unable to be heard. Before Barbara had stopped to think she heard herself saying angrily: 'Be quiet! The wretched woman has to earn her living!' Her hosts were stunned into silence, and Barbara, realizing what she had done, sat embarrassed as the woman she had supported sang very badly a popular bawdy song called 'I've got Ants in my Pants'. On a matter of principle she was right, but the intellectuals never invited her out again.

She remained, however, in Beaverbrook's set, and continued to enjoy their company. One of F. E.'s favourite party tricks, which he demonstrated to her when they all went to Cowes, was diving into the sea with a lighted cigar and bobbing up out of the water with it still alight. Later, when he became Secretary of State for India, Lord Birkenhead invited Barbara to a glittering reception he and his wife gave at India House. It was the first time she had seen the shimmering beauty of Indian women, wrapped in their diaphanous saris like exquisite flowers. The jewelled turbans of the Indian princes and that peculiar, spicy scent that permeates all Indian gatherings made her long to visit India and study their philosophy of life.

Over the years Barbara has travelled five times to India and is just as intoxicated and enchanted by its beauty today as at that first glimpse fifty years ago. Through her friendship with Lord and Lady Mountbatten, she has many close friends there, not least of all, Prime Minister Indira Gandhi, whom she met in 1958. Both women admire each other and in a letter written in recent years to Barbara, Indira Gandhi said: 'You are beautiful outside, because you are beautiful inside.'

Another member of the Beaverbrook circle was Sir James Dunn, the Canadian financier, who had been knighted during the war. Like Lord Beaverbrook he was a self-made millionaire and delighted in all the worldly trappings that great wealth brings. Tempestuous, unpredictable, extravagant and ruthless, he was like a tornado from the prairies of Canada. He was just the kind of explosive challenge that Max Beaverbrook enjoyed. To Barbara he was a new breed of man, the first she had met from the New World, and she found his audacity refreshing.

Jimmy Dunn had rented a large house at Roehampton to be near his friend Max Beaverbrook. With his touch for showmanship he gave the most spectacular parties of the day and filled his lawns with celebrities - actresses, ballet dancers, politicians and statesmen. The women had to be pretty and the men celebrities in their own right. This heady mixture never failed, and his huge floodlit parties were famous.

Some time after he met Barbara, Sir James, who was in the middle of a divorce from his wife, asked her to marry him. Polly was horrified and Beaverbrook was furious. 'The one thing I cannot offer you', he said angrily, 'is marriage.' Barbara however had no intention of accepting Sir James. She thought him very old at fifty-four, and besides she would never think of marrying an already married man.

At the same time, when Sir James begged her to join a big party at Deauville, she longed to accept. Deauville was *the* fashionable resort, the El Dorado of the gamblers at the tables and on the race-course. Reluctantly Polly agreed she could go if she took her own chaperone with her. Sir James, frantic to have her, willingly accepted another guest. Barbara had been introduced by the Marquess of Queensberry, whom she had met racing, to his wife with whom she had become close friends. Irene Queensberry had been on the stage and at the age of sixteen had played the lead in a musical comedy called *Mr Manhattan*. She was small and beautiful with large expressive eyes, and, always ready to do something new and exciting, agreed readily to be Barbara's chaperone.

They all set off in a howling gale in the *Mairi*, a rather precarious yacht which Sir James had rented from Lord Birkenhead. With them were Duff and Lady Diana Cooper, who was on her way to America to play in *The Miracle* in which she was to be a huge success, and Sir James's son, Philip. When they emerged from Southampton Water into the open sea, it was very rough, and Diana Cooper, who was terrified on any ship however large or small, insisted the yacht turn back, because it was too dangerous to go any further. On this occasion she was perfectly right, for the yacht made port in France three days later with everything on board smashed. The party went over instead by cross-channel ferry and arrived at Deauville to find another very large party of twenty-six occupying a great deal of the hotel. They were all sophisticated, amusing, but very much older, people, with the exception of a young man called Noel Coward who was fresh from the success of his review *London Calling*.

Noel Coward hated Deauville as much as Barbara did. It rained and rained, and both were unhappy and shocked by the other guests who were all gambling and drinking. In fact the luxurious Casino, filled with distinguished men and beautiful women all somewhat abandoned in their behaviour, was to be a background to many of Barbara's books including *An Angel in Hell*, *The Lights of Love*, and *A Gamble with Hearts*. Noel Coward expressed his view of Deauville in *Present Indicative* when he wrote:

All the correct adjuncts were there: champagne, beautifully gowned women, high-powered gambling, obsequious *maitre d'hotel*, moonlit terraces - a perfectly arranged production with all the parts well cast according to type. I think, perhaps, that there must have been something wrong with the dialogue. The author must have had a common mind, because soon I became irritated and bored and wanted to go home.

Barbara and Noel were to become life-long friends:

I thought Noel was cynical and we quarrelled at luncheon until he called me 'Queen Gloom' and I burst into tears. After that he was sweet to me and we became great friends - all through the years until he died he never changed and was always the same - kind, sympathetic, witty but never - to a friend - cruel.

When I wrote my biography of the twenties *We Danced all Night*, Noel wrote to me: 'I have enjoyed every page, which filled me with nostalgia. What a long time we have known each other! And how nice and satisfactory that is. My thanks and congratulations and my love, as always, Noel. XXX'

When she wasn't with Noel, Barbara wandered about Deauville alone, feeling curiously out of place. She must have seemed out of place to others too, for friends she had known in London came up to her and one of them said, 'You have no right to be here with that crowd. If you were my daughter I would give you a good spanking and send you home!'

In the meantime Barbara realized that her 'chaperone', Irene Queensberry, was becoming very flirtatious and intimate with Sir James. She did not mind, but it made her feel even more out of everything. One day when she felt so tired in the afternoon that she went to lie down, Irene led them all into her bedroom to see if she wanted to go to the polo with them. Barbara was horrified, as to curl the fluffy sides of her hair she had put them into hinz pins.

'I must have looked awful!' she exclaimed.

'No', Irene answered, 'only very young.'

She must, in fact, have looked like an angel from an Easter crèche among that raffish crowd.

On the last day of the holiday, Irene and Jimmy told Barbara they were running away together, Irene quite cheerfully abandoning her husband and her daughter. Incredibly they asked Barbara to go to Paris with them, but she refused, and Jimmy then arranged for his son Philip to take her home.

Barbara and Philip set off in a cross-Channel steamer and before they reached London he had asked her to marry him. She refused, and though he sent a beautiful present on their arrival, this was the last she was ever to see of him. The Marquess of Queensberry blamed Barbara for what had happened to his wife and never spoke to her again.

It was after she came back from Deauville that Barbara virtually broke away from Max. To begin with she was very busy enjoying herself with Hugo Baxendale, and dancing with a large number of younger men. Then Deauville, and the exotic life she had seen with the adventurers, had made her rather shy of the whole crowd.

I drifted away from Max. I never broke off, I just did my disappearing act, made myself elusive and difficult to see. I learnt afterwards that Max had had a love affair with one of my friends which rather surprised me. It only lasted a short time and eventually he had a really passionate love affair with the most beautiful woman in London who was in fact madly in love with him.

From all I heard, he was never very kind to her and often actively unkind and I sometimes wondered whether I was responsible for that. There is nothing worse than being disillusioned over one's first love affair.

Max never spoke to me about it or reproached me in any way for leaving him, but he did what was to him a typical revenge. He told the editors on his newspapers they were to publish anything I wrote, but there was to be a black mark against my name socially. I was not to be mentioned in any of the gossip columns.

It was only as the years increased that everyone was to realize, as Lord Mountbatten did, that Max could be a very persistent and very cruel enemy. So actually I got off lightly, and when we met again in 1945 he could not have been kinder or sweeter, and being with him was just like the old days.

10

*'To a man you may be framed in dreams, but a woman
sees the cheap material and the unfinished seams.'*

Barbara Cartland

Now that she was on the Mayfair merry-go-round Barbara's modest little
wardrobe on her £50 dress allowance needed a face lift. She could not go to
the couture dress-makers as some of her friends did and, clever as she
might be at buying hats from a shop in Brompton Road for two and
sixpence and trimming them herself, she needed lots of afternoon and
evening dresses as dancing was, and always has been, hard on clothes.
Polly and Barbara solved the problem by buying them second-hand.

It was through Sybil Eyres Monsell that they were invited to a friend's
house for a sale of clothes in aid of the Red Cross. They attended it and
Barbara bought a pretty silk afternoon dress for £3. Polly was sorely
tempted to buy a long sable stole with many tails and a muff to match, but
at £30 she thought it too expensive. For the rest of her life she oftimes
sighed 'I wish I had bought those sables.' It was to become another
Pollyism.

From her first adventure into the second-hand clothes market Barbara
now realized that many of the best-dressed women in Society sold their
clothes, however rich they were. It was a way they could keep abreast of
fashion and placate their bill-picking husbands. Tucked away in Belgravia
and Mayfair were several discreet little shops where people bought and
sold clothes. Mary Leigh, in South Molton Street, which only closed its
doors a few years ago, was considered the best and some women sent their
maids there twice a year with suitcases filled with last Season's dresses. It
was rumoured that some younger members of the Royal Family disposed
of their clothes at Mary Leigh's, any distinctive trimmings that might
make the dresses recognizable being removed before the sale.

When my daughter Raine [Countess Spencer] was presented at a
Garden Party at Buckingham Palace immediately after the war the
country was still in coupons. Of course we went along to Mary Leigh
and found a lovely Molyneux dress for three and a half guineas. She

looked quite lovely. Several of her evening dresses when she came out were also from there.

Mary Leigh was originally begun by a woman who was married to a Captain in the Royal Navy. When he was demobilized after the First World War and sold his uniform she was appalled how little he got for it. 'I can sell things for more than that', was her reaction, and she promptly went into business. Over the years Mary Leigh changed hands and one owner asked Barbara for help:

> She told me that she was so upset as she had been married for twelve years and did not have any children. I gave her vitamins and eventually she had six. Six children all out of my vitamins, so you see one always pays back for what one gets. When I had a hysterectomy at the London Clinic I sent all my nurses to spend £5 at Mary Leigh and they came back delighted with lovely dresses they had bought.

So for £3 Barbara could buy some of Edwina Mountbatten's dresses, besides those belonging to other famous beauties like The Hon. Mrs Richard Norton and Paula Gellibrand. She was also given a lot of clothes. Through Geoffrey Rodd she met the Dowager Lady Michelham who lived in great style at Arlington House, one of the great London houses. She had dinner parties where thirty guests were served off gold plates. At one dinner party Barbara blushed bright pink when the canteloupe melon on her plate disappeared under the table as she tried to cut it. It was retrieved by a disdainful footman with powdered hair and another slice placed in front of her.

Lady Michelham gave Barbara many of her expensive gowns when she was tired of them, but there was, as always, a snag! Most of them were brown or beige, a colour Barbara had already begun to hate and which she now loathes. Mrs Kerr Smiley gave her an evening gown with pink feathers down the sides, but Barbara was tall and the dress made her feel shy as she thought it showed too much of her very elegant legs!

In the beautiful gowns she now owned Barbara began to look more *soignée*. The wide-eyed innocence was never far from the surface but there was a new veneer of sophistication. One of her most successful buys was an evening dress in shades of pink chiffon, with the pointed hemline which was all the rage. It had belonged to Mrs Dudley Ward, who was then mistress of the Prince of Wales. Barbara liked the dress so much that when she married in 1927 she had it copied for her bridesmaids.

Through their very clever buying and sense of style Polly and Barbara were very *chic*. Although Polly had been offered financial help many times from Frank Greswolde Williams, a rich friend who had known her for many years and, on the death of Bertie, wanted to marry her, she always refused. On one occasion when he handed her a cheque she tore it up in front of him. She did however agree that he should buy Barbara, who was his godchild, a dress from Revilles in Hanover Square for her to wear in a musical play in which she appeared at Covent Garden in aid of charity.

When mother and daughter went to Revilles Barbara sat entranced as the dresses were paraded in front of her on a bean-slim model with honey-gold hair cascading over one eye. She was Sylvia Hawkes, reputedly the daughter of a London ostler, who had taken Mayfair by storm with her beauty. She was later to become successively Lady Ashley, Mrs Douglas Fairbanks, Lady Stanley of Alderley, Mrs Clark Gable and Princess Dimitri Djordjadze.

With the constant worry about money Polly became ill with heart trouble. When the doctor told Barbara, 'I'm afraid there is nothing I can do for your mother, you must be prepared that she may die', Barbara was furious with fear and anger. Polly could *not* die. 'I don't believe you and I don't think you should say such a thing', she stormed at the doctor. 'I think you had better go as we have no longer any need of your services.' It must have been the only time a qualified doctor had been so summarily sacked. As Polly lay there looking very fragile Barbara pleaded, 'You can't die Mummy. You know we can't do without you. What would happen to Tony and Ronald . . . and me? We would all turn out badly without you and you would hate that to happen. You've *got to* live . . . please Mummy.' Polly listened and went on living until 1976 when she died aged ninety-eight.

In the summer of 1925, Polly decided that it was time Barbara was presented at Court. When she first arrived in London Polly was still mourning Bertie and so the years had slid by. Unless she had been 'presented' Barbara could not go to the garden parties at Buckingham Palace like all her friends. Somehow, Polly thought, she would get the money together to buy the dresses. Court etiquette required that though débutantes no longer kissed the hand of King George V and Queen Mary they must still wear the correct court dress - a white evening gown with a train and three white ostrich feathers in their hair. Barbara's one concern was whether the feathers would hold in her newly shingled hair or flop off at the crucial moment.

Barbara had by now been asked to help a young Cambridge undergraduate called Norman Hartnell who had recently opened a shop in a top room in Bruton Street. He needed publicity and was so delighted to be able to make her presentation dress of white chiffon and sequins that he gave it to her and only charged Polly cost price for hers. Polly, however, considered her violet satin gown with a train embroidered with amethysts and diamonds very expensive at £12, and complained all the way to Buckingham Palace. Norman Hartnell always said that Barbara was his first customer and he never forgot how many clients she sent him, undoubtedly helping him reach the top and design for Royalty.

Polly's sister, Edith, The Hon. Mrs Alfred Maitland, also a war widow, was presenting her eldest daughter, Lottie, and they went with Polly and Barbara to Buckingham Palace where seven or eight hundred presentations were made every year. Like a flock of white cygnets the well-drilled débutantes filed past the King and Queen in the red Throne Room. It was a moving and especially English spectacle that Barbara was always to remember - in particular a handsome, gold-braided diplomat, covered in decorations, who came up to her as she was moving away from her second curtsey saying, 'You look lovely and I adore you!' She was terrified he would be overheard!

Barbara wrote some poems that year, and one was called 'Enchantment', from which I have chosen the opening lines. It shows that despite the sophisticated world in which she was now living, the fairy-like world she had known at Amerie Court had never been forgotten.

> Your headlamps like two golden moons
> Shine on the silver way,
> The wind is singing your faery tunes;
> Drive on till you find the day.

At about this time, while convalescing from appendicitis, and bored from being idle, Barbara decided to try her hand at writing a play called *Blood Money*. Noel Coward had warned her that it was well nigh impossible for anyone who had not been in the theatre since the age of ten to write a decent play, but typically she set out to prove him wrong.

The play was to be produced at the Q Theatre near Kew Bridge, but the script was held up for approval by the Lord Chamberlain for three weeks as it was said to require 'special consideration'. Jack de Lion, the producer, made many personal calls to the Lord Chamberlain's office explaining that if the play could not be produced in time this could mean not only financial loss, through breaking contracts with the artists, but in all probability closing the doors of the theatre for good.

In the end Barbara herself went to see the Lord Chamberlain. It turned out that all the fuss was about was that she had used the title of a living

Indian prince and therefore the play could be libellous. Lord Cromer explained patiently, 'You must give the character a new name.' 'You choose one for me', Barbara said audaciously. 'That's not really my job', Lord Cromer replied. But good-humouredly, taking down a book he suggested that it was changed to Prince Abdul Singh. Only Barbara could have persuaded Lord Cromer, who was treated with awe by everyone in St James's Palace, to help her with her play.

Despite all the mysterious publicity, which only whetted the public's appetite, nothing could save the critics' waspish pens. *The Stage* wrote: 'The story of *Blood Money* is paltry and the character drawing mostly exaggerated and out of focus. [The theatre] has licence for the play owing to the censor being out of town in which case it is hoped its consideration did not duly interrupt any much harassed official needful of rest. The piece as it stands could pass through Palace Yard without the flicker of an eyelash and there is no law against dull epigrams.'

If she was upset at her first theatrical failure it was not in Barbara's character to sit down and cry about it. 'Noel was right', she laughed and promptly turned it into a novel, re-christening it *Sawdust*. The literary critics were fulsome with the *Inquirer* writing:

The writer of *Jigsaw* appears to have made distinct advance in her second novel. The plotting is firmer, the descriptions of the scenery and incident are better done. She has a romantic fancy and though her characters may not yet be deemed impressibly real they are not wooden puppets and their interactions are mostly natural. The tale will no doubt win more readers and should lead on to still higher work.

As soon as she was well enough, Barbara was back on the dance floor. The Charleston, imported from America, had just become the rage and caused a furore in the popular press. Mrs Wilfred Ashley, stepmother of Edwina Mountbatten and a noted hostess, wrote in the *Westminster Gazette*: 'I think that acrobatics in a ballroom or indeed any so conspicuous dance as this is in the worst taste. I regret to say that the Charleston is now danced at private dances. Modern dancing needs pulling up.' Barbara was invited to add her comment and prissily wrote:

It is only the very objectionable Oxford-trousered, tight-waisted kind of young man who is to be seen dancing the Charleston, and the girls who dance it wear ultra-short, tight frocks, and make up their faces to excess. It is all hideously vulgar. When the Charleston is done correctly the feet should never be lifted from the floor. This high kick is quite wrong.

──11──

*When you reach the horizon there is always another
beyond it.*

Barbara Cartland

In the following year Barbara was to find the Duke who was to be the
prototype of her ducal heroes throughout the years in her romantic novels.
The Duke of Sutherland, whom she had met with Max Beaverbrook at one
of his parties, came into her life again and asked her to stay at Sutton Place.

Sutton Place near Guildford in Surrey, which in recent years was owned
by the late Paul Getty, was, and still is, one of the most beautiful and best
preserved early Tudor houses in England. Barbara was captivated by this
lovely red-brick mansion, and it has appeared in many of her novels,
including her recent *The Vibrations of Love*, where she writes of the
vibrations of a house felt by the heroine. These were exactly what she felt
when she first walked in to Sutton Place.

There was a large party at the house. Eileen, Duchess of Sutherland, was
extremely beautiful and quite pleasant to Barbara but sharp and rather
disagreeable to her husband even in front of the servants which Barbara
thought, adopting Polly's standards, showed bad manners. The Duke of
Sutherland was a handsome man, six foot two inches in height with
piercing blue eyes. He looked like a magnificent Chieftain, especially when
wearing a kilt. The first weekend at Sutton Place - with the peacocks
moving majestically about the yew-hedged gardens, the indoor tennis
court where Barbara played and the amusing dinner parties where the
conversation was a pale imitation of the intelligent talk at Hurlingham -
was in a way a revelation.

Barbara was aware, because he had told her so, that the Duke was in
love with her. She did not know then, but she learnt later, the real tragedy
in his life.

He had fallen in love when he was very young with one of the most
beautiful women in England, Mary Curzon, who was later to become the
Countess Howe. Born in the obscurity of a poor country vicarage, she had
an amazing beauty, which Michael Arlen called 'the golden-white beauty
of the world's last aristocracy', so overwhelming that at eighteen she was

hastily pushed into marriage with a distinguished and titled cousin.

They were both unhappy, yet when Geordie Sutherland, the most eligible Duke in the whole of *Debrett*, and much younger than she was, fell in love with her, although she flirted prettily with him her heart was untouched. It was then that Duchess Millicent, the Duke's mother, intervened and told him that he must find himself a wife. The Duke, feeling bitter and disillusioned, like a 'Barbara Cartland hero', said 'As I cannot marry the woman I wish, you choose.' The Duchess Millicent invited three beautiful girls to stay at Dunrobin Castle, the Sutherlands' seat in Scotland. The Duke proposed to the first one he saw. There was a magnificent wedding attended by most of the Royal Family, but after they were married it was discovered that of all the girls he could have chosen to be his wife, the one he had married was barren.

Although Barbara was not aware of this at the time, she knew that the Duke was unhappy and she wished she could do what he wanted to make him happy. But Polly's insistence that she did not become involved with married men was stronger than her heart. She said 'No' to Geordie but he continued to pursue her.

After that amusing and happy weekend at Sutton Place, the Duke invited her to Summerfold, a small but attractive house he owned in the Surrey hills. It was built like an Italian villa high up on the edge of a forest with the ground falling away beneath it. From the terrace one could see for miles over the countryside as far as the sea. It was so enchanting that it was difficult, when the Duke took Barbara there, for her not to be carried away by the romantic surroundings.

He motored her down to Summerfold early before his party arrived and they sat in a wood of silver beech, which had always been connected in Barbara's mind with fairies, nymphs and knights in white armour. He told her how much he loved her. Barbara however still managed to say 'No', and later when the rest of the party arrived, including Lord Birkenhead and the Earl of Dundonald, they spent what was to Barbara a very different weekend to any she had known before. Geordie had brought down from Scotland the spirited little Dunrobin ponies, on which he rode out shooting, and all the party, including Barbara, rode in the woods. 'F. E.', with his usual passion for exercise, played round after round of golf and three sets of tennis, and naturally dominated the conversation at the dinner table.

Although Barbara continued to refuse the Duke over the years, he became one of her closest and dearest friends, and she loved and admired him until he died. Dunrobin, which is a fairy-tale castle in Sutherland, has been the background for many of her novels, and years later when she went annually to Scotland with her second husband Hugh and her two sons, they lunched there every Sunday.

The Duke of Sutherland was also to be the godfather of Barbara's first child, Raine, and when she 'came out' he gave a lavish dance for her at Sutton Place. He was a loyal and devoted friend and the whole of Barbara Cartland's family adores his last wife, the Duchess Clare, to this day. The only tragedy was that the Duke never had a son of his own.

Another man who figured in Barbara's life at this time was a good-looking young actor who came from a distinguished family. Barbara, who had never known anyone in the theatrical profession well, was at first intrigued, but she was quickly disillusioned by the lack of glamour *behind* the footlights. Once again she found herself refusing a proposal of marriage, this time because she knew she could never bear to live a life which was centred on one person's individual attraction to the public. But what she learnt back stage was extremely useful, and of course became material for a number of her novels, including one recently published called *Lights, Laughter and a Lady*, in which Barbara wrote of the Gaiety Girls. She knew quite a number of them in the late twenties, girls who married into the aristocracy, like Rosie Boot who became the Marchioness of Hertford.

All this time, however, Hugo Baxendale was still in attendance and although she knew she should be brutal and send him away she found it impossible to do so. Having known him for so long it was very difficult, without being really unkind, to make him understand that she did not want to marry him. She did, in fact, try but he would not listen.

Hugo had acquired a small but attractive farmhouse in Surrey, and he had also bought a very pretty antique ring which he intended for Barbara's engagement finger. It was, unfortunately, an emerald, and Barbara had always been suspicious of this stone believing it to be unlucky, and over the years has proved herself right. It was difficult not to see Hugo, as Barbara had also become a friend to all his family and they were always asking her to stay for weekends. Hugo had a brother who lived in Sussex, a sister who lived at Bosham near Chichester and another brother who was part of the artistic set in Chelsea.

It was through Hugo's brother that the sculptor Charles Jagger, who was just in the middle of executing the enormous War Memorial at Hyde Park Corner, asked Hugo if he would be allowed to sculpt Barbara's breasts because he thought they were so beautiful. 'I though it was a compliment until I realized he wanted to sculpt me naked! Then I was extremely shocked and refused immediately.'

Where Hugo was concerned, it was Barbara's instinct, which was to grow and grow stronger and stronger, almost like the voices of St Joan of Arc, that if she married him she would be unhappy. She had not formulated in her own mind exactly what she was looking for but she needed a man she could look up to and admire and who would be a great success in his own field. She says, 'I never wanted to be a success myself. I wanted to be in the shadow of the throne, the woman who inspired and helped someone famous like a very important and distinguished Duke or, better still, the man who was to be the Prime Minister.'

But Barbara was to find, as so many people do, that life inevitably has a strange quirk about it and fate never allows everything to run smoothly. Her Duke was married, and the Prime Minister, who she visualized would help the Nation and the World through her, was not to appear yet. In the meantime she was left with Hugo, who was insistent that they should marry immediately. This time she did not turn to Polly, who had shown for some time her disapproval of the way she had continued to see a man she had no intention of marrying. Barbara thought she must cope with the problem herself, though suddenly she felt unable to do so.

Actually, although she was not really aware of it at the time, Barbara was beginning to feel ill, run down and somehow depressed. She longed to have someone strong, comforting and protective to look after her, and one day when she walked into the Ritz to have luncheon with some friends, she was sure she had found him.

There was every reason in the world why Barbara Cartland should have chosen Alexander McCorquodale, the fiftieth man to propose to her. He was desperately in love with her and was eminently eligible. 'Sachie' McCorquodale was not a duke, a marquess or even a peer, but he was a physical replica of a Cartland hero - Scottish, dark-haired, with good looks and a hint of brooding and a virile strength beneath his impeccable manners. He was also rich, or to be more accurate, the only son of a very rich father. His uncle was Lord Horne of Shirbroke who had commanded the First Army during the War.

The McCorquodale family came from Scotland and had made a fortune as the largest printing group in the world - they were government printers and produced all the postal orders, cheque books and pensions and did all the posters for the railways and owned *Bradshaw's Guide*. Although 'Sachie', as he was called by his friends, lived in London in Berkeley Square, the family seat was an impressive, beautiful Queen Anne mansion – Coombe Hall, in Shropshire. He had served in the Argyll and Sutherland Highlanders and was a first-class game shot and an accomplished salmon fisher. As an owner driver he also won several gold medals in the annual London to Edinburgh trials. In his 30-98hp Vauxhall he once drove the

542 miles from London to the family shoot in Scotland with only two short stops of a few minutes each.

For some months Barbara had been in turmoil within herself. She was not satisfied with the life she had been living. Through Ronald's influence she had begun to realize that life held more to it than the superficiality of the social roundabout. When she became ill with a septic throat, Alexander McCorquodale was never far away from her thoughts, sending her flowers and charming gifts.

In one of her unpredictable moments she agreed to marry him. Polly took a more realistic view of this new proposal. Though she liked this twenty-nine-year-old Scotsman in many ways, and approved of his promise to give Barbara a lovely house in Mayfair and her own Rolls Royce as a wedding present, deep down she had her own misgivings. Barbara's happiness was uppermost in her mind when she solemnly asked her: 'Is he really worthy of you darling?'

Sachie was a terribly sweet, kind person. I was ill with this wretched septic throat and filled with poisons. You know when you are ill things are always out of focus. I *was* in love with Sachie, and I really believed it would be a happy marriage. I realized that many of the exciting young men I had met during the last five years were really quite unsuitable as husbands. It never entered my head that I was about to enter into a marriage that would break up within five years.

I had always dreamed of marrying a powerful man. Sachie was not that but I was quite determined I would be a wonderful, wonderful wife to him.

The weeks before her marriage were very exciting as Polly geared into action, helping her daughter buy a suitable trousseau without spending too much money. Barbara continued her gossip writing and even managed to give a broadcast on 'How to Buy a Trousseau'.

For her wedding Barbara wore the first tulle wedding dress seen since the War. Although it was made by Norman Hartnell, she designed it herself. It was a typical Barbara Cartland heroine dress made from layers of tulle frills. After that Barbara set a fashion for tulle wedding dresses which were breathtakingly lovely. She wore the long, wide satin train Polly had worn at her wedding. Hartnell added white fur round the sides and a lot of *diamanté* embroidery. It really was a masterpiece and worthy of a museum. Polly wanted it back for sentimental reasons and later gave it to Raine who in one of her tidying moods threw it out, and it was taken away by a daily woman!

At Polly's wedding her train had been carried by two pages in white satin knee breeches and court dress. Barbara had four, with ten bridesmaids in pink, and a matron of honour. 'All my little bridesmaids looked like rosebuds', she says. 'They were shaded from pale pink to dark and carried roses for St George's Day.'

On the eve of her wedding on 23 April 1927, Barbara looked back at the years in which she had enjoyed herself and realized that her first ambition, to know people, had come true. Apart from the many people she had met through Max Beaverbrook, including Tim Healey, the first Governor General of the Free State of Ireland, Geoffrey Rodd had popped backwards and forwards from his ship and introduced her to a miscellaneous collection of celebrities, from Prince George of Kent, the younger son of the King and Queen, to 'Baby June' who was a lovely, plump little dancer at the London Pavilion. Many years later she became the second wife to Lord Inverclyde. Through Geoffrey Barbara also met Mr Hwfa-Williams who had initiated the Sandown Race Meeting and made roller-skating the rage, at which Barbara became very proficient.

It was on a roller-skating rink that she met Jocelyn Lucas, who had asked her to stay at his father's house in Newmarket, and proposed to her on the racecourse in a howling blizzard. (Barbara said 'No'.) For some reason she could not ascertain, she was frightened of him as a man and made sure that she was never left alone with him. Later Jocelyn became a very popular M.P., inherited his father's baronetcy and had the only pack of hunting sealyhams in the country. He too was a friend of Barbara's until he died.

> I cannot think why I was frightened of him as a man, but I was, and when I write of my heroines being afraid, I can describe their feelings very accurately.

Geoffrey always had a very strange effect on Barbara's life, invariably saying that her current young man was not good enough for her. He had a vitality that equalled her own, which always swept her away on a cloud of excitement. Barbara had enjoyed every moment of her dashing suitors and 'dancing days' but now had no regrets that she was giving up her freedom and getting married.

The marriage took place on St George's Day at the fashionable St Margaret's Church in Westminster. The bridesmaids were headed by six-year-old Lady Patricia Douglas, daughter of the Marquess of Queensberry, and the new Lady Dunn, now radiantly happy, came with Sir James to the wedding. The wedding had all the social trappings of the time with a blue carpet - a few guineas more expensive than the red - and a full choir that sang divinely. Goodyears the florist had banked the church with roses.

When Barbara signed the Marriage Register in the vestry after the ceremony, Sachie introduced her to his cousin, Hugh McCorquodale. They had been to the same school, Harrow, and were always together in the office. Hugh had been in Scotland, otherwise Barbara would have met him before. As they shook hands, Hugh fell in love!

The list of wedding presents as published in the *Tewkesbury Register* was impressive. Sachie gave Barbara a sable coat and a fitted dressing case. Her mother-in-law presented her with a diamond spray. Ronald gave his sister a gilt three-tiered looking-glass and a card case and her brother Anthony a travelling cushion which were all the fashion at that time. Two of the men who had loved her, and with whom she was to remain on good terms for the rest of their lives, were the Duke of Sutherland, who gave her an exquisite gold cloth, and Viscount Elmley who gave a Worcester china coffee set.

These were all on show at the home of Sir Bolton and Lady Eyres Monsell in Belgrave Square. They gave Barbara her wedding reception there and had been unbelievably kind friends to the whole family over the years. Ronald and Tony, who were the same age as their children, had often stayed with them at Dumbleton Hall in Worcestershire. Once when Polly was in the country, Barbara stayed at Belgrave Square for three months, although Sybil Monsell said she was a very ineffective chaperone, never seeing Barbara who was dancing all night and sleeping most of the day.

Barbara and Sachie's honeymoon had been planned with all the romanticism of one of her novels. The newly-weds set out in Barbara's new black and white Rolls Royce with a lady's maid and a chauffeur. They planned to motor round Europe taking in the South of France, Florence, the Italian Lakes and across to Venice. St Moritz was added later as an afterthought.

It was a journey of 5,000 miles and Sachie insisted on driving. He and his bride sat in the front seats while the chauffeur and the lady's maid were relegated to the back. The maid became squeamish and the chauffeur disgruntled, and while the bridal couple in front may have been deliriously happy zooming across Europe, the back-seat passengers were clearly not enjoying the honeymoon. The maid was the first to give notice, followed by the chauffeur!

Now they were on their own, the tour took on the aspect of a motor rally and Sachie was in his element. But poor Barbara was still far from well with her septic tonsils.

It was, as everyone told Barbara, the worst spring for forty years. In Venice she tried to feel romantic in a gondola with the wind lashing the lagoon and thunder drowning 'Maria, Mari'. In Como she shivered, and, bored with a lounge-full of old women at the villa D'Este - *the* honeymoon hotel of Europe - Barbara and Sachie bought a halma board to play in bed.

Having won three games, I was nearly asleep after this desperate dissipation when I heard a strange noise from the floor. I switched on the light and saw to my horror the halma box moving slowly across the carpet. It was nothing supernatural but a large, well-fed black beetle carrying the box on its back!

In Switzerland, in an effort to reach St Moritz, the couple got stuck on the St Julian Pass in snow, 7,000 feet above sea level, and had to be dug out by the keeper of the pass at about five in the morning. Sachie found a 'dear little hotel' where they stayed. When they wanted blue trout for breakfast the proprietor fished for them out of the kitchen window from a glacier stream.

Many years later Barbara wrote an article on honeymoons in the *Evening News*. Although the young bride she described was fictitious it was, indirectly, and exaggerated, partly a description of her own feelings.

She had dreamed of a strong silent cave-man - a man of deeds but of few words - a man who underneath a deep reserve was passionate, commanding, conquering. Finally she thought that she had found him in her husband. She mistook inertia for reserve, lack of interest for silent strength and inexperience for hidden passion. She was miserably disappointed.

Back in London, Barbara plunged into the excitement of creating her first home - a charming little house in Culross Street, off Park Lane. It had once been two houses that were now made into one, and most important it had a room large enough for dancing. With her passion for bright colours Barbara chose jade green as the main colour scheme in the drawing room, and Nile blue in her bedroom with curtains of coral pink. The sunshine yellow bathroom caused such a furore among decorating circles that it was described in detail in the *Tatler*. For their bridal bedroom she had bought an ancient Spanish four-poster bed carved and gilded, thus beginning her hobby of collecting antique beds.

Today at Camfield Place Barbara sleeps in that same gilded four-poster with its handsome coral pink damask curtains and a cupid, wings outspread, high on top of the canopy. All through the last sixty years the height of the bed has varied according to whether Barbara was rich or poor, so the ceiling was high or low. Now it is a magnificent height and the centrepiece of her beautiful bedroom of the same Nile blue and coral pink, two colours she adopted as her own after visiting the Temples and tombs in the Valley of the Kings at Luxor.

As soon as they moved into Culross Street Barbara had her tonsils removed and was extremely ill. Her surgeon, Sir Thomas Parkinson, insisted she must rest, and she lay in bed reading every volume written by Jane Austen and all the books of Anthony Trollope.

Later throat specialists all agreed that her operation had been badly done and she would never be able to sing again. Something Barbara proved wrong in 1978 when she sang an 'Album of Love Songs' with the Royal Philharmonic Orchestra. The oldest woman ever to make her first album!

—12—

When I am in love, all the fairy tales come true, for he is Prince Charming and a magic wand has made me beautiful for him.

Barbara Cartland

At the end of the first year of their marriage, Barbara and Alexander McCorquodale were in debt to the tune of £17,000.

> We spent without thinking, quite recklessly and although Sachie's father gave him £1,000 as a wedding present, he did not increase his allowance of four thousand a year. Out of this we bought a house in London and furnished it, rented another in the Orkney Islands, bought a Rolls Royce and engaged four servants. Of course, his money wouldn't stretch that far.

It was Barbara who bearded her father-in-law and told him of their debt. He was perturbed that she had not produced a child and with her usual forthrightness she assured him it was not her fault! As a spoilt bachelor,

Sachie had never been clever with money, and Barbara was caught up and carried along in the whirlwind of her new role as a Society hostess.

Meanwhile the *Tatler* announced a new portrait of Barbara, 'Mrs McCorquodale an accomplished hostess is one of London's leading social figures this Season.' The jade green salon bulged with guests as Barbara proceeded to 'get to know everyone in London', just as she had promised Ronald that first night they walked in South Kensington together.

Sachie and Barbara travelled a great deal that first year. They went to Madeira, and cruised the Mediterranean on the *Homeric*. In Constantinople they saw great poverty and encountered a few frightened White Russians whom Barbara was to write about years later in *Pride and the Poor Princess*. In July they visited Norway in her father-in-law's yacht. Barbara hated the cold, the rough sea, the glaciers, and it didn't cheer the party up when she said: 'If this be the pleasures of the rich, give me a penny bus!'

It was Christmas 1928 when Barbara was twenty-nine that she became pregnant, much to her wild delight. She had always wanted to have children and had written many articles on the theme that children were a necessary part of fulfilment in marriage. She believed that 'If the union of spiritual and physical love evokes in the act of conception the ecstasy which is as near as we get to the Divine - the child will be beautiful.'

For the next nine months Barbara concentrated on everything of beauty around her in her belief that through this she would produce a perfect child. She listened to beautiful music and looked at fine paintings. In her bedroom she hung a picture of a beautiful baby so that she could gaze on it last thing at night and first thing on awakening in the morning. Guided by Ronald she read many of the classics to improve her mind.

She would not read an improper book or see a violent film which she thought could induce the wrong or bad thoughts that might affect the unborn child. She neither smoked nor drank except for the occasional glass of champagne. She also kept herself physically fit and when she had to give up dancing she took long walks. It was as if her whole existence were geared towards that unborn child. A quest for perfection.

Although he was pleased about the baby, in his dour Scottish way, Sachie did not share his wife's rapturous excitement about the preparation of the blue and white nursery with its pink chintz curtains and cot trimmed with crisp pink organdie tied with blue posies and ribbon bows.

Perhaps I was being over romantic about my baby, but I was so thrilled at having a child and went off to buy a pram as if I was going to a sacred shrine. When I came back I said to Sachie: 'What do you think I've done today Darling. I've bought a pram.' He replied: 'If you had done it through the office you could have saved ten per cent.' I was cut to the quick. 'How can he think about our precious baby like that?' I asked myself.

In September the baby was born - a girl weighing 7lb 10¾ oz. It was a very difficult birth as her own birth had been. Barbara was given no chloroform, and the baby was born with the cord round her neck and took over half an hour to breathe. Though the baby's features were rose-bud delicate her entire body was covered with eczema and she had to be washed only in oil for the first six months. At night-time she wore tiny white gloves on her hands to stop her from scratching the inflamed sores which covered her body.

Eczema was a blood disorder that had been handed down through the McCorquodales and later both the baby's half-brothers, Ian and Glen McCorquodale, the sons of Barbara's second marriage to Sachie's cousin, Hugh McCorquodale, were to suffer from it too. When Ian was a young child his legs had to be bandaged, and it was not until he sunbathed in Canada many years later that his skin peeled and he was almost cured.

Several of Barbara's friends had babies at the same time, a fact duly recorded in the *Daily Sketch*:

September was a bumper month for babies and now Lady Weymouth has a son and heir. . . . Below I give the runners and weights, so to speak.
1   Lady Alington's Mary..........9lb 4ozs
2   Mrs McCorquodale's Raine........7lb 10¾oz
3   Lady Diana Cooper's Julius........7lb 4ozs
4   Princess Bismarck's daughter.....7lb 5ozs
5   Lady Dunn's Ann..........7lb 10ozs
6   Lady Maud Carnegie's James.....5lb 12ozs

The christening at St Margaret's Westminster was one of the social events of the Season. In her romantic way Barbara chose the unusual Gaelic name, Raine. Friends were fascinated to see that Raine did look exactly like the picture of the baby which Barbara had gazed upon during her nine months of pregnancy.

Barbara had done this first because she had read that the ancient Greeks believed in pre-natal influence on their unborn children and that the places where the women had their babies were always decorated with beautiful statues. Barbara believed firmly that from the moment the child was conceived the mother should make every effort to influence its mind and body and she explains quite simply:

When I 'came out' the most beautiful girl of the Season was Blossom Forbes-Robertson. She had perfect classical features and it was difficult to imagine anyone more lovely, but actually she had to wear a glass eye as she had an empty eye-socket. The daughter of Sir John Forbes-Robertson the famous actor, Blossom's mother, Lady Forbes-Robertson was playing the part of a one-eyed woman for seven months while she was carrying her baby! I was terribly impressed with this story and it made me determined that my child would be as beautiful as Blossom but with no flaws.

Raine was dressed in a long, lacy christening robe with little diamond thistles running up the front among the lacy frills. Dr Wilson, the Bishop of Chelmsford, officiated, and the four godparents were Lady Berwick, a friend of the McCorquodales, Lady Stonehaven, an older woman who was a great friend of Barbara's because she was psychic and they had some very interesting discussions together on psychic matters (she was, however, unfortunately in Australia where her husband was the Governor-General), the Duke of Sutherland, and Sir Francis Davis who had been Bertie's General in the War and was a very old Worcestershire friend of the family. He had given Barbara away at her wedding.

Already Raine McCorquodale was making the newspaper gossip columns, and these first cuttings are the beginning of the volumes that Barbara began for her, like the ones she has painstakingly kept for herself all through the years. The scrapbooks now tally into many volumes and are stored in the library at Camfield Place. Samples of the first fulsome entries are, *Modern Weekly*: 'At bye bye time Raine sleeps under a pink silk quilt trimmed by a blue bow in which a pink rose is tied. Even her nighties are rose coloured and made of softest washing satin.' *Glasgow Evening News*: 'One of the smartest babies in the Park this season is Raine, six months old daughter of Mrs Alexander McCorquodale. Even at this tender age she has undoubtedly inherited her smart mother's flair for clothes and coos proudly while attention is called to her pretty frocks. Raine lives at present mostly in her mother's Park Lane house and receives her guests while her mother entertains in her Queen Anne drawing room.'

Because of the eczema, when Raine was eventually put into dresses, the material had to be gossamer fine. Even now Countess Spencer and her two brothers still suffer occasionally from this skin disease.

Though she had given up her gossip paragraphs, despite being married, Barbara wanted to continue with her literary career. Her mother-in-law was particularly keen that she give up writing 'your immoral novels', so Barbara decided to make a book of fairy stories which she dedicated to her. They were romantic stories about changelings, fairies, gods and goddesses and some very imaginative poems. The book started with a poem, of which the first two lines were:

Would you sail away from a gloomy world
To the land of dreams come true?

It was doubtful whether Mrs McCorquodale appreciated Barbara's fairy world, but when they had a glimpse of it, men found it irresistibly attractive. One man who took her to the Russian ballet said to her afterwards, 'I have never been so thrilled as watching you. You were like a child who had unexpectedly stepped into fairyland.'

With Barbara's writing done in the mornings, or at odd moments before dinner, this left the afternoons free for seeing her friends. The drawing room in Culross Street was brimming every afternoon. In the evenings if they were not entertaining at home Barbara and Sachie were out to dinner-dances at nightclubs.

The last big party of 1929 was held at the Kit Kat Club. Barbara had been consulted about this dinner-dance to be given for the Queen Charlotte Hospital and immediately suggested that a pageant would add a novel touch. Eventually the idea evolved of the 'Queen Charlotte Birthday Dinner', and Barbara asked 'Peter' Baxendale, Hugo's sister-in-law, to design the costumes. The pageant began with an 'oyster', followed by Lady Dunn as 'white wine', her daughter, Lady Patricia Douglas, as 'mince-pie'; Viscountess Castlerosse was the 'fish', Viscountess Scarsdale the 'goose' and Barbara was 'champagne' in a dress of gold tissue covered with Cellophane, a new transparent product made from wood pulp which had just come on the market.

When Barbara asked Lady Curzon to be Queen Charlotte she refused frostily pointing out that Queen Charlotte was an extremely ugly woman. It had never occurred to Barbara that she might have been offensive, as she herself had represented both Mary Queen of Scots and Ellen Terry in previous pageants and had made no attempt whatsoever to look like the ladies in question. In fact when Ernest Thesinger, who knew Ellen Terry well, saw her waiting to go on stage he said, 'One thing Ellen never had and that was plucked eyebrows.' With that he seized some brown grease paint and drew thick, broad eyebrows on Barbara's delicate ones. She hated the effect and rubbed them off before making her entrance but she says she still felt more like George Robey the comedian than the lovely Ellen Terry. Finally Binnie Hales took the part of Queen Charlotte and looked both regal and beautiful.

Fancy dresses and 'freak' parties were all the rage, too. At one party given by the Duchess of Sutherland the Prince of Wales had appeared in two different comic costumes, Winston Churchill had been an illustrious Cardinal Wolsey and Lord Ednam a buxom nurse. At another party given in a big studio, decorated to look like a French café, Barbara was shocked to be greeted by her host dressed as a can-can girl. His naked shoulders were powdered and his face heavily made-up as he frou-froued round the room shrieking in a falsetto voice to his friends. It was the first time she had seen men dancing with men and she was horrified. This was not the kind of thing which happened in her romantic novels and she left as soon as she could.

Through Ronald Barbara was introduced that year to *Experiment With Time* by J. Dunne, who had designed the first military aircraft in 1907. He set out to prove through recording one's dreams that when a person is asleep he or she is released from the imprisonment of the third dimension and thus able to experience images from the past, the present and the future. Barbara experimented with dreams just as Dunne directed, and on three separate occasions she dreamt very clearly of things which were to occur within the next twenty-four hours.

Though it had been a year of bubble and gaiety Barbara was already deeply involved with 'the world behind the world'. Despite her hectic social life she had learnt a lot and progressed in her inner search for her real self.

She was to need all the courage she could muster for the difficult years ahead.

And there are those
Through whom the stream flows gently
Often dim and grey, but never still.
Its flow unceasing, ceaseless,
Till - as dawn breaks in a sable sky -
The purpose of its moving stands revealed,
The path of God - the leaping flame of life.

Barbara Cartland

Barbara's life has never been an easy one. It has been threaded with a series of shocks that have erupted every time she began to feel secure. Perhaps they were meant to play their part in her evolution through this life, and since she believes in reincarnation she has always been able to deal with them in her own way. Her faith is deep and abiding.

The arrival of her baby had meant complete fulfilment as a woman to Barbara. While Sachie had a decided fondness for his daughter, of whom he was very proud, Barbara doted on Raine, even if the baby spent most of her time with an experienced old-fashioned and loving Nanny.

All babies were vaccinated against smallpox soon after birth, but Barbara had stubbornly refused to have Raine done. She perceptively felt that it was not right and fought against her doctor's, her in-laws' and even Polly's advice.

Barbara and Sachie went off gaily to Egypt for a holiday. In Luxor Barbara found Howard Carter sitting outside the tomb of Tutankhamen which he had discovered in 1922. He showed her the gold sarcophagus of the Pharoah and she understood from that moment some of the hidden secrets of the Valley of the Kings and the Temples. She was not able to express them until she wrote *The River of Love* in 1980. When Barbara and Sachie returned to Cairo they learnt that Raine was seriously ill, and they returned immediately to England.

Raine was only six months old when her Nanny noticed one morning that the baby was turning black for no obvious reason. Only a bottle of brandy, and the quick wits of the Nanny, who contacted the family doctor, Sir Louis Knuthsen, saved her. She was taken to hospital and given X-rays which showed that she was suffering from an enlarged thymus gland, a peculiar ailment among children for which there was then no known explanation. All that was known at the time was that there were no two children in the same family who suffered from the illness. The gland increases for two years until it becomes normal again and the child is out of danger. These few years can be critical because any sudden shock or fright could cause the child to collapse and die.

Raine survived - with the help of £15,000-worth of radium which was strapped to her chest half a dozen times while she slept. Back in England Barbara had to face the question whether Raine was to be brought up as a near invalid for the next three years or allowed to lead a normal life like other children.

All the arguments for bringing up the child in the country were presented to Barbara but these she deliberately put aside. 'And if I do keep her isolated away from all the noise and excitement of London what happens when a rabbit pops out of a hedge and the child dies of shock?' she asked the doctor. 'I shall bring her up as if she was an ordinary healthy child and trust in God.'

With hindsight it is interesting to speculate what would have happened had Raine been given a smallpox injection when only a few days old, considering the enlarged thymus gland? It could well have been fatal for her. Today Barbara has no valid explanation for her stubbornness except that at the time all her instincts told her that vaccination would be wrong, and in the case of her only and beloved child she was taking no chances.

In every respect Barbara was a conscientious mother and she now began to take a positive interest in child welfare quite apart from that of her own baby. Appalled by the effects that the new slimming craze was having in producing unhealthy babies she wrote an article in the *Daily Mirror* called 'Mothers Must Help' in which she condemned the selfishness of young mothers who, through intensive slimming, were now producing tiny, often misshapen babies which would be handicapped for the rest of their lives. As a result she received dozens of letters from doctors, midwives and nurses all congratulating her on spotlighting this insidious new illness of pre-natal undernourishment.

Had not Max Beaverbrook told her that she must find a platform on which to launch herself into being a personality? Now, in addition to her fund-raising work, she had found a deeper and more worthwhile one - public health. The article in the *Daily Mirror* was to be a spear-head for Barbara Cartland's relentless campaign for better health, to be waged over the next fifty-five years.

Although she was deeply immersed in the social whirl, which she had so aptly written about in *Jigsaw*, Barbara had never been taken in by its scintillating values. Donations to charity were more acceptable to the rich gift-wrapped, in the glamorous balls and pageants that were being staged, than dipping their hands directly into their pockets would have been. 'Charity has become a ladder with which to climb the social tree,' Barbara wrote at the time.

She was to organize many charity events, but Barbara's triumph was the pageant she produced and designed on the jingoistic theme 'Britain and her Industries' which was staged at the Royal Albert Hall. All that flow of energy was now siphoned into cajoling the various industries to donate the cost of the dresses. Barbara did the designs, which were then executed by the theatrical designers, Nathans. As all the dresses had to be on a large scale, so that they would not be dwarfed in the vastness of the Albert Hall, the models had to be taught how to walk in them gracefully.

As the Mayfair lovelies lined up the inevitable back-biting began. Sylvia Ashley as 'coal', paid for by the Coal Board, had one of the most eye-catching outfits with slinky black sequin tights and a black oil-cloth train thirty yards square. Her long legs and cool blonde beauty set off the costume to perfection so much so that Doris, Viscountess Castlerosse, as 'paper', in a massive crinoline of coloured paper which hid her famous legs, was so jealous that she had to be given a dressing room at the opposite side of the hall to that of Sylvia.

Barbara, as planned, of course, stole the show when she sailed out in a huge construction - a canvas-covered trolley painted to look like sea and bearing on its white-crested waves a model liner lit up in every porthole. Somewhere amid the construction was her pretty face, bubbling with fun. The dress had been given by the White Star Line, and there were more than a few jealous looks, as she was not only the most spectacular exhibit but also had three attendants. Even the four beauties representing knives and forks, paid for by the Sheffield industries, who wore huge silver knives and forks on their heads, could not compete with a winking and blinking ocean liner.

The tableaux ended with all the Industries grouped around the red, white and blue figure of Lily Elsie wearing £100,000 worth of jewels. As a glorious finale, up through a twenty-two feet column in the centre of the hall came St George - Captain Paul Bennett, V.C., M.C. - dressed in golden armour. Bennett had been in the same regiment as Barbara's father and was considered to be one of the most glamorous of the young war heroes. His presence as St George was a stroke of genius and the whole of the Albert Hall broke into a euphoria of wild excitement.

As the organizer Barbara was presented to the Prince of Wales.

Changing into a ball gown she later sat with him in his box and talked about the events of the evening. The Prince, not known for his generosity, had given a large Wedgwood dinner service to be sold for the British Legion. Never at a loss for words Barbara remarked to the Prince that she did not think the dinner service was a very pretty one.

'What do you think I am getting rid of it for?' he answered petulantly.

Barbara was given the sought-after social accolade of the twenties when the Prince invited her to dance with him. They made a striking couple as they took the floor. The popular tune of this time was 'I've danced with a man who's danced with a girl who's danced with the Prince of Wales', but this was better!

The *Daily Telegraph* was complimentary about the pageant and wrote: 'It was a parade of exciting, fantastic contrasts, constructive, imaginative and brilliant.'

As a result of this pageant the well known revue producer, C. B. Cochran, asked Barbara to present some of the 'Industries' at the Midnight Revue he was presenting for charity in July at the London Pavilion. This was not only the first but the most successful of many midnight performances, and £12,000 was collected and presented by Lord Louis Mountbatten to the Prince of Wales at the finale at three-thirty that morning.

The presentation of the pageant at the London Pavilion, which lacked the space of the Albert Hall was not without hazards as the 'Industries' manoeuvred in the cramped wings, each fiercely protective of her dress. On stage, squeezed together, they looked like a tin of sardines. Captain Bennett nearly came a cropper, as he scarcely had enough room to come up through the trap door. The chairman was Lady Louis Mountbatten, and the organizer that indefatigable American Mrs Frank Braham, who had been a protégée of Sarah Bernhardt.

Ray Braham's secret lay in the fact that like so many of her countrywomen she understood women. She showed the climbers how they could mount the rungs of the social ladder; she aroused, too, the competitive sense of those who disliked their friends 'going one better'. She appealed in the right way to those who had to be coaxed into generosity. What was more she 'delivered the goods'. She made people pay heavily for publicized charity, but she took them into the intimate circles of 'big names' and saw that their actions were recognized by the Press. Hers was a formula that has been proven right through the years and to a lesser degree applies today, except that now the climbers go one better and employ their own public relations experts to project their charitable 'good works', with always the hint of a peerage lurking in the background.

One paper wrote of the Midnight Revue: 'Sir Oswald Mosley and the prominent Socialites were among the millionaires and duchesses in the stalls.'

In 1930 Barbara met one true woman friend who was to remain close to her all her life. She has always found women difficult, and because of their not surprising jealousy, she has had some unpleasant and somewhat treacherous encounters with women who had at first pretended to be her friends. One evening she was taken by wealthy Edward Hulton, later to be the brilliant young editor of the *Picture Post* magazine, to Ye Kinde Dragon Club, a popular nightclub at that time. At the nightclub was Captain Alec Cunningham-Reid, who saw them and came up to talk to Barbara and to introduce his young wife, the former Mary Ashley.

Barbara had met Alec Cunningham-Reid at *thés dansants* at the American Embassy, where she danced with him and learnt that he was political private secretary to Wilfred Ashley, the old friend of her father and mother. In 1927, a month after Barbara's own wedding, he had married Mary Ashley at St Margaret's, Westminster. Although Polly had known the Ashley girls - Edwina and Mary - from the days when she stayed at Broadlands, Barbara had not met them until they were grown up. The papers were always full of Edwina's brilliant marriage to Lord Louis Mountbatten and the enormous fortune they had both inherited from their grandfather, Sir Ernest Cassel. In his will he had left Broadlands and Classiebawn Castle in Ireland, where Lord Mountbatten was staying at the time of his assassination, to the elder granddaughter Edwina, and to Mary, The Hall, a rambling Victorian shooting-lodge at Six Mile Bottom, near Newmarket in Cambridgeshire.

Mary had a disconcerting childhood as she had been unhappy with her stepmother, and this not was surprising. Barbara has still not forgotten when she was a little girl, and Molly Forbes Sempill came to stay at her parents' house, Amerie Court. On several occasions she was heard to say: 'I much prefer my Pekingese dogs to children.' From that crushed, unhappy childhood, Barbara now found that Mary had grown into a bewitching beauty. She was completely unlike her sister Edwina and had inherited the Ashley colouring of flaming red hair and a white translucent skin. Although not a classic beauty like Lady Diana Cooper, she had an aura of innocence and vulnerability like Rosetti's Beatrice. On the night Barbara first met her she was wearing a sheath of white lace and an aquamarine necklace which set off her striking colouring.

From the moment they met there was an affinity between the two women which was quite different to anything Barbara had known before with the rest of her species. Years later people used to say, 'Why are you such friends with Mary?' and Barbara's answer was always the same. Mary was not only extremely clever, but had a sense of humour which Barbara had not found in any other women, not even in her scintillating sister, Edwina. Right up to the present day Barbara finds Mary, Lady Delamere, more amusing than anyone else she knows, and Mary feels the same about her.

When I went to visit Mary, Lady Delamere, at The Hall, while researching this book, though she has undergone two severe cancer operations, she still has an irresistible charm and wit. Her intelligence obviously comes from Sir Ernest Cassel, one of the brilliant men in King Edward VII's circle.

In addition to being so beautiful, Edwina and Mary were extremely well educated, both speaking French and German fluently. Unlike Lady Mountbatten, who collected people, Lady Delamere has a great appreciation of the arts and she has always been an avid reader. 'It was Barbara's intense vitality that first attracted me to her. She was bubbling over with life', she told me. 'Something she still has to this day. This is what my husband and I first noticed. . . After all, she was a lonely, rather battered woman after her marriage broke up but we found her so attractive and welcomed her into our life. She had this wonderful *joie de vivre* and vitality that just flowed out of her.'

Mary and Barbara had so much in common that they telephoned each other nearly every day and met continuously. In the years ahead it was Mary who turned to Barbara when she was having marriage troubles and it was she who supported Barbara through all the shocks and difficulties which were at that moment just over the horizon. Barbara and Sachie stayed frequently at Six Mile Bottom for the shooting and were constant guests at the large house parties at Number 12 Upper Brook Street, where Alec Cunningham-Reid, who was always known as 'Bobbie', arranged amusing parties in the Squash Court.

As Lady Delamere played with her present dachshund, she told me how Barbara figured in the life of Fritz, a favourite in a long history of dachshunds she has owned. The incident took place just after Barbara's divorce some two years after they had first met:

I had taken my small dachshund called Fritz with me to the South of France where we had taken a villa for three months, and I could not imagine living without him. When it was time to go home I was distraught as to how we could get him back without quarantine. I telephoned Barbara frantically who, as usual, came up with an idea. She asked one of her beaux, Geoffrey Rodd, to help. He was a great charmer who had been in the Navy, and he flew over in his private plane. The vet in Cannes put the dog to sleep with an injection and we packed it in a shoe box. My husband and I had gone ahead to Six Mile Bottom where Barbara joined us, and just imagine the fun of seeing the plane land in an adjacent field with Fritzie still fast asleep in the box.

Well then we had to change his name and he became Gustav. My cousin Marjorie, Countess of Brecknock, who was a great tease, used to give me a heart attack when she visited me by asking 'Where is L.L.F.?' (Late Lamented Fritz). I used to say 'If you're talking about Gustav he is playing in the garden.'

—————14—————

I thought that love would come to me,
As a gently twinkling star,
But this is like a violent sea
Or an all consuming fire.

Barbara Cartland

Glen Kidston - dashing, handsome, rich and charming - was one of London's most eligible bachelors. He had been in Barbara's social life for several years. Glen, who had been away for some time, suddenly returned like a meteor to tell Barbara he intended to buy the ill-fated 'plane in which Captain Alfred Lowenstein, the Belgian financier, had fallen into the Channel three years earlier.

'You can't do that!' Barbara exclaimed.

'Why not?' Glen asked.

'Because it's unlucky!'

Glen laughed. 'It's lucky for me in that it's a very good aeroplane, and cheap!'

Barbara instinctively felt there was something wrong about this aeroplane and begged him to change his mind, which was as easy as asking the tide to turn the other way.

One cold, misty morning in April, while Sachie was away on business, Barbara drove down to Croydon with one of Glen's friends to see him off to Africa. As they went into the aerodrome she saw the aeroplane waiting like a huge, sinister black bird, and she felt herself shiver.

Then Glen walked towards her smiling, and for one moment he seemed to become larger and more vivid, more vibrant, as if he had stepped out of time and space. It was something which was to happen to her several times in the future, but for the moment she did not understand what she was seeing and feeling. Then he was beside her, and there was nothing she could say but, 'Goodbye, take care of yourself!' He laughed. 'That's what I'm saying to you.'

A party of his friends, and there were quite a number of them, cheered as the aeroplane set off down the runway. Then it rose black against the grey sky and grew smaller and smaller until it vanished. Soon afterwards Barbara was to think that she had been right about the aeroplane and that tragic and emotional experiences of human beings imprint themselves on and are absorbed by inanimate objects.

A month later Glen crashed into the side of a hill in Africa, and Barbara learnt that the 'plane had been overloaded. Glen's body was brought back and buried at his home in Wales.

Several months later, Barbara received from Lady Darnley, Glen's elder sister, six photographs of herself in Nile blue leather frames that Glen had with him in the aeroplane. The frames bore the marks from the mud into which the aeroplane had crashed, but the pictures themselves were untouched! It was inevitable that she should be haunted by the idea, however far-fetched, that the photographs had been responsible for the overloading.

Glen was only the first of several men who loved her whom she was to lose through their absorption in flying, and it was inevitable that Barbara should become interested in it too. When two Air Force pilots, Flying Officers E. L. Mole and E. C. Wanliss, came to see her about gliding, the more they talked about their idea, the more fascinated Barbara became. Hand-launching had become popular in Germany owing to strict restrictions imposed by the Versailles Treaty on aeroplane flying, but these pilots had the idea it would be possible to attach a glider to an aeroplane. If the aeroplane was towing not merely one glider but quite a number of them, it would save fuel and when they reached the right altitude they could glide down for any distance required. This appeared to be a new cheap proposition for commercial flying. Barbara decided to build a glider that could be towed up to 10,000 feet and let it fly the Channel landing on a French aerodrome.

Barbara ordered the glider to be built at a cost of £150, and the three inventors of the idea kept quiet about what they were planning. But somebody must have talked, and a month later the *Daily Mail* announced an offer of £1,000 to the first glider to fly the Channel both ways. Barbara sent somebody to the office to find out the details and they discovered the *Mail* had no idea as to how it could be done, but 'just thought it might be possible'!

Gliding experts from all over the country started to scheme to win the prize, and the contractor engaged on making Barbara's glider decided to compete himself. It was Barbara's idea that now instead of bothering with the Channel she and her two pilots should deliver the first Glider Airmail across country. But to make sure of his Channel success, when Barbara and the two pilots arrived at Manston Aerodrome on 20 June the contractor insisted on leaving first. When the release cable, and there was only one, dropped back onto the ground they attached it to their aeroplane and to the red and white 'Barbara Cartland Glider'.

It was a perfect day, calm and sunny, and like the amateurs they were, to show up the tow-rope they tied their handkerchiefs along it, so that it could be easily seen from the ground. Barbara, wearing a red suede coat and red helmet edged with white fur, got into the aeroplane with Flying Officer Wanliss, with the release hook just above her head. Flying Officer Mole was in the glider.

They rose slowly, then proceeded across-country towards Reading. A cricket match stopped in astonishment to wave at them as they passed, and Barbara has always said she is sure she is the only person who ever stopped a sacred English cricket match in the middle of an over!

They reached Reading Aerodrome, a distance of about a hundred miles, where the Mayor was waiting to greet them. As Barbara stepped out of the aeroplane an on-looker seeing what she was wearing cried: 'Here comes Father Christmas!' Full of smiles, Barbara delivered the world's first Glider Airmail letter to the Mayor. For the flight on to Heston, where they were offered the hospitality of the aerodrome, they had an escort of five aeroplanes commanded by the Master of Semphill, who was Vice-President of the International Commission for the Study of Motorless Flight.

The 'Barbara Cartland' was to take part in several air rallies that summer, and on one, when carrying a passenger from London to Blackpool, was an easy winner against an express train. Barbara's glider also set up a record for British gliders with a falling height of four and three-quarter miles, but on landing from one flight the 'plane was blown over three times. Though the pilot escaped injury what remained of the glider was taken to the scrap heap. But Barbara had proved her point that it was a practical and inexpensive way of transporting goods or mail.

The Air Ministry thought otherwise and stopped aeroplane towing as being too dangerous. Gliders then returned to hand launching, but Germany did not forget what had been proved by the experiment and used aeroplane-towed gliders in the invasion of Crete.

People had forgotten Barbara's involvement in this pioneering work until in 1958 she was the subject of *This is Your Life* on television with Eamonn Andrews, and one of the 'surprise' guests was Group-Captain E. L. Mole. On the stage he said: 'During the last War, I was put in charge of the development of military gliders at the Ministry of Aircraft Production. Hundreds of these were subsequently used on D-Day, so I would like to say how grateful I, and the Air Ministry, are to Miss Cartland for supporting the original project so courageously.'

In 1984 America suddenly woke up to the fact that Barbara had been instrumental in developing air technology, and at a special ceremony at Kennedy Airport she was awarded the Bishop Wright's Air Industry Award.

Because Barbara was always looking for something new and exciting, her next project was to help the Marquess of Donegal at Bray to organize a full-scale motor rally. She persuaded Sir Malcolm Campbell, who had won the world speed record in 1929, to be one of the judges, and supported by the glamorous Bentley brothers, the rally was a huge success.

Barbara had been a friend of another great motoring hero of the time, Sir Henry Segrave, who with Malcolm Campbell was trying to be the first to reach 200 m.p.h. at Parradine Sands, Carmarthenshire. Sir Henry Segrave eventually won the World Speed Record in 1929 by doing 231 m.p.h. at Daytona Beach, Florida, but he was killed the following year. Barbara never forgot him, and she often told the story of how one evening when he came to dine at Culross Street he was laughing at having been summonsed in Bond Street for driving too slowly and causing an obstruction of traffic. 'She had the best pair of legs I've seen in years!' he explained.

Another quest for excitement in 1931 resulted in Barbara being involved with something which was new at the time. Lord de Clifford asked her to organize the first woman's motor car race in Great Britain. All the competitors - and Barbara had great difficulty in finding them - were to drive supercharged M.G.s.

Although Barbara had only just started to drive, taught by Sachie, she entered the race simply because the whole idea behind the stunt was to show the public that women could drive as well as men - something Barbara did not believe to be true, at the time or now! Lord de Clifford went as Barbara's passenger, while his wife Dorothy partnered the winner, Princess George Imeretinsky, who was later to be the fourth Mrs Ernest Simpson.

Raine had now grown into a very pretty child and was known as being the most photographed baby in the Park. She was just one year of age that autumn when she went to her first party which was held by Lady Plunket at Londonderry House. Dorothé Plunket was the daughter of Fanny Ward, the American actress who was the first person to have her face lifted. It was renowned that Dorothé was also connected with the handsome, dashing Marquess of Londonderry. True or not, the London-derrys always treated Dorothé as one of the family, and she was close friends with the charming, shy little Duchess of York.

It was at this party that Raine, dressed as a fairy and held by Nanny was noticed by Princess Elizabeth, later the Queen, who rushed up to her and exclaimed: 'Oh, what a lovely fat baby! What is her name?'

'Raine, Your Royal Highness', Nanny replied.

The Princess burst out laughing. 'What a funny name!' she said and ran off to play with the older children.

Dorothé Plunket became a dear friend of Barbara. Sylph-like, she could dance as well as any professional dancer, and she gave exhibition dances at charity balls, matinées and private parties. Barbara always thought of her as the spirit of happiness for she affected everybody she met with her own joy of living. But again an aeroplane, like an ugly dark bird, shut out the sunshine of somebody Barbara loved. In 1938 Dorothé and her husband were burned to death in America when the aeroplane in which they were travelling caught fire.

It was in that year that Barbara was worried about Raine going into Hyde Park in case her pram should be overturned during the riots and disturbances caused by open meetings on unemployment. She did not then understand, as she was to do later, the sheer horror of the distressed areas in the industrial Midlands, but she was upset by the National Hunger March, when 250 marchers bore a petition with a million signatures demanding the abolition of the 'means test'. She was appalled at the sight of the gaunt men, with their lined faces and the unhealthy tinge which comes from lack of fats, having violent skirmishes with the police.

Polly had been to Portsmouth to meet Tony, who was returning from Egypt in a troop ship. He had been for two years *aide-de-camp* to the General commanding the troops in Cairo, General Sir George Weir, and had been a great success. Unfortunately he had had a fall from his horse onto the tarmac parade ground and was now being sent back to England on a stretcher.

While Polly was waiting for the ship to arrive she wandered round the dreary little shops in dockland and saw in one what she thought was a rather pretty china figure that she could give to Barbara as a present. When she entered the shop and saw it at close hand she did not think it was good enough, but looking around saw high on a shelf a small statue of what she thought was Buddha. 'I'm not very keen on selling that', the woman told her.

'Why not?' Polly asked.

'It's considered very lucky', was the reply, 'and anyone who wants a bit of luck around here borrows it from me for a few pence a time.'

This made Polly want it even more. She bought it and gave it to Barbara with the shop-keeper's instructions, which were: 'It's to be put in an important place where it can be seen, and treated with proper respect!'

Barbara put it on the mantelpiece in her bedroom in the new house which she and Sachie had moved into in Green Street. Nanny had found the nurseries too cramped for Raine in Culross Street. Twenty-seven Green Street was far more palatial with its four floors, the windows at the back looking over a very attractive private garden. Barbara however never felt as happy there as she had at Culross Street, and she suspected, although he did not say so, that Sachie felt the same.

One evening at dinner with a number of friends present he said unexpectedly, 'I'm leaving early tomorrow for a cruise on the *Homeric*.'

Barbara was surprised. He had not mentioned it to her before, but it was impossible to question him too closely while there were people there, and he went to bed early before the guests had left. That night, lying alone in the large, attractive bedroom which housed the same four-poster bed which had been in Culross Street, Barbara found it hard to sleep as she wondered why Sachie was going away so unexpectedly and why he had been so secretive about it.

Suddenly she was acutely conscious of the statue, which by now she knew was Shou Hsing, God of Happiness, standing opposite her at the far end of the room on the mantelpiece. She felt magnetically drawn to the figure, then as she asked for his help the answer was very clear: 'Go downstairs! Go downstairs!'

At first she could not believe it. It was something she never did at night as her bedroom was on the second floor and as there was a lift she seldom used the staircase.

And yet the message was repeated again and again until finally, although she thought she was being ridiculous, she put on her dressing-gown and went downstairs. Barbara had no thought of where she was going except where her feet were taking her, and she found herself in the small room at the front of the house on the ground floor which Sachie used as his sitting room.

As she switched on the light it looked very much as it usually did, except that on the desk there was a black leather, gold-edged wallet which Barbara had given him as a present. She looked at it, thinking it seemed very fat, which meant, she thought, it was filled with money for his journey, and she was sure it should not be left lying about. She picked it up and saw the fatness was not entirely due to the amount in it, there were also two letters on bright blue writing paper addressed in a woman's flowery hand-writing. Almost as if she was compelled to do so, Barbara opened the letters.

What she read came as such a shock that for the rest of the night it was impossible for her to sleep or to think clearly. The letters were from Glen Kidston's younger sister, Eleanor Curtis, whom Barbara had never actually met because she lived with her husband and children in the country. In one of her letters to Sachie she had written: 'Do not let us be in a hurry to run away, darling, because if we play our cards cleverly I think you will be able to get hold of your daughter, and I shall be able to get my children.'

To Barbara it was as if an enormous gulf she had not known was there had opened at her feet. She had never guessed, or even suspected, that Sachie was not completely happy in his marriage, and although she had flirtations, she had never concealed them from him, nor had he seemed in any way jealous. He had, in fact, always appeared delighted that men like Glen and his other friends should admire Barbara, and he often laughed about them to her, giving them nicknames like 'Warthog', 'The Weasel', 'The Bishop', 'Big Boots', and 'The Buffoon'.

The London house was always filled with guests, and it was at his invitation as much as Barbara's that the men were asked to the Orkneys to shoot and fish, to France, or anywhere else that he and Barbara were going. She had often thought that he was proud that she was such a success and that even his closest friends fell in love with her. But while she had laughed and danced and found quite a number of men attractive, she had never been unfaithful to Sachie, and it had never crossed her mind that he might be unfaithful to her. And yet, here was clear evidence of it, and also that Eleanor Curtis was accompanying Sachie on the *Homeric*, even if he had been going on the ship for business reasons.

She could not bring herself to face Sachie before he left the house, or to make a scene so early in the morning, when obviously the servants would be helping him to pack and the car would be waiting to take him to the station. Instead, after he had gone, she thought it over and decided that the only decent thing to do would be to go and see his parents, even before discussing it with Polly. That afternoon she went to Berkeley Square and told Mr and Mrs McCorquodale what she had discovered.

'If Sachie no longer loves me and wishes to leave me', she told them, 'I am perfectly prepared to divorce him, but I must make it absolutely clear that in no circumstances would I give him custody of Raine!'

Brave words, but they were intended to frighten Sachie with reference to Raine more than anything else. Barbara was sure in her heart that Sachie did not really want to leave her or break up their home, and this was confirmed when he sent her a letter from the first port of call starting in the usual way - 'My Own Darling One'.

The McCorquodales were upset in a restrained manner, and begged Barbara to give them her word of honour that she would do nothing until Sachie returned from his cruise on the *Homeric*. She promised to do what they asked, and kept her secret, except from Ronald. He was adamant that on no account should they tell Polly at the moment.

A little more than a week later, Barbara learnt by sheer chance that she was being watched by a detective. Forced to take action, she went to a solicitor who said that the letters were complete evidence of adultery, but Barbara was still very anxious not to do anything irrevocable. As soon as she heard that Sachie was back in England staying with his parents she wrote to him and asked if he would see her. She received a formal refusal from his solicitors. She then, through them, asked if she could have a meeting with him, in which she was going to suggest that they patched everything up and remained together, if only for the sake of Raine. This was again refused, and from that moment everything Barbara had built up so carefully and lovingly crashed into ruins.

The next three years were to be a time of such desperate unhappiness that she has never wanted to talk about them, and she shies away from the subject now as if it still has the power to hurt and frighten her. It was not only that she was upset at losing Sachie, whom she still loved for the same qualities for which she had married him, but she also lost his family who she had believed liked her for herself. The whole McCorquodale clan, and they were a very large one, turned on her as if she had done something unforgivable in even mentioning the word 'divorce'.

In a way, this was understandable, as at the time Barbara left school the divorce figures for the country were 0.01 per cent of the population, and in aristocratic circles the belief was that there should never, in any circumstances, be a scandal. Barbara was to find out the hypocritical truth of this when, after the gossip columnists mentioned that she was having a divorce, the Countess of Pembroke told Ray Braham that Barbara must not help her at a large charity ball that was being arranged. At the time the Earl of Pembroke, whom Barbara knew quite well, had run away with the Honourable Lois Sturt and from the South of France was begging his wife to divorce him. The Countess, who was a close friend of Queen Mary, and often with her, refused to do anything of the sort, saying: 'You are my husband, and if you wish to come back your home is waiting for you.'

After several years, during which the Earl continued to beg for a divorce, he became ill. He then returned to Wilton, where the Countess welcomed him as if nothing had ever happened. This was considered the correct behaviour for any injured wife, and had Queen Mary's approval. It was, of course, before the 'winds of change' arrived in the shape of Mrs Ernest Simpson.

Sachie employed the toughest and most feared divorce solicitors of the time. Their tactics were a kind of mental harassment which Barbara had never known existed. Detectives followed her wherever she went, sleeping in the next bedroom when she stayed at an hotel, watching her in restaurants and night clubs, and questioning her friends, and almost every day she received a legal letter that was aggressive, provocative and extremely upsetting. Sachie had one trump card that was more powerful than anything else - money - and the first thing that happened was the financial means of keeping up the house in Green Street ceased. The house-keeping bills were not paid, nor were the servants' wages.

Polly came to the rescue by finding Barbara, after a long search, a cheap, but very attractive place in which to live which consisted of the first and second floors of a house on the corner of Half Moon Street and Curzon Street. The rooms had previously been the lodgings of the Regency bucks, and Barbara liked to feel their ghosts were sympathetic and that in their own way they protected her. Protection was certainly something she needed because, for the moment, the social life which had filled her days had collapsed, as the majority of older people were shocked that any woman, however innocent, contemplated going through the divorce courts.

It was then that Ronald really came into Barbara's life and to him she clung as if he were a lifeline in a tempest. The first thing he did was to move into Green Street, before Polly found the flat in Half Moon Street, leaving his own flat in Paddington so that he could be with her and make sure she was chaperoned by one of her own family. It was Ronald who realized what she was up against in that the McCorquodales, determined that Sachie should not pay the large alimony which was hers by right, were using every possible weapon to prove that Barbara was not the innocent petitioner she alleged and were trying to bring counter-charges.

The moment Ronald heard that the McCorquodales had briefed one of the more admired advocates of the Bar, Sir Norman Birkett, K. C., on Sachie's behalf, he persuaded a friend, Sir Patrick Hastings, to take Barbara's case free of charge. Sir Patrick, who was a great orator and one of the highest paid King's Counsels, was also a Socialist. As soon as he heard what was happening, he was convinced that this was the effort of a rich man to 'get off the hook' without paying his just dues, which is exactly what it was.

It was Ronald who helped in the small cases that came first, one after another, in other courts, for unpaid bills, the subjection of witnesses and other irregularities, all of which, due to Ronald, Barbara won. He made her see that whatever happened, they still had each other and nothing, however bad, however unpleasant, could touch the feeling of closeness that had been theirs ever since they were children. It was Ronald's support that made Barbara say courageously to her solicitor, 'There is nothing more they can do to me except shoot me, but if I fail I will go down with flying colours!'

It was also entirely due to Ronald that Sir Patrick said to Barbara, 'You are one of the best witnesses I have ever had!' This was not merely because Barbara had only to tell the truth, and was supremely confident that the truth and Polly's prayers were invincible, but also because Ronald, with a brilliance that was so much a part of his character, had rehearsed every trick question which she was likely to be asked in court by Sir Norman Birkett. He made sure she phrased her answers in the correct manner. At a time when Barbara was deeply unhappy, frantic with fear that she might lose Raine, frightened as she had never been frightened before for herself, for the future and of course from a monetary point of view, it was Ronald who brought out the faith that had always been in her and made it a living, breathing and powerful force.

Despite the terrible difficulties of raising money Barbara and Ronald went to northern France for a holiday, staying at a cheap hotel and lying on the sands talking about themselves and the spiritual side of life. It meant so much to Ronald from a Christian point of view, and Barbara, who had been vaguely groping with her belief in reincarnation and the Chinese knowledge of 'the world behind the world', was suddenly vitalized by the wonder of it. Ronald gave her a book that had just been published called *A New Model of the Universe*, by P. D. Ouspensky, which told her a great deal of what she longed to know. It made her aware that she was not alone and never would be. She also read two huge volumes of *Isis Unveiled* by Madame Blavatsky, and she and Ronald argued fiercely on spiritual matters which were so real to them that the menacing of the law seemed somehow to pale into insignificance.

Barbara won her case, and the jury after only fifteen minutes returned a verdict of guilty on Sachie. Eleanor's husband immediately sued for divorce citing him as co-respondent. All the posters of London carried the message: 'NOVELIST VINDICATED'.

It had been a bitter, unpleasant, cruel battle in which the odds were most unfairly tipped against Barbara simply because she was poor. And yet right triumphed in the end, but not without leaving her with deep scars which would never completely heal.

The Judge, the famous Lord Merrivale, said: 'Here is a husband, a man evidently with great means and great resources and one of the heads of a very well-known business, and he is charged by his wife with adultery. If she establishes that he has committed adultery, upon that charge of hers, and there the matters stands, she is entitled to a decree of divorce, and she has those rights which under our law a married woman has in respect of property and pecuniary wealth. Of course, in this case of great wealth they are very substantial rights.' But the case had cost an astronomical amount of money; the damages Sachie had to pay Eleanor's husband, besides the cost of everybody else involved, meant his personal fortune was all spent.

Eventually, after an illness which kept him in hospital for nearly a year, he did not marry Eleanor, but returned to live in great comfort at his father's magnificent house, Coombe Hall in Shropshire, as well as retaining a comfortable flat at 25 Berkeley Square. Barbara was left with the mean sum of money allocated to her in the marriage settlement, which was £500. She had however the only thing that really mattered, and that was custody of Raine, although she never at any time denied Sachie and his parents any access they wished. The trauma of the last months had made her mind up about one thing. She would never again be entirely dependent upon a man, however much she loved him, and she would work her fingers to the bone to make enough money to keep herself and her child.

One joy that came out of everything, apart from the happiness of finding in Ronald the spiritual guide and teacher she sought, was that she found out who were her real friends. First came the Cunningham-Reids, whose unfailing love and loyalty sustained her all through the miserable years, and who made their home hers, whenever she needed it. Then came Comyns Beaumont, one of Fleet Street's most intelligent editors who offered Barbara the position of social editor on the *National Graphic*, an interesting political magazine that was just coming into prominence.

Other journalistic jobs came her way simply because people remembered she had been kind to them when they had come for interviews or written up her drawing room in Culross Street. Soon she was writing eight to ten thousand words every day, and there was no more dancing until dawn. Although she was never short of attentive escorts, she now told them she had to be home soon after 11.00 p.m. so that she could keep up with her work. In addition to the publicity jobs and the journalism, which provided regular payment, Barbara was also writing more romantic novels. In them she could escape into the fairy-tale world which had once been hers as a child and was now translated into the real love which was to make her novels different from those of any other author because the heroine was pure.

Barbara's talent for publicity resulted in her being asked to give the Embassy Club, which had fallen on bad times, a new lease of life. In the twenties, under the guiding hand of the most famous maître d'hôtel, Luigi, it had been the night club mecca of Europe. On Thursday nights it had been the smartest, most exciting and glamorous place that could be found anywhere in London, and being there was just like being at a private party. The Prince of Wales was always to be found in 'the Royal Box' which was just on the left inside the door, and everybody watched as he arrived with the beautiful Mrs Dudley Ward, the Mountbattens, General 'G' Trotter, Major 'Fruity' Metcalfe, and other intimate cronies who, of course, knew and were known by everyone in the room.

But new places had been opened and the rich clientele became bored, especially after a misguided attempt to attract attention by replacing the pretty, unobtrusive decorations with a stark *art nouveau* interior with lights coming from the ceiling.

Barbara was given *carte blanche* by the Chairman, the Hon. Wilfred Egerton, but was asked not to spend more money than she could help. She transformed the place by introducing the colours of her bedroom, Nile blue walls and coral pink sofas, combined with soft, eye-level pink lighting which is the most flattering of all to women. On the opening night, when Barbara persuaded Anna May Wong, the Chinese film star, to do a cabaret act, the Embassy came alive again. Back in his favourite seat was the Prince of Wales, but now with him was the beautiful Thelma, Lady Furness, who was a close friend of Barbara's. At another sofa table were the Cunningham-Reids with Charlie Chaplin.

The Countess of Portarlington, an indefatigable dancer, was swinging round the room in the arms of her faithful young man who was known as 'Didsy Wee', and her husband, Lionel Portarlington, was going from table to table forcing himself, like a cuckoo in the nest, on the prettiest girls, who much preferred to be alone with the man they were with. It all provided what any journalist would call 'first class copy' and Ambrose's band, engaged by Barbara, were playing the romantic tunes which made even the most cynical man believe he was falling in love.

Unfortunately Barbara, with all her flair, had not yet learnt to be commercial. She was paid by the club at so much a head for everybody who came, but she had not taken advice over her contract. Once the club was regularly full and people were being turned away, especially on a Thursday night, they thanked Barbara profusely for what she had done and told her that she was 'no longer necessary' to them.

Barbara did not waste time regretting. That was something she has never done at any time in her life. She laughed and said lightly: 'One learns by experience.'

In May 1932 Barbara published *A Virgin in Mayfair*, her fifth novel, which was compared with Elinor Glyn's *Visit of Elizabeth*. Of course the 'Virgin' was Barbara herself, and she depicted what she had felt when she first arrived in London and found the social world had deep undercurrents that were very different from the quiet life she had lived in the country.

James Agate, the waspish book critic of the *Daily Express*, whose scathing reviews caused much heartache among authors, wrote:

> The minutes spent in turning the pages may not be a serious waste, but I suggest that the time spent in writing this and all those other books is considerable and would be better employed in say spring cleaning Belgravia, or even in learning French. It is typical of our infantile intelligentsia that it cannot get the simplest phrase correct.

A few nights later Barbara met James Agate face to face at the theatre and in her usual courageous way confronted him: 'You reviewed my book and you certainly gave me the stick!'

'Oh, it was your book that Reggie Pound [the features editor of the *Daily Express*] sent me to review', he replied. 'I knew I was asked to do something about it, but I couldn't remember what!'

As Barbara remembers wryly: 'So much for "influence at Court!"'

Barbara's flair for hitting the headlines was now well established, and Sir James Dunn, who still figured a great deal in her life, had found the inventor of a new process for cleaning clothes quickly. He asked Barbara to publicize it. She chose the name 'Six-Hour Cleaners', designed a jazzy trade-mark in red and white, and personally sent out five thousand letters to prospective clients. Until then, clothes had been dab-cleaned with petrol by maids at home, but this new technique was to revolutionize the whole of the cleaning industry. Jimmy paid Barbara £50 for her work during the first year of the 'Six-Hour Cleaners' with the advantage of having her own clothes cleaned free of charge. He actually offered her a hundred pounds' worth of shares if she liked to buy them, but as Barbara was struggling on a shoe-string to keep her own and Raine's heads above water, she could not afford it. Later Jimmy sold the 'Six-Hour Cleaners' at a very large profit, and once again she had proved herself to be uncommercial.

There were several other things that Barbara did that year, including popularizing a swimming-pool on the roof of the Piccadilly Hotel. Of course it poured with rain and while Princess Arthur of Connaught and several other distinguished guests looked at the bath, the only person who ventured in was a débutante, thus making her début at a bathing party instead of a ball!

By August, Barbara was tired and somewhat depleted of ideas. It was therefore a joy to be asked by the Cunningham-Reids to go with them as their guest to the South of France. It was also to be an important milestone in her life.

—15—

I felt you when you walked into the hall
Then I saw your portrait on the wall
And knew you were the man I'd sought
Through centuries of thought
And in my dreams.

Barbara Cartland

After all her unhappiness Barbara found the light-hearted gaiety of the South of France in the summer stimulating. Although she had spent part of her honeymoon there, this was quite different, with swimming-pool parties, dancing under the stars and rushing wildly over the smooth blue Mediterranean in fast speed-boats.

This, incidentally, resulted in Barbara buying for the first and only time in her life a pair of trousers. Finding it impossible in the speed-boats which Alec ("Bobby") Cunningham-Reid enjoyed to be modest in a skirt, she went to the cheapest Emporium in Cannes and bought herself a pair of navy-blue serge trousers with full bell-bottoms and a pretty coloured jumper.

At Monte Carlo a great floating stage in the Summer Casino held every night a show costing millions of francs, yachts filled the harbour there and at Cannes, while villas were rented at enormous rents. The most amazing villa on the whole coast was Maxine Elliott's *Château l'Horizon* at Juan-les-pins. When Mary told Barbara they were taking her there for lunch she was excited, and she found reality exceeded even her expectations.

The villa itself was decorated with beautiful antique furniture coupled with twentieth-century luxury - a cocktail bar and a huge swimming-pool which had a fast slide down into the sea, an exotic rock garden and a sun-bathing balcony.

Maxine Elliott, one of America's most famous actresses, had not only made money, but, unlike many others of her profession, had kept it and doubled it. She had been a great beauty in her time and she and Ethel Barrymore were the only actresses ever to have a Broadway theatre named after them. Maxine had attracted Edward VII, and the Marquess Curzon of Kedleston had asked her to marry him, but she had lost her heart when she was forty-two to a younger man Anthony Wilding who was the New Zealand tennis champion, but he had tragically been killed in 1915 in the second battle of Ypres.

It was after the war that Maxine built the *Château l'Horizon* and grew enormously fat because she really cared for nobody except a bad-tempered, smelly little monkey called Kiki. He made messes all over the villa, bit anyone who attempted to touch him, and had a terrifying habit of springing unexpectedly on one's shoulder. Barbara disliked Kiki, and pleaded with Mary, who was good with animals, to keep him away from her.

After a large luncheon party Maxine said to Barbara: 'I want you to play backgammon with a charming young man of whom I am very fond.' She then introduced Barbara to the Viscount Rattendon, who was fair, blue-eyed and one of the most attractive men she had ever met. They sat down under an awning beside the swimming-pool and played a very strange game of backgammon, finding it hard to concentrate on the game because there were long silences when they just looked at each other. It was one of those special moments that are sheer 'Barbara Cartland' and laughed at by other people, when one person's vibrations touch another's and they know without words that person is of great importance because they have met before in previous lives.

'Nigs', as the Viscount was called, was going back to London the next day, but Barbara knew it was only a question of time before they would be together again. But before that could happen she learnt with surprise that he had been married before, to Blossom Forbes-Robertson, of whom she had thought all the while she was expecting Raine because of the pre-natal influence which had resulted in her having only one eye. Even before she was aware that Blossom had been his wife she realized Nigs had been deeply hurt by the break-up of his marriage, as she had been by hers, and strangely enough, they were both in exactly the same position of having to wait for six months before they received their decrees absolute.

This was a cruel, almost Chinese torture imposed by the law on the parties in a divorce. The innocent party, having been awarded the decree was then watched by the detective of an anonymous man whose name is never mentioned, known as the King's Proctor. If, during the six months, he or she was found to have committed adultery or behaved in anything but an exemplary manner, the divorce was declared to be null and void, and the petitioner and the respondent remained married. It was unjust, and people's lives were completely ruined by the findings of the King's Proctor. It meant, as far as Barbara and Nigs were concerned, that they had to behave with the utmost discretion until they were finally free.

Barbara has always believed that as they were so much in love with each other they would have been married almost immediately they met. But in the ensuing months she learnt something about Nigs that was very upsetting. His father was the first Earl of Willington, Viceroy of India, and when Nigs left Eton, he went straight out to be with his father and mother in New Delhi. He joined the Bengal Lancers and was appointed *aide-de-camp* to his father, but, with his very fair skin, in the heat of India he developed eczema. This, as Barbara knew from looking after Raine, could be extremely painful and tiresome, but Nigs was told by his doctor: 'Don't worry, we have a wonderful new cure for eczema in the shape of radium.' He had several treatments and the eczema vanished, but it was not until later, when he met and was married to Blossom, that he learned to his horror that they had used radium on him without protection with the result that he was incapable of fathering a child.

All his life Nigs had a flair for 'backing the right horse'. He helped Edward Molyneux, the most successful of all British designers, when he was first starting his climb to fame, and he went in with the Rootes Brothers, makers of Humber and Hillman cars before they became manufacturers. In a tiny village in Sussex, turning the handle of a cinema projector, he had discovered a young man called F. G. Miles who became the pilot of his aeroplane. This eventually turned out to be an unfortunate find on his part, because Blossom eloped with F.G. Miles and with him invented the Miles-Hawke aeroplane which was a success in 1935. She also personally designed the little Sparrow-Hawke, which did the fastest time in the King's Cup Race that year.

Barbara learnt with a sense of shock that the man with whom she had fallen deeply in love could never have any children. She had Raine, but she longed more than anything else in the world to have a son. When Nigs begged her to marry him she therefore prevaricated. It was a ghastly decision to make. She loved him and he loved her. But could they ever find real happiness when just as Barbara longed for children, so did Nigs? When they were both free Nigs took Barbara to look at houses in which they could live, but every time he said, 'And there is a nice nursery for Raine', they were both silent because it was so painful. Finally Barbara knew it was no use and she had to be firm and say 'no'.

Desperately hurt by her refusal Nigs rushed off and became engaged to a girl much younger than himself, telling Barbara defiantly: 'She doesn't mind whether I can give her a child or not!' On his wedding day he sent Barbara a huge bouquet of red roses and a letter so tender and loving that it made her cry. Six months later he was back in the divorce courts, but Barbara never saw him again until he was eighty-two and came to luncheon at Camfield Place with his fourth wife.

It was strange all those years later to see somebody who had meant so much to her, though they had parted. Nigs was still very good-looking. When he was leaving he called Barbara to his car. 'Look what I have here', he said pointing to something on the dashboard. She looked at it and saw it was a St Christopher. 'You gave it to me', he said, 'and I have never been parted from it.'

The terrible thing was - she did not remember!

Back at work, which Barbara knew was the only way she could survive so many different emotional shocks, in 1933 she had her first international newspaper 'scoop'. She learnt from one of her young men that there was a prisoner in the Tower of London whose name was Lieutenant Norman Baillie-Stewart. Barbara told her story to the editor of the *Daily Express* and, rather nervously although he believed her he was, he said, taking a great risk: with nothing but Barbara's word for it, he had the story splashed all over the front page.

By lunch-time that day the War Office was forced to issue a statement and Barbara's revelation became world news. Baillie-Stewart was subsequently court-martialled for selling Army secrets to a German spy called

BARBARA CARTLAND.

Wishing good luck to the pilot of the
Barbara Cartland glider which, in 1931,
carried the first Glider Air Mail from
Manston Aerodrome to Reading

One of the earliest Barbara Cartland
publicity stills. The quill pen was a romantic
whim of the photographer because, even
then, Barbara dictated her novels as she
does today

(Above left) *Barbara's 'headlights' were how her huge eyes were once described. By the 1930s she was acknowledged as one of the great beauties of the London social scene* (Photo: Dorothy Wilding)

(Above right) *Hugh McCorquodale, Barbara's second husband. He loved her from the moment he saw her signing the Register in the Vestry at her wedding to h cousin, Alexander (Sachie) McCorquodal*

This photograph, was hailed at the time a 'the most beautiful picture ever photographed of a mother and baby'. Rain is two years old (Photo: Dorothy Wilding)

(Above) *Over four hundred years old, River Cottage at Great Barford, Bedfordshire, was bought as a honeymoon retreat. Barbara and her children spent most of the war years here.* (Below) *At Polly's new home, Littlewood House. Barbara is flanked by her two handsome brothers, Ronald (left), now an M.P., and Tony on leave from the Army. Raine and Ian complete this happy snapshot*

A Happy Christmas – 1940

Family Christmas cards have always been a tradition in Barbara's life. (Above left) This one was taken at River Cottage in 1940. (Above right) The Christmas card for 1942 showed Barbara in the uniform of a Junior Commander in the A.T.S. Hugh, inset, was in the Home Guard. (Below) Christmas 1944. Raine has blossomed into a pretty fifteen-year-old, Ian is seven and Glen five years old

(Above) *Barbara, a Voluntary Junior Commander in the A.T.S., and children collecting books and magazines for distribution to outlying searchlight posts.* (Below right) *Barbara in her wartime uniform when she joined the Women's Voluntary Services.* (Below left) *Barbara as a County Cadet Officer in the St John Ambulance Brigade*

(Above left) *Barbara and her daughter, Raine: both beautiful, vital and provocative.*
(Above right) *With her striking colouring, Barbara was to become one of the most photographed women in London. Lord Mountbatten once remarked that in early photographs she resembled his wife Edwina. (Below) When Raine married Gerald Legge, heir to the Earl of Dartmouth, the event was hailed as the wedding of the year. Raine, in her restyled 'coming out' dress looked strikingly like a Barbara Cartland heroine. Sixteen bridesmaids complete the wedding group*

(Above and below) *Holidays at the family estate on the Helmsdale River in Scotland were always fun, and Ian and Glen learnt to shoot grouse and catch salmon there*

(Above) *Egypt has always fascinated Barbara and is used as a backcloth for several of her novels. Here she is seen with Ian, who is on the camel.* (Below) *Barbara with Glen at the Taj Mahal, snapped by Ian in 1968. This, her first trip to India, inspired her novel* The Karma of Love. *Since then, Barbara has made six trips to India and counted Mrs Indira Gandhi as one of her most treasured friends*

Marie-Louise. Barbara was given £50 for her 'scoop' - a great deal of money to her at the time.

That spring, Barbara published her seventh novel: *Just Off Piccadilly*, the story of a feckless dance hostess who survives the dangers of the smart Mayfair set before ending up on the final page in the arms of the man she loves. A journalist on the *London Weekly* wrote that it was a 'good warning as well as a good tale'.

All through the year Barbara and Ronald had saved up to have a holiday together in Austria that autumn. Vienna was entrancing as they drove through the streets in an open taxi, and from her stay in Austria Barbara took her background for *Not Love Alone*. This became her pattern for fifty years - regular foreign travel which was translated into the pages of her novels. It meant that her geographical backgrounds as well as her historical ones were always correct. When Grenada was invaded by the Americans in 1983, anyone wishing to knew about the 'haunting Isle of Spice' had only to look up Barbara's *Secret Harbour* to read a vivid description of that tropical paradise.

On her journey to Austria with Ronald, Barbara had a strange esoteric experience in its Cathedral, St Stephens. She felt that there she had found the real spirit of Vienna, and as she sat in a pew watching all sorts and conditions of people, praying before a miraculous picture in the Chapel of the Immaculate Conception, she saw the figure of a Cardinal etched on the darkness of the Church wall in the same way as she had seen the Michelangelo angel when she had been a girl at Bath. It was so clear that she could see every feature of the Cardinal's face. There was an expression of compassion and a faith which transcended all the cruelties, the bestialities, and the stupidity of mankind. He remained with Barbara for a long time, and she found it difficult to think of anything else.

This was one of two esoteric experiences she had in Austria. From Vienna she and Ronald went to Seeboden, a small village on the banks of a warm lake in Carpathia. They did not like the rooms they had booked and instead moved into a small villa from which they were expected to wash in the lake. They spent the mornings swimming and sun-bathing. In the afternoons they would walk up the steep sides of the mountains, drinking coffee in attractive little villages and visiting the churches with their distinctive and beautiful wood carvings.

One day as they walked round the lake they were caught in a thunderstorm and the beating rain and blinding flashes of lightning were frightening until, as suddenly as it had begun, the storm subsided, and the sun shone with a dazzling brilliance. As they hurried home to change their soaked clothing they saw on the other side of the lake a magnificent castle.

It was white with a dark, round roof surmounted by a flag floating in the breeze. Against the background of the green hills and the snowy peaks of the mountains, shimmering against the blue sky it was breathtakingly lovely. Barbara felt it was one of her fairy-tale palaces come to life, and they determined to try and see the inside of it. 'We can but try to get in', Ronald said. 'We'll go tomorrow. . . '

The next afternoon they set off, but failed to find the castle. The following day they tried again, and eventually discovered its ruins - the Gothic archways and the remains of a tower, the foundations of a great courtyard, the first steps to a twisting staircase. Nowhere were the walls more than ten feet high and all covered with moss and ivy!

Why, Barbara asked, had they seen for over an hour the castle as it had been in all its splendour? Years later she was to think it was perhaps a bitter warning that the plans they were making so happily for Ronald's future, a future in which they both whole-heartedly believed, would never be fulfilled.

During the summer Barbara was asked to join the *Sunday Referee* who reported: 'Miss Cartland has made a very special study of modern social problems and her writings are stamped by a deep human sympathy, wide general knowlege and keen fresh vision.'

For Barbara it meant a small regular income to add to her journalistic freelancing. In addition, she wrote a number of articles and a few short stories, and began a book she had longed to write for some time explaining her own philosophy. It was called: *Touch the Stars* and was a *compôte* of the thoughts and feelings that she had discussed with Ronald over the past few years. Emotionally and spiritually it had been a period of enormous self-development. Her esoteric reading had been broadened under Ronald's guidance and her own search for the truth.

Alas, the women who bought over ten thousand of each of Barbara Cartland's novels were not interested in her philosophic theories. She sold less than five hundred copies of the book, despite several good reviews. As had often been the case, Barbara was just ahead of her time, and in today's climate, when young people are searching for an alternative to orthodox religious theories, it might well have been a success.

Later she was to publish in *Lines on Life and Love* this poem which expressed her whole philosophy:

> One thing I know, life can never die,
> Translucent, splendid, flaming like the sun.
> Only our bodies wither and deny
> The life force when our strength is done.

Let me transmit this wonderful fire,
Even a little through my heart and mind,
Bringing the perfect love we all desire
To those who seek, yet blindly cannot find.'

In October, when the Parliamentary seat for King's Norton in Birmingham became vacant, it seemed as if everything they had dreamed of was about to come true. It was a seat Ronald had always wanted, as in the old church at King's Norton was the vault where their grandparents were buried, and the priory where their great-uncle, Howard Cartland, the head of the family, lived, stood on the boundaries of King's Norton and King's Heath. Ronald was working in the Conservative Central Office, and the moment he knew of the vacancy he rushed to see Barbara in Half Moon Street.

'It's Fate', Barbara told him. 'You must put your name forward. I'm sure it is the right thing to do.'

Ronald was doubtful as to how he could possibly afford it, because a Member of Parliament only received a salary of £400 a year, and he had to pay his election expenses, which usually amounted to over £1,000. But he was soon carried along by Barbara's enthusiasm, though still worried whether holding the position was possible when his conscience told him he could never be a 'party hack' paid for by the Central Office with his hands tied.

Everything soon fell happily into place when Howard Cartland agreed to guarantee Ronald £500 for his election expenses and Barbara was certain she could do almost the same. Polly promised a small allowance of £100 a year, which was all she could possibly afford. On 3 November Ronald went to Birmingham to meet the Selection Committee of the King's Norton Association who had already turned down no less than twenty candidates. The Committee recommended him to the executive and finally on 7 December, after he had spoken to the whole Association, he was unanimously adopted. Throughout all these meetings Ronald held the audiences spellbound. He had, as Barbara had always known, that strange, magnetic quality of power which radiates from every natural leader. Listening to him Barbara was sure that her intuition was right and a brilliant Parliamentary career lay ahead of Ronald. That one day he would become the Prime Minister of England, as he had wanted since he was a small boy.

Brother and sister had never been closer, and just as Barbara had turned to Ronald for advice and support in her difficulties, he now turned to her. To Polly it was as if all her sacrifices had been worthwhile. It was what she had always envisaged for Bertie. Now his son was taking his place. The night after Ronald was adopted they all returned to the Priory, where Uncle Howard opened a bottle of champagne to celebrate. The family retired to bed at midnight, but Barbara and Ronald sat on Polly's bed and talked until 3.00 a.m. because they were all too excited to sleep. There would be difficulties, financial strain, and hard work ahead, but that night they were, all three of them, ready to take on the world.

In the next two months there was an almost overwhelming number of meetings to be held in King's Norton, and Barbara realized that as Ronald had no wife to work for him it meant the whole election campaign must fall on her and Polly. The obvious problem of finance had also to be faced, but both Barbara and Ronald's faith was to be justified. Barbara through sheer hard work had had a good year, and was able to give Ronald his deposit of £150 and the guarantee of an over-draft of £300.

The campaign opened on 4 November. Ronald was to stay at the Priory, but his great-aunt Annie Cartland was seriously ill following a stroke, and as there were two nurses in the house there was no room for Polly and Barbara, who stayed in a small, dirty and extremely uncomfortable hotel in the constituency. They both canvassed all day, and at night Barbara opened Ronald's meetings, being followed by one of his speakers, then as soon as Ronald arrived they left the hall, and rushed around to the next meeting where they held the audience until the candidate arrived.

There were, luckily, local dignitaries to help in this game of 'my leader follows' which worked very well. Lord Carlow, one of Ronald's closest friends and the son of the Earl and Countess of Portarlington, a brilliant young man who spoke six languages and was learning Japanese as a seventh, loaned Barbara his car and chauffeur. The car was a large Hispano Suiza and seemed somewhat incongruous. But strangely enough, no one queried it, and Barbara went from house to house begging them to give Ronald their vote and leaving leaflets without anybody being anything but very pleasant.

Barbara was, however, appalled at the poverty in Birmingham, just as Ronald had been shocked the first time he visited Shoreditch when he was working for his friend Lord Knebworth, who was the candidate. He had never got over the poverty he had seen there and what appeared to be a national lack of interest in the people concerned. In Birmingham, Barbara learnt, Austins, one of the biggest industries in Ronald's constituency, the others being Cadbury's and Triplex, paid £3.10s a week to their workers, who were stood off usually for three months of the year, and could only obtain the dole if they had nothing left in the house to sell.

Friday 14 November 1935 was polling day, and it was pouring with rain.

The family started their activities in low spirits having been warned over and over again that 'Labour goes to the polls in the rain - our side can't be bothered. Pray for fine weather!'

Barbara and Polly hardly saw Ronald as they made one tour of the committee Rooms while he made another. The Labour Party was in tremendously high spirits and backing itself for an easy victory, making no effort to disguise the fact. Barbara reached the town hall at about midnight. She watched the tellers at the long table, keeping to one side of the room; on the other side Mr G.R. Mitchison, a well-known socialist and Ronald's opponent, strode up and down while his wife, hatless and in high Russian boots, sat on a bench beside their Labour agent. Everyone was tired and tense. When the result was announced at ten minutes to one it seemed almost impossible to believe that the goal had been reached and the fight was over. Ronald had a majority of 5,875 votes.

Outside the town hall a small crowd was waiting to see the night's results, but they made up in enthusiasm what they lacked in numbers. They burst into cheers as Ronald appeared, and, rushing across the square lifted him high on their shoulders. It was raining and the streets were damp and greasy, but they carried him all the way to the Conservative Club rushing up the steps of those dignified precincts as if nothing could stop them.

The other members were about to leave. Mr Neville Chamberlain was standing in the hall, his hat in his hand, the not-yet-famous umbrella on his arm. He gave way before a noisy, excited crowd and stood aside while the 'baby' of the Birmingham members spoke a few words of thanks from the doorway of the Club. It was about five o'clock before they got to bed (Ronald had wanted to be with his mother and Barbara that night and had therefore moved to the hotel where they were staying), still with tears of gratitude in their eyes for what had been a tremendous fight - politically and emotionally.

To find you I would climb the highest mountain,
And dive into the sea of deepest blue.
I would walk the sandy deserts and the frozen Northern snow,
Until I find my Heart and Soul and You.

Barbara Cartland

During the dark years of the divorce, besides Ronald there had been another man always at Barbara's side, supporting, helping and comforting her - Hugh McCorquodale. This was certainly a brave act on his part because he defied his whole family who were, in Scottish fashion, a very close-knit clan. They shot and fished together, having house-parties on their large estates, and Hugh, who in London lived at his club, went home every weekend to Forest Hall, the big Georgian house in Essex which belonged to his father.

He was the third son of Harold McCorquodale and his wife Gracie, holding a very special place in their hearts because he had been so badly wounded at Passchendaele that it was a miracle he lived. He received the M.C. for his bravery during the battle, when he was hit by a dum-dum bullet from a sniper. It passed through his right shoulder and out through his back, exploding as it went and collapsing his lung and smashing three ribs. He lay in no-man's-land for forty-eight hours, until he was carried in on a man's back, collecting further shrapnel wounds in the process. When he was eventually taken to a base hospital they said there was no chance of saving his life, and he was put, as was the fashion in those days, in a tent to die by himself. He remained without food and in a state of semi-consciousness for four weeks, and his parents crossed the Channel to say good-bye to him. But, owing to the fact that he was only eighteen and very strong, and that he was taken to a rich hospital where they did not interfere with him, but gave him heroin and port every time they dressed his wounds, his system was able to readjust to the shock and begin its own healing process. Had he been moved he would undoubtedly have died.

He went to five different hospitals on his return to England, and when finally he left the surgeons said: 'Never let anybody fiddle about with you, because there is nothing they can do, and it's only by the grace of God that you are alive.' He suffered very badly with bronchitis, and every so often he would have a particularly bad attack during which another piece of shrapnel worked its way out of his body.

He was medically a 'bad life' but it made him in consequence gentle, patient and tolerant. He was also capable of loving at least once in his life very deeply, and he had fallen in love with Barbara on the day she married his cousin. His love had never swerved but increased year by year.

Sachie and Hugh, being the same age, had always been close, and it had been automatic that Sachie would expect Hugh to spend a great deal of time with them at Culross Street and later at Green Street. It was Sachie who had asked Hugh to go with him and Barbara to visit the battlefields, Sachie who invited him automatically every year to stay in the Orkneys or at Cound Hall and to dine with them whenever he did not have another engagement. In fact they were very much like brothers, and Hugh was closer to Sachie than he was to his own. Hugh was therefore extremely upset by the divorce and distressed that Barbara should have been treated so harshly by his own family even though he did not blame Sachie, but those who had advised him.

It was inevitable, after all she had been through, that Barbara should find it possible, when she was alone with Hugh, to talk of her real feelings and to drop the mask with which she faced the world.

In his own way, just like Ronald, Hugh helped her to forget the past and look ahead to the future, but it was not until 1935, after she had had quite a number of other proposals of marriage, that she realized that the only person she could really contemplate as a husband was Hugh. Laughingly she used to say: 'How could I possibly explain all I have been through to a stranger?'

What she really meant was that it was an immense joy to find somebody who understood and did not criticize, except kindly, and who made her feel that though what she had been through had hurt her, at the same time it had developed many qualities she had not known she possessed before. 'I had known Hugh,' she says 'for eight years, and although he had been in love with me all the time, on my side it was a case of friendship and a deep affection developing through trials, difficulties and unhappiness into a firmly rooted love.'

Ronald, who was already devoted to Hugh, was to grow even fonder of him as the years went by. It was also very important that Raine had a great attachment for him and he was to become her beloved 'Uncle Hugh' for the rest of his life. Working together for Ronald's triumphant winning of the Parliamentary seat of King's Norton had mentally fused brother and sister so closely that they were inseparable, almost as if they were twins.

Marriage could damage that relationship, but Barbara knew that in marrying Hugh their relationship would not change because Hugh appreciated and understood what she and Ronald meant to each other.

Because of her strict religious beliefs, Polly thought of marriage as an eternal commitment, but she was willing to concede that the marriage of Barbara and Sachie had irrevocably broken down. Therefore her daughter's happiness was more important than ecclesiastical dogma. She saw in Hugh the rock on which Barbara would be able to lean in the years ahead, if he lived.

Barbara knew the risk she was taking in marrying Hugh, as she had been told by his family and her doctor Sir Louis Knuthsen. 'You will be lucky if you have five years together.' Once again her instinct told her that he was not only the man she had been looking for, but also that in some miraculous manner he would survive. 'And right I was. We had twenty-seven years of perfect happiness until Hugh died when the scar tissue from the wounds he received at Passchendaele touched his heart.'

At the time of her wedding Barbara received two letters that have remained close to her heart all these years. The first was from Hugh, written at his Club and posted in time to arrive early the next morning. In his neat, masculine hand-writing he had written:

. . . Darling, I am getting older, yet you, the loveliest creature God ever made, loves me and wants to marry me. It's so wonderful I can't believe it's true. . . I fear it may be a dream, and I shall wake up and find I was just dreaming. . .

A second letter arrived on the day of the wedding, written by Ronald from Trent Park where he had joined Sir Philip Sassoon's Christmas house-party. It expressed yet again the extraordinary relationship between this sister and brother:

Darling,

I must send you this morning all my love and thoughts and good wishes for the future. You know what you have meant to me these last five years - much more than I can ever tell you - support, inspiration, courage, faith and love - I've sought them from you often, never in vain. Now, after today, it can't be quite the same - our relationship. But I'm not unhappy about it. I'm glad. Because I know you are doing the right thing, the wise thing, and the thing that is going to make you happier and even more lovable to all of us in the future.

Darling, I'd hate you to marry anyone but Hugh. I am genuinely delighted that after all this long time you are going to marry him. I can't think of anyone I've met who will look after you and care for you as he will.

Don't ever lose the memory of these last few years; the struggles as well as the victories - and don't forget darling, all the happy hours we've spent together. I don't think they're finished. There are many more for us in the future. But I want you to know that after them all, and because of them, I can say you've earned all the love and happiness there is for ever; I know by marrying Hugh that love and happiness will be yours more and more.

Bless you both - always,

R

In order to avoid publicity Hugh and Barbara were married quietly on a foggy morning on 28 December 1936 at the Guildhall in London. It had been closed for the Christmas holidays and so was far less likely to attract the Press than if they had chosen to be married at fashionable Caxton Hall in Chelsea. The wedding was followed by a service of blessing in the Church of St Ethelburga. The only people present were Ronald, and Theodore Matthew, later to be Attorney General, who acted as Hugh's best man. The service was quiet, beautiful and intimate - the exact opposite of Barbara's first wedding, and this is how she wanted it to be. There was not a Press camera in sight.

Hugh's carefully laid plans that the honeymoon would begin by flying to Paris were thwarted because of the weather, and he had to re-arrange everything hastily. Due to fog Croydon Airport was closed down, and instead the bridal couple took the Golden Arrow. Even this was difficult to arrange as the trains were booked out, and only because of the McCorquodales' association as printers with the British Railways were they given a compartment of their own on the train, a private cabin on the cross-Channel steamer and a coupé on the Paris Express.

The journey was long, but looking back Barbara always said it was one of those strange blessings which come when you least expect them. They had hours in which to talk things over and to start their new life together in a very different way from anything either of them had known before. 'They were hours of great joy, of almost a spiritual ecstacy because of what we discovered about each other in words, which at that moment were more important than anything else,' says Barbara. 'Later, I used to feel it was then I really understood the depth and wonder of Hugh's love for me, and I think he felt the same. Anyway, I am quite certain that the fog at Croydon laid the foundation stone of our marriage.'

Their honeymoon begun at the Ritz Hotel was so blissfully happy that for the rest of their years together, except for a break during the war,

Barbara and Hugh always returned to Paris and stayed at the Ritz, re-capturing its rapture and joy. From Paris they continued down to the South of France, where one of the first people they met was Mrs Wallis Simpson, lunching at the Carlton with her American hosts, Herman and Katherine Rogers. They had invited her to stay while she was waiting for her divorce to become absolute, and thus to be free to marry the Duke of Windsor, who had renounced the throne for her.

Barbara had been one of the first of Ernest Simpson's friends to whom he had introduced his new American bride on her arrival in England. She had also been one of the first people to realize when the Prince of Wales transferred his affections from Thelma, Lady Furness, to Wallis Simpson. Thelma had told Barbara that she was going to America on family business and that she had asked Mrs Simpson to 'look after' the Prince in her absence.

Barbara, who was very fond of Thelma, was worried when whispers began to go round Mayfair that the Prince was becoming infatuated with the American wife of Ernest Simpson. Barbara was quite certain these rumours were untrue, because although Wallis was *chic*, had a brittle wit and was an outstandingly good hostess and housewife, she could not believe that she could compare with the sweetness and beauty of Thelma who, with her twin sister, Gloria Vanderbilt, had been described by Cecil Beaton as being 'like two magnolias'.

One day Barbara and Mary Cunningham-Reid were having lunch at Claridges at a table just inside the door, which Barbara still uses, when Wallis Simpson came in looking unusually glamorous in a cape of silver foxes, which were all the fashion. She talked to Mary and Barbara for some minutes, then moved off with her escort to another table. When she had gone Mary said: 'Did you see what she was wearing?'

'Her cape?' Barbara asked.

'No, the diamond clips', Mary replied.

Barbara, who had been talking animatedly to Wallis, now realized that she had been wearing at her neck two very large diamond clips, and as she thought of them Mary exclaimed, 'The centre of each one contained the pear-shaped diamonds from Queen Alexandra's earrings. I would have recognized them anywhere!'

Barbara, being fond of Ernest, had always thought that, compared to him, Wallis was somewhat superficial however charming she might be. She had in fact been very shocked when a young house decorator had shown her secretly the plans Wallis had told him to draw up for modernizing Buckingham Palace. According to Wallis's plans, there was also to be dancing in the Mall, and many other innovations which would certainly have upset Queen Mary. But what horrified Barbara was that the American-born woman, who aspired to be the Queen of England, did not appreciate the interior of Buckingham Palace as designed and decorated by George IV, or even the magnificent furniture and pictures of the period, which were unique. These were all to be swept away, or rather, altered and rearranged for a 'new look' that would certainly not have fitted in with the dignity and the position which Buckingham Palace held in the Empire. Besides this, Barbara had also learnt that a special honour was to be awarded to a number of women who were to be nominated as 'Queen Wallis's Ladies'. Among these women was the famous Society hostess, Emerald Cunard, someone whom Barbara had never liked.

Barbara's ecstatic happiness on her honeymoon is expressed in the engaging letter she wrote to Polly from Cannes:

I am frightfully happy, darling, and Hugh is so nice I feel it can't be true. I want you to promise me that my being married won't make any difference to the wonderful times we as a family have at Littlewood. I have learnt in the past years since my last marriage that I have the most wonderful family in the world, and that I can't do without your constant help and love. You have been a marvellous mother to me, darling, and I do appreciate all you have done for me, and your great loyalty through all my troubles.

Promise that you will always go on in the future, helping me and my children. Every day I grow to realize more and more how right you are in all your principles and ideals. I tried hard to find another way of living and thinking, but I know now that what you have always fundamentally believed in and lived up to, in spite of all temptations, is the real and perfect way.

Back in London Barbara slipped silkily into her new marriage. Though Hugh McCorquodale was not as rich as Sachie, he was able to give her the financial stability and comforts that had been missing since her first marriage had broken up. Whereas Sachie had lived wildly beyond his income, Barbara felt safe with Hugh when he took over the money affairs of the household. Though he was generous she knew he would see that they always lived within their means and there would be no awful financial shocks, such as Polly had experienced, and as she had experienced herself. In fact Barbara swore when she married Hugh that she would never again be in debt, except to a bank. From that time her bills have been paid as they come in, and she can say happily, 'If I die tonight I will not leave a single debt!'

In their new flat Barbara set a fashion with her dinner parties for men. As she matured she had found dancing less interesting than intelligent conversation, and she began to arrange intimate dinner parties to which she invited a number of well-known men, and at which she was the only woman. They would sit at the dining-room table sometimes until two o'clock in the morning, arguing on every important subject under the sun, but predominantly about politics. Most of the guests were much older than Barbara, Ronald and Hugh, and their quick wit, their brilliant turn of phrase and their originality made her remember the dinner parties at the Vineyards when, very young, she had sat wide-eyed, listening to Max Beaverbrook's brilliant friends, and being mesmerized by them.

During the bitter controversy of her first marriage Barbara had decided that she would never be entirely dependent again on anyone, and now with eleven novels to her credit her career was booming. She was accepted as an established and successful author. In the first year of her marriage to Hugh her production stepped up to three books, with the engaging titles, *Dangerous Experiment, Desperate Defiance* and *The Forgotten City*. This last book was a complete break-away from the romantic novels that Barbara had been writing previously. It was the beginning of many attempts to express within her books her quest for spiritual enlightenment. It tells the story of a Scots girl's adventures as she runs first to Brittany and then to Tunis before she finds happiness. This book became years later one of the 'Library of Ancient Wisdom' which Barbara brought out to help people, as she had been helped, by the occult.

The extravagances of her marriage to Sachie had left their mark, and she translated this into an article called 'An Open Letter to my Daughter when she's Twelve':

> ... You are learning that money is unimportant and only brings happiness when you give it away. It took me many years to realize that one should be far more apprehensive of being rich than of being poor. Nearly every rich person I know is desperately unhappy, their money chains, encompasses, and often embitters them.

In addition to her writing Barbara continued with her fund-raising for various charities. In order that her 'outside activities' should not impose on her family life she created a work pattern that was to continue right through her life. All the telephoning was done in the mornings - and fund-raising relies a great deal on personal contact. Her writing was therefore slotted into the afternoon with an almost military discipline, enabling her to turn out anything between six and eight thousand words a day, as she still does. Professional to her pink enamelled finger tips she has always known how to discipline herself.

This is not to say that she does not enjoy writing - she loves it! It is part of her life, and when she is writing she escapes into the same fairy-tale esoteric world that she knew as a child. She often says that she feels more relaxed, happier, and better in every way after she has dictated for nearly three hours, than at any other time of the day.

On 11 October 1937 the long-awaited son was born. Barbara was always to say: 'I don't think I've ever been so thrilled by anything as having Ian'. All through the nine months of waiting she had hoped and prayed for a son, despite the fact that everyone had been persistently certain that she was having a girl. *Pearson's Weekly* once asked five well-known women what mattered to them most. Ellen Wilkinson, M.P. answered 'work'; Ursula Bloom replied 'love'; Daisy Kennedy 'happiness'; Jessie Matthews 'having someone to love and be loved' and Barbara Cartland 'men' - just men!

Barbara wrote at the time:

It's no use telling English women, American fashion, that daughters matter as much as sons. It is deeply ingrained within us from babyhood that men are more important than women. Every father longs for a son whether the child be heir to the name of Smith and a few sticks of furniture, or to a dukedom and vast acres. Boys come first in English family life. I, personally, am prepared to find it both natural and commendable that they should. It is an indisputable fact that Englishmen make the best husbands, and the reason for this, which sounds at first a strangely contradictory one, is that Englishmen are the most selfish men in the world.

The Englishman expects so much more of his wife than a man of any other nation because he has been brought up to believe himself the more important sex, and yet ninety-five per cent of the women married to Englishmen are happy. And this is because, as the superior being, it is both his right and his desire to cherish, love and protect the 'little woman' who belongs to him.

Although these views were expressed fifty-two years ago, in our discussions together over the past year, I found that they remain as evergreen fresh in Barbara's attitude to men as when she first wrote them down. Ideas of women's liberation and the equality of the sexes have made little impression on her, and certainly play no part in her evaluation of the sexes. To her, men always have and always will be a race apart, and the birth of a son was all that she needed to complete a year of great happiness.

Barbara had finished her seventeenth novel *But Never Free* a few days before her son Ian was born. It was published the following January and the title was taken from a verse which sprang to her mind as she mapped out the plot: 'Must I go through tears and pain, Climbing to distant peaks I cannot see? Is man a creature born to grope in vain, Driven, directed, led, but never free?'

In the New Year of 1938 Barbara and Hugh made the first of many travels together. Like Agatha Christie, who often wove the plots of her detective novels round the experiences she gained from being able to accompany her husband, Sir Max Mallowan, on his archaeological 'digs' in the Middle East, Barbara was intrigued when her husband suggested that she travel with him on his business trip to Khartoum where McCorquodale & Company Limited had printing works.

They left England on a damp, grey, and foggy day in January and arrived in the balmy air of Khartoum, which at 95 degrees Fahrenheit was pleasantly warm. Khartoum, with its *beau geste* buildings, docile bullocks patiently working the water wheels, white and red uniformed native servants guarding the white Palace, wide avenues radiating out like spokes in the Union Jack - as planned by Lord Kitchener - white minarets silhouetted against the blue sky and the pipers of the Black Watch marching across the parade ground in a pink haze of dust, delighted Barbara. To the novelist's eye it was rich material indeed, and after a few days a plot was already fomenting in Barbara's head.

One week after her arrival, just as Barbara was settling down to the unfamiliar roar of lions greeting the dawn in the Khartoum Zoo next door to their hotel, she received a cable from Mary Cunningham-Reid saying: 'CASE BEING HEARD AT END OF WEEK MUST HAVE YOU WITH ME PLEASE FLY HOME DARLING.'

This referred to a very unpleasant settlement action brought by Alec Cunningham-Reid against his heiress wife, which had been pending for some time, but which Barbara thought would not come up for hearing for some weeks. Barbara was most anxious to be with Mary, who had stood by her so staunchly at the time of her own divorce, but she was unable to fly back as there was not another aeroplane for three days, which meant that the case would have finished by the time she arrived in London. Barbara was consoled by the knowledge that Mary was in good legal hands as Sir Patrick Hastings, who had taken her own case, was defending her.

Barbara and Hugh decided to return by Abu Simbel and travelled 250 miles by the desert railway to Wadi Halfa. There they boarded a steamer and went down the Nile to Cairo to meet up with Barbara's brother Tony who was stationed there as *aide-de-camp* to General Sir George Weir, G.O.C., Egypt. Tony had just returned to Egypt after a long spell in hospital in England where he had been seriously ill. In the fall from his horse in Cairo he had almost severed his spinal cord at the base of his neck, but under the care of the Catholic nuns in a nursing home at Eastbourne he had recovered and was back on duty.

Cairo has always cast its own spell on people, and Barbara found life there fascinating. It has always been a city of extremes with the glamour of rich living and the pitiful plight of the poor. The streets are thronged night and day with a miscellaneous collection of Arabs, Muslims, Bedouins and Egyptians, all intent on some secret business of their own. She has used it as a background for two of her novels - *The Marquis Who Hated Women* and *Moonlight on the Sphinx*.

In 1937 British relationships with Cairo had never been better, and Barbara and Hugh were plunged into a social whirl, with Tony delighted to introduce his famous sister to his friends. One of Barbara's memories from this visit was the dinner party given on the last night by Sir George and Lady Weir:

It was just a small dinner party, ourselves, Tony, Pamela Wavell and her father, General Sir Archibald Wavell, who was commanding the troops in Israel and Trans-Jordania and was in Cairo for a conference. The General arrived for dinner without his daughter as there had been some misunderstanding about the invitation and we all waited for nearly three-quarters of an hour while Miss Wavell was fetched from the hotel where she explained she had been having a bath!

I wondered what an English cook would have done in the circumstances but Tony, who, as A.D.C. was, of course, in charge of the household, said the Egyptian Chef wouldn't mind. If the food is spoilt they throw it all away and start again.

Shortly after their marriage Barbara and Hugh bought a four-hundred-year-old thatched cottage in Great Barford in Bedfordshire. Barbara had said to Hugh: 'Fond as I am of your family, I think it a terrible mistake, and enough to ruin any marriage, if we stay with them every week-end, and I know you loathe being in London. We will therefore have a tiny honeymoon cottage of our own where we can go away and be together without having a great number of social interruptions.'

She had no way of knowing then that in a few years' time this cottage would be the only home she and her family had away from the bombs that were falling in London, or that having said she had no wish for any social commitments, they were in fact few and far between in Bedfordshire.

The rumblings of war were already in the air. As early as March 1938 Ronald, whose fearlessness in speaking his mind was already becoming legendary, warned his audience at the annual meeting of the Division Unionists Association in King's Norton of the possibility of war:

I tell you quite frankly that we are faced today with forces in the world, which if they go unchecked, must threaten peace, if not in the immediate present, certainly in the eventual future. There are in this country some who hold the view that dictatorships and democracies can exist side by side. That might be so - although personally I doubt it - but what might be the cost of democracy? Might it be at such a cost that in the end the very essentials of democracy have to be thrown over-board? I hope the Government will not hesitate to call upon all sections of the community for sacrifice during the next few years in order to make this country safe.

On a national scale visionaries like Winston Churchill cautioned the House of Commons of the imminence of war, but few were willing to listen. He was frequently to be referred to by his Parliamentary enemies as 'the old war horse'.

It was not only rumours of war to which the Government under Neville Chamberlain would not listen, but also to new ideas. Ronald was the first Member of Parliament to ask for holidays with pay and family allowances. People were horrified! At a luncheon party Barbara was told by a fellow guest 'Winston Churchill, your brother and you ought to be strung up on lamp posts for being Bolsheviks.'

All through that halcyon summer of 1938 London danced its way through the Season in a frenzy of defiance as the war clouds gathered. One of the dances - which prophetically was to end an era in history - was given by Lord and Lady Louis Mountbatten at their penthouse in Brook House for an eighteen-year-old débutante, Sarah Norton. When she inherited Brooke House in Park Lane from her grandfather Sir Ernest Cassel, Edwina Mountbatten felt ill at ease with its pomposity and had it pulled down and a modern building erected instead. On the top was the most spectacular penthouse in London. Though the house was conspicuously new with a silver lacquered entrance hall, the famous Van Dycks looked just as at home there as they had in the Cassel mansion.

Barbara stayed there with Mary when the house was in the process of being completed and was amused by the pink crêpe de chine sheets on her bed trimmed with exquisite lace, while when she lunched with the

Mountbattens and the King and Queen of Sweden, they ate off card-tables with food served on odds and ends of china that had just been taken out of the packing-cases.

Sarah Norton's dance was a night of champagne, beautiful women and heady romance. All the great beauties of the English aristocracy were there, but the most striking was Princess Marina, the Duchess of Kent, who wore a crinoline of black lace with her hair swept up in the Edwardian mode.

Barbara enjoyed every moment of it, especially so because as well as Hugh, Ronald also was a guest, and as usual unexpected in what he said. When a woman friend came up to Barbara and gushed: 'Barbara you look twenty-five', Ronald overheard her and remarked, 'That's the rudest thing I ever heard!' When the woman looked astonished at his frankness he added, 'Barbara is thirty-seven. I should be sorry if she hadn't more character in her face than she had twelve years ago.'

In the autumn, while Hugh was happy to go shooting and fishing on his father's estate in Scotland where, many, many years later the Prince of Wales was to become captivated by salmon fishing, Barbara and Ronald went on holiday together in Switzerland. They chose this time a small hotel near Interlaken, surrounded by pine forests with the lake of Brienz shimmering like blue enamel a thousand feet below. In the distance were the snow-capped mountains surrounding the Jungfrau and the only noise was the sound of mountain streams. Here they walked and talked the days away with an incessant urgency, almost as if they both guessed that the sands of time were running out. It was true that their complete and selfless contentment together was now on borrowed time.

They returned to London to find an undercurrent of nervous tension. Feelings ran high across the whole country as the Prime Minister, Neville Chamberlain, groped his way out of his fatal appeasement at Munich. Commenting on this Noel Coward said bitterly to Ronald: 'Neville Chamberlain has just discovered what every chorus boy discovers in his first year on the stage - the heady quality of applause.' For the general public the hysterical relief of Munich was followed by a dull sense of apathy. Neville Chamberlain's umbrella had become a joke round the world, and though no one believed any longer in his veracity, everyone wanted to be lulled into a sense of security.

Barbara and Hugh moved into a large, airy flat overlooking the gardens of Grosvenor Square. Cinema audiences were enthralled with the new film, *Gone With the Wind*, the Rajah of Sarawak's three beautiful daughters - Princess Gold, Princess Pearl and Princess Dawn - filled the gossip columns, and swing music, with the big bands, had come to stay.

Behind the Parliamentary scenes a small group of caring Members took it in turn to meet at each other's houses to discuss the situation - how long the peace would last. The most distinguished members of this group were Anthony Eden, Leo Amery, Lord Cranborne and Duff Cooper, while the younger ones included Jim Thomas, Bob Boothby, Richard Law and Ronald Cartland.

Through her insatiable curiosity and Ronald's reportage, Barbara was one of the best-informed women in London and knew of the secret desire of these men that Winston Churchill should be given office at this critical period, despite the opposition of the pro-Chamberlain Members. 'Winston will never get into Neville's Cabinet unless there is war', Ronald said to Barbara.

On Wednesday 2 August the Prime Minister moved an adjournment of Parliament until 3 October, and it was opposed by the Opposition. They were, of course, slapped down immediately, but Ronald, coming out of the Chamber into the Lobby, said to Winston Churchill: 'I suppose there is nothing more we can do.' 'Nothing?' roared Winston. 'This is the time to speak, to act, my boy!'

Ronald went back into the Chamber and at 8 p.m. rose. He made a speech which is remembered to this day because it was so positive and overwhelming, for, as Barbara explains, 'The life-force flashed out of him to hold the House spellbound.' This is what he said:

> I cannot imagine why the Prime Minister could not have made a great gesture in the interest of national unity. It is more important to have the whole country behind you than to make jeering, pettifogging party speeches which divide the nation. We are in a situation where within a month we young men may be going to fight, we may be going to die!

After he had spoken Ronald left the House, and that night he rang Barbara to say: 'I want you to be prepared for a shock in the morning newspapers.' They carried the banner headlines:

PREMIER ATTACKED BY SUPPORTERS
BITTER DEBATE YIELDS ATTACKS BY CHURCHILL
AND KING'S NORTON MP

Ronald then went to camp in the New Forest with the Worcestershire Yeomanry, of which he was a member, for a week's special course, after which he motored down to Caister-on-Sea to be with Barbara

Nervous of going abroad with the children, and as she was having another baby, Barbara had taken a house at Caister-on-Sea. Hugh was in Scotland shooting. Sitting on the beach watching Raine and Ian building sand-castles Ronald told her that war was inevitable, and his own future in jeopardy. He had received five hundred congratulatory telegrams, but many of the older people in his constituency were horrified by what he had said.

On Friday 1 September German troops crossed the Polish frontier. Hugh had returned and he and Barbara decided to pack up and drive with the children the one hundred miles across country to their cottage in Bedfordshire. On Sunday 3 September, sitting in her flower-filled sitting-room like millions of other women throughout Britain, Barbara heard Neville Chamberlain's gloom-filled voice on the radio saying: '. . . this country is now at war with Germany!'

Ronald was wrong by only two days!

—17—

I am so happy that we had those days,
Wind in our faces, and a cloudless sky.
I am so happy that we had those nights,
Do you remember how the moonlight made you sigh?
Every note I hear, each shaft of sun,
Reminds me of something we have done.
Music which echoes down the years,
Music of laughter with a touch of tears.
Your hand in mine, the times we talked together,
Those hours are mine, for ever and for ever.

Barbara Cartland

In December 1939, Mary Cunningham-Reid asked Barbara, who was awaiting the birth of her third child, to come and stay at Six Mile Bottom.

This was a great relief to Hugh who had thought London was now too dangerous for her and the children. Although life had been led in slow motion during the last three months of the 'phoney war', everybody lived in apprehension of the Germans beginning their air offensive which, in fact, did not occur until the following May.

Barbara was delighted at the idea of being with Mary, who was by then divorced and therefore alone. During the day Mary had taken on the gruelling task of voluntary nursing at a Cambridge Hospital, but in the evenings she was free. She and Hugh had always enjoyed each other's company and she was one of the few 'outsiders' who was allowed to call him 'Uncle Hugh'. So it was a joy to be at Six Mile Bottom all together. Despite it being very tiring at times for Hugh he greatly enjoyed the first-class shooting he had at the weekends. As all the young directors in McCorquodales had been in the reserves of their regiments, Hugh, being the only one unable to rejoin owing to his war wounds, had become Chairman. Every day he left the house before seven o'clock in the morning, journeyed either to London, Wolverton, Newton-le-Willows, or Crewe, to supervise the work of printing the most hated, and yet the most prized possession of the war - the coupon books. There were coupons for food, for sweets, for clothes, for petrol, besides a multitude of government forms which increased every week.

Hugh was, however, stronger than he had ever been before and this was because Barbara had cured his bronchitis, which had sometimes been agonizing at night, with honey. Two spoonfuls of comb honey, morning and evening, had been effective where every doctor's medicine had failed.

'I remember this all happening', Mary Delamere told me. 'There was Hugh and Barbara, Raine and Ian, Nanny and the nursery maid, Barbara's own maid and of course the midwife. In those days she stayed with the mother for a month, arriving well before the birth and remaining for three weeks or so after. Barbara was in terrific form and we all had a wonderful Christmas with the countryside under deep snow. Barbara and Hugh and the children gave this old house a special Christmassy feeling.'

What worried Barbara was the question of a specialist. She was now thirty-nine, and she had had an extremely difficult time with both Raine and Ian. In the usual muddle of war, Sir William Gilliatt, the Royal Gynaecologist who had delivered Ian, had been put in charge of a hospital for geriatrics in Surrey. He told Barbara he would try to get her a famous Cambridge gynaecologist whom he knew, but warned he was a very independent man. Barbara went to see the specialist in question, who told her he only took very difficult cases. 'My daughter was born with the cord round her neck'. Barbara told him, 'My son was an "hour-glass" contrac-

148

tion. I promise you this one will be a pink elephant with five legs!' He laughed and promised he would look after her.

A spacious bedroom on the first floor was given over to Barbara for the confinement and at twelve minutes to midnight on 31 December, with the help of two doctors and two nurses, she gave birth to her second son.

Outside there were three feet of snow, and while the champagne popped downstairs in the drawing-room Barbara saw in the New Year struggling with a retained placenta. Hugh waited until mother and child were comfortable before telephoning Polly at 3.00 a.m. to announce the good news.

When Barbara saw her new son, who was to be named Glen, he was extremely large and solemn looking and she told everybody that she was sure that he had been reincarnated many times and must be what the mystics call 'an old soul'. Reincarnation was close to her heart and she had recently written a most unusual novel called *The Black Panther* on the theme of reincarnation. The hero was a thinly disguised description of Sir Philip Sassoon, the millionaire politician who was a friend of Ronald.

On 4 January Polly went to Victoria Station to see Tony off to France, just as she had done years before when she waved her husband off at Southampton.

Mummy had done it all before. She couldn't help remembering as she experienced the same shivering fear, the same desperate fight for self control. 'Don't worry, don't worry, don't worry' were the last words Tony said to her as she walked away and began the lonely journey back to Littlewood. All Tony's things were lying about but when she got home she couldn't touch any of them that night. She turned out the lights and went upstairs to bed.

Ronald was thirty-three on 3 January and five days later he telephoned Barbara, and she knew as soon as she heard his voice what he was going to say. He, too, had been ordered to France as his regiment, the Worcestershire Yeomanry, now the 53rd Field Artillery Anti-Tank Battery R.A., was joining the British Expeditionary Force which was waiting on the Belgian border. He had wangled himself into the Yeomanry without a medical because he knew no doctor would have passed him for military service. He had been shot in the leg by a shotgun when staying with the Monsells as a boy and although over a hundred pellets had been taken away, many more remained. But Ronald said: 'I will ask no young man to risk his life for me', and was determined to play his part in the war, even though as a Member of Parliament he was automatically exempt.

As soon as Barbara was well enough the family returned to London. Everything was quiet and there had been no bombs. Thousands of children were being evacuated, especially from the East End, and each railway station was the scene of bewildered children clutching an old teddy bear, with their name tags pinned on them, as they were shepherded into trains taking them into the countryside to be billeted with an unknown family.

Ronald arrived back in London on 10 April, the day after the Germans invaded Norway and Denmark. He went straight to the House of Commons, and after long talks with Anthony Eden, J.P.L. Thomas, Richard Law and other Parliamentary colleagues he returned to Barbara's flat depressed by what he had heard. 'The complacency and apathy everywhere is even worse than I feared', he told her. 'Factories working short hours with weekends off; Ministries in a hopeless muddle; petty jealousies obstructing effort; and among certain members of the Government the conviction that they can "muddle through" without sacrifice. . . . '

Ronald stayed with Barbara at Grosvenor Square and the next day they lunched together at Claridges. Ronald looked thin but handsome, and as usual the tempo rose, and it was an excitement to be together. There was so much to say, yet so much left unsaid.

On Friday 12 April the newspapers reported German troop movements on the Belgian border, and Ronald decided he must return immediately. He had missed the boat train, but hired a car to take him to Dover. There was only time to telephone Polly, who was desperately upset as they were to have met the next day, for a quick goodbye. Outside it was a dull, grey, windy day and as Ronald stood in Grosvenor Square and looked up at the flat he saw Barbara silhouetted in the window with baby Glen in her arms.

It was the last time that brother and sister were to see each other.

Memories of the summer of 1940 will always remain indelible in people's minds. It was as if the sun had become a huge arc-light flooding all Europe in a fierce glow before the curtain rose on the holocaust. The English countryside had never looked more beautiful. From France Tony wrote to Polly a letter which is symptomatic of the sheer boredom and frustration he and thousands of fellow officers were feeling at that period.

B.E.F.
May 3rd 1940

My darling Mummy,

What do you think of the war? Our disgraceful set-back in Norway appalls me. Why they have sent a lot of untrained and unequipped Territorials to fight the Germans - I do not know. Here are all the regular troops kicking their heels and a lot of war playboys mince about Norway getting badly defeated. It really is time we got down to brass tacks and really took the war seriously.

At Westminster the failure of the Norwegian expedition was disastrous and on 10 May Chamberlain resigned after a fierce attack in the House of Commons. Leo Amery denounced him in the words of Cromwell to the Long Parliament ending in the cry: 'In God's name, go!' Winston Churchill was sent for by the King.

That morning Barbara opened a letter from Ronald in France - bold, courageous, inspiring as always:

This is just to send you my love and bless you always. Don't be anxious if there is a long silence from me - the fog of war is pretty impenetrable.

We shall win in the end, but there's horror and retribution ahead of all of us. We can't avoid it.

What a waste it all is, but after the months of desolation we shall gain and retain what you and I have always understood the meaning of - Freedom!

On 15 May 1940, the Netherlands Army surrendered. Two weak French divisions posted at an unexpectedly critical point of the line near Sedan broke under the strain leaving a gap through which the main body of the German tanks poured. The bulge grew larger every day and soon the Germans threatened to break right through to the Channel ports just as had been feared. When King Leopold, in his capacity as Commander-in-Chief of the Belgian Army, in turn surrendered, the B.E.F. was immediately cut off from its allies and wedged between the Germans and the sea.

Barbara and Hugh were at the cottage at Great Barford for the weekend. They had as usual been spending the week in London as there still appeared to be no danger. She wrote some years later:

I shall remember those hot, dry, sunny days all my life. The lilac was in bloom, huge bushes of white, purple and mauve: the may trees were crimson and the blossom was heavy on the cherry trees.

Beyond the wattles which bordered the tiny lawn was the slow moving, silver-grey river. Behind the cottage the gargoyles on the fifteenth-century grey stone tower of the church stood sentinel at the end of the winding, sleepy little village.

It seemed to me that a great quiet lay over everything, as if the earth itself held its breath. I walked up and down the garden, waiting for the telephone to ring.

In a world devoid of the instancy of television, people had to rely on their daily newspapers and regular wire bulletins to keep them in the picture. Barbara was uncommonly well informed through Ronald's friends in Westminster and her important journalist contacts in Fleet Street. Meanwhile, Polly was busy with Red Cross work at Malvern, but every day Barbara telephoned her. Polly's courage as always was magnificent, and they were both filled with hope and faith that Ronald and Tony would be alright.

These were agonizing days for Barbara as she listened to the hourly bulletins waiting for news about her brothers. All the memories of the years came flooding back as she walked in the garden alone with her thoughts . . . Ronald as a little boy playing at politics and applauding himself at the end of a speech . . . Ronald driven by an inner flame going without food to buy books that would enrich his mind . . . Ronald being carried shoulder high through the wet, slippery streets of Birmingham at one o'clock in the morning by the 'Brummies' who had elected him to represent them in Parliament . . . Ronald who had sat with her night after night when she was numbed by the shock of her divorce. His belief in the divine purpose of life and his conviction that this world is only a preparation for the next. Ronald, looking across the wide sweep of the Severn Valley from the top of the Malvern Hills, with the sun lighting the towers of Worcester Cathedral, and saying to her: 'Our job is to do all we can to keep England great in a difficult world.'

Once Barbara had entered his room while they were on holiday in Austria. Ronald had been lying sleeping like 'a crusader on a tomb'. When Barbara told him this he answered without hesitating:

'That is how I shall be in Westminster Abbey.'

With anyone else it would have sounded boastful but with Ronald it was different. He was so sure of his future. So convinced of his destiny.

And Tony so completely different. With his devastating charm and irrepressible gaiety . . . the sparkle at the party. . . the caring host. . . the clever organizer. Tony falling in and out of love. The warm-hearted Tony so proud when Ronald gained his crown. 'I had dinner with "Major Ronald" last night - very well and in terrific form. I think it's splendid him getting on so well and so quickly', he had written to Polly.

Those days of waiting are etched on Barbara's mind. As she talks about it today some of Ronald's last words come to mind. 'And you ask', he had written, 'what do we want out of life? That question should only be asked by you of yourself. It can be answered only by you. In other words - or a written word - "faith".'

The miracle of Dunkirk began on 27 May when into that flat pancake of the French coast poured the whole of the B.E.F. Every road scoring the landscape was thick with transport and long lines of weary, red-eyed, dust-begrimed soldiers. And overhead always the merciless strafing from the German Air Force. From the south coast, in the greatest secrecy, an armada of ships set out to bring back what remained of the B.E.F. There were 222 naval ships and 665 other vessels, some so small that, packed with men, they almost sank. Men sick and hungry, their wounds neglected, their bodies drenched with blood and sweat.

All that week-end Barbara never left the cottage and was waiting by the telephone. Three times Winston Churchill the Prime Minister, the busiest man in the world, rang Polly personally to ask if there was any news of Ronald. Hugh, anticipating the worst, had decided on the Monday morning not to go to the office, so he was with Barbara when she opened the newspaper to read the heavy black headlines: 'LAST MAN OUT OF DUNKIRK'.

It was not until Thursday 6 June that Polly, alone at Littlewood, received two telegrams from the Under-Secretary of State for War.

Both Ronald and Tony were missing.

—18—

In the deepest darkness, there is always a flickering light if one looks hard enough.

Barbara Cartland

Forty days after Dunkirk the Germans entered Paris, and Mussolini summoned up courage to enter the war on the side which appeared to be already victorious. This left the British Forces in the Mediterranean area outnumbered by land, air, and sea and Hitler began massing his victorious army in and about the Channel ports, assembling a large fleet of transport ships and barges for the invasion of the British Isles.

One morning the telephone rang. It was Irene Dunn to tell Barbara that the Prime Minister had been in touch with her husband. 'It is top-secret', she said, 'but Winston is sure we will have to repel a German invasion, and he intends to evacuate all the women and children from the south of England up to the north.' Irene then went on to tell Barbara that Jimmy, who was in Canada, had booked cabins for her and her two daughters, her grand-daughter and various other members of the Dunn family to come out and join him. He had also booked a spare cabin for Barbara and her three children. 'Jimmy says you must come for the children's sake', Irene nagged.

Barbara was stunned at the information, and so was Hugh when she told him that evening. They had twenty-four hours in which to make up their minds. That night after they had been to see their children, asleep in the nursery, Barbara and Hugh talked until dawn. Both were horrified at the idea of being parted, although they knew it would happen anyway if Barbara and the children were sent north.

What was so disturbing was that there had just been a report that small babies, apart from a direct hit, were often killed by the blast of a big bomb, and Glen was only five months old. The newspapers had been full of terrible stories from France of the German tanks mowing down refugees, children being dive-bombed as they came out of school and the homeless crouching panic-stricken in ditches or hiding in woods. 'Supposing something happened to the children', Barbara said at last. 'Would we ever forgive ourselves if we had had the chance to save them and refused it?' There was no need to answer her.

The next morning Barbara rang Irene and accepted Jimmy's invitation, and after that it was a nightmare, buying trunks, getting passports, packing, saying good-bye, all of which left Barbara feeling everything was unreal and she moved in a disjointed dream. The party left London on the morning of 16 June. Having obtained a special pass to go on to the docks from Anthony Eden, Hugh was able to come with them, and allowed to board the ship to see Barbara off. The train journey was horrifying and when they reached Liverpool they were herded like cattle into a customs shed where they had to stay for two solid hours with no possibility of buying food for the children and nothing to sit on except dusty, dirty forms meant for luggage. Barbara looked at Hugh. 'Shall we not go?' she asked. He did not reply and after a moment she added, 'If this is voluntary evacuation, what must the compulsory sort be like?'

Eventually they embarked. The ship was the *Duchess of Atholl*, one of the big, comfortable passenger ships of the Canadian Pacific Line. Barbara, despite the protests from Irene and the rest of the party, insisted on sharing a cabin with her children, although she had one for herself on another deck. She knew that if there was a question of anything going wrong she wanted to be with them and did not trust them with anyone but herself. They sailed late that night and the next day Barbara learnt they were carrying 1350 people on board, a large majority of them children with the women escorting the children and some women who were pregnant. There were just fifty-two men on the ship apart from the crew.

The next day they found the ship was alone without an escort and Barbara had time to look around and see who else was aboard. Irene's party had been joined by the American-born Countess of Jersey, former actress Virginia Cherrill, and the beautiful, exotic Russian dancer, Tilly Losch who had become the Countess of Caernarvon. Rather detached from them all was Liza Paravincini, daughter of Somerset Maugham, who sat composedly reading Tolstoy's *War and Peace* throughout the voyage.

Everyone on board talked continually of money as each person had only been able to take out £10 with them which meant that Barbara only had £50 in all for her family, including Nanny. She was confident however that Jimmy would look after her and that Hugh would be able to repay him in England anything that was spent in Canada.

Before they left the Irish Channel there was tremendous activity. A destroyer rushed backwards and forwards, they altered course, received more signals and altered course again. It was not difficult to guess that they were in danger from German submarines and Barbara learnt with dismay that in the event of the ship being struck, there were not enough lifeboats on board for everyone. About the third day out, the ship ran into rough weather. This, coupled with the continuous zig-zag movements to avoid submarines, made everyone sea-sick.

On arrival in Canada, at Jimmy's instruction, the whole party set off for a hotel in the fashionable Metis Bay. Barbara however was only concerned with one thing and that was that on reaching Quebec there would be telegrams or letters from England saying that Ronald and Tony were alive, but there was nothing except letters from Hugh saying how much he was missing her. Alone in Metis Bay with the children, the full shock of what the last two weeks had meant suddenly hit Barbara and she suffered a severe haemorrhage which left her weak and depressed and so enfeebled that her hair began to fall out. For the first time her courage faltered. 'I felt an unreasoning, blind despair. I felt trapped, desperate and helpless.'There were constant cables from Hugh, but no word of Ronald and Tony. I was so sure I was going to hear, and the agony of loss began to steep over me.'

She remembered then that just after Dunkirk she had a dream about Ronald which she dismissed at the time as just a nightmare. She had seen him clearly in the darkness in what seemed to be a room, or it might have been just nothing. He was very pale and his eyes were closed. He had a hole in the very centre of his forehead. It had been a brief dream and she had hardly thought of it the next day, yet now it began to haunt her, and she felt perhaps it had been more prophetic than she had realized. Yet if Ronald were dead, as he had said so often, they would both be aware of it and he would come to her as he had always promised to do.

To add to Barbara's troubles, the three children, beginning with Raine, had bad attacks of hay fever and then went down with measles. In Canada patients with measles had to be sent to the fever hospital, and Barbara was frantic in case the children should be taken away from her. She told everyone they had eczema, and she painted their faces with calomine lotion and kept them in their bedroom at the hotel with the blinds drawn so that their eyes would not become damaged.

Before she left England, although she had so much to do, Barbara had been in touch with officials in Ronald's constituency to say that any children who came from King's Norton were to get in contact with her immediately, and Hugh had said the same to all those at the McCorquodale Works. Thousands and tens of thousands of people had applied for their children to be sent abroad, but Hugh told Barbara they were now receiving evasive answers as to the possibility of getting a passenger ship and the sailing dates were being altered over and over again. Now Barbara learnt that the government plan to evacuate children abroad, which was to be put into operation almost immediately after Barbara left England, was to be postponed. The sinkings of vessels in the Atlantic made it imperative for passenger ships to be escorted by a war ship, but with the capitulation of France, these could not be spared.

The evacuation scheme was actually to be closed down two months later after the sinking of the *City of Benares*, which was packed with children, a great number of whom lost their lives. It was obvious by the end of July that sea evacuation was to prove impracticable and that only an infinitesimal percentage of children would have the opportunity of going overseas. In fact, counting those who had gone to Australia, South Africa, Canada, the number evacuated abroad totalled seven thousand when all schemes, privately and government sponsored, were stopped.

Before this Barbara had already made up her mind. She had made a mistake and was not afraid to admit it. If children in Birmingham had to face the invasion, her children must do the same. She should never have accepted Jimmy's kind invitation, but should have stayed in England even though, as Winston Churchill had said: 'We shall fight on the beaches. We shall fight on the landing grounds. We shall fight in the fields, on the streets and in the hills.' 'I have made a terrible mistake', Barbara wrote to Hugh, 'and you must get me home.'

Hugh replied that things were very difficult in England. The Battle of Britain had started and bombs were falling every night. He would however, he said, do his best to see if his family could return, but he reminded Barbara that she had signed a form to say she would not try to return to England for six months.

One day a letter arrived from Hugh saying that fifty incendiary bombs had set the wood adjoining his father's house in Essex on fire, two bombs had fallen on McCorquodale factories and there were terrible reports of the treatment of prisoners by the Germans, which were of course profoundly upsetting for Polly. On top of this Barbara was desperately short of money - she had not yet seen Jimmy, who was so busy with war work, and did not like to ask Irene for more.

A kind Canadian friend she had met through Lord Ellibank found her a flat in Montreal where she could go when they left Metis. Taking with her one of the maids who had been looking after them at the hotel, she moved gratefully to the city, thinking that once she was in the centre she might get plans moving to return to England.

Barbara's courage had returned to her and she was starting to make the best of things as she always did in any situation in which she found herself. Distressed and unhappy she may have been, but she was still fighting for what she thought was right and just. Hugh had been sending her large parcels of clothes and medicine and other things the children had needed, so that she needed almost no money. It had been announced that evacuees could have things sent from home without paying duty. She found, however, when she went to collect the parcels that there was a duty on them, and she sat down immediately and wrote to the Head Customs Officer in Ontario pointing out that to charge duty on such articles was giving evacuees something with one hand and taking it away with the other. What was more they could not afford the duty! Once again she won a battle and the duty was refunded to her and all personal parcels from Britain came in free.

The Customs House was to be of help to her in another way. It was when she was there one morning, accompanied by Raine and Ian and trying to look after them and carry six parcels, that a man offered his help. She accepted gratefully and he introduced himself as being English. His name was Philip Saunders and he was the talented inventor of the Saunders Valve. When he realized that Barbara was an author he asked her if she would write his biography, which he had wanted for a long time. He offered to pay her £250 for it, which at that moment was a godsend. She wrote it with her usual speed and he was delighted.

In the meantime Hugh had written that he thought it would be a mistake for her to come home as it would be too dangerous. But by this time Barbara had become absolutely convinced that she should not take privileges, nor should her children, in war-time. She had even written to Nigs Rattendon and he answered by return giving her an introduction to the Prime Minister, Alexander Mackenzie King, and to J.W. McConnell, President and owner of the *Montreal Star*. Barbara telephoned for an appointment with Mr McConnell and went to see him at his office. She knew little about him except that he was the richest, and certainly the most philanthropic, man in Canada and had placed one million dollars at the disposal of the R.A.F. for their immediate needs.

Tall, handsome, and with vivid blue eyes, he asked her with a simple directness:

'What can I do for you?'

'I want to go home', Barbara replied.

'Why?'

She told him how she had made a mistake and that the government scheme for the evacuation of children, which had been a large one, had been closed down. Ronald was missing, his constituency in Birmingham had been bombed, and she knew it was absolutely and completely wrong in her position for her and her children to take privileges in war-time. She must have been very convincing because without any more palaver Mr McConnell said, 'I understand', and added, 'You do realize that the Canadian Government have passed a law prohibiting their ships from carrying women and children in war zones?' Barbara nodded. 'Nevertheless, I will see what I can do', he said.

There was no need to say more. Barbara was suddenly buoyantly reassured and confident. He even asked her if she had enough money and said that if she was in any difficulty to come to him. He was so kind and unexpectedly generous, she felt it was impossible to thank him adequately.

A week later Mr McConnell telephoned her to say that he had spoken to the Under Secretary of State for External Affairs who had promised he would give Barbara permits to return home. She had won yet again. As she wrote to Hugh: 'I nearly fell dead with joy.' Barbara sent off her passports and asked to be allowed to return as soon as possible, then waited apprehensively.

In the meantime it was impossible to sit idle, and when a Canadian woman friend, whom she had met at Metis, suggested that she should do a short lecture tour for the powerful association of the Canadian Women's Clubs, she agreed, feeling this was a chance to tell the women of Canada what the war meant to the ordinary people of Great Britain and to counteract some of the isolationist propaganda which was flooding into Canada through the American radio stations.

For the next two weeks she had an insight into Canada which she might never otherwise have had. Barbara had never travelled by herself before and she now found herself in strangely different surroundings. One night she was the guest of the Prime Minister of Halifax, a province which is twice the size of the British Isles, and having a morning cup of tea brought to her by the Prime Minister's wife in a Crown Derby teapot which she had washed up herself; another night she stayed at a small lumber house where the sheets were flannel and the steam heating came from underneath the floorboards, and Barbara felt she was being cooked during the night. At St John's, Halifax, she entered a huge ballroom at the Admiral Beatty Hotel to find a thousand women knitting and counting stitches. It was a daunting sight for even the most experienced speaker.

Wearing a black cocktail dress she had brought with her and a silver fox fur, she held audiences in rapt attention wherever she went. Barbara talked in her usual personal way, without notes, about her own friends. Eily Donald, for example, who worked all day in her decorating business and at night went out with an ambulance picking up casualties. She spoke of Eily's son, Donald, a boy of seventeen in the Royal Navy who had been badly burnt in the raid on Stavanger in Norway. When his mother saw him, his face was smothered in black anti-burn grease, his hair and eyelashes burnt away, and his lips so swollen he could hardly speak. 'Was it awful, darling?' his mother had asked him. 'Rather like acting in a film', he told her, and with a flash of spirit added, 'without the love interest of course!'

Barbara being Barbara, despite the seriousness of her messages which every audience found very moving, she attracted men. One tall, good-looking doctor followed her back to Montreal where he came to see her. Unfortunately it was Nanny's day out, and Glen, who was usually a very good little boy, for some reason began to protest. He screamed from the moment the doctor arrived until he left - so it was not a very romantic meeting.

One thing Barbara had arranged was for Raine to go to a day school in Montreal, and in her spare time, Mam'selle Romand, a Parisian, took her for walks and spoke French to her. Barbara was insistent that Raine should have a really excellent education, something she had never received from the various schools she had attended, and most of all that she should learn languages. Mam'selle Romand's lessons were to bear fruit years later when Raine addressed a meeting of the Senior Architects and Surveyors of Paris for an hour in perfect French and without notes.

Hugh had written to say the bomb damage was heavy and Barbara decided to take First Aid lessons. It was her first contact with the St John Ambulance Brigade which was to mean so much to her in the future. At that moment all she realized was what splendid work the Brigade was doing in Canada and that the Royal Canadian Mounted Police were all first aiders.

News became worse. The sinking of the U-boats had increased alarmingly and a pocket battleship, the *Graf Spee*, was at large in the Atlantic. It had attacked a convoy, and an armed merchant ship, the *Jervis Bay*, had sacrificed herself with great gallantry to save the little ship she escorted, giving it time to escape into the darkness. Hugh cabled Barbara: 'Very concerned increased sea danger. Think advisable to postpone return for a month.' The telegram came at the same time as Barbara received a special permit to travel home in a Canadian ship.

Jimmy Dunn came to see her, begging her not to go, and every Canadian she knew told her she was almost a murderer. She began to have nightmares that Ian was drowning and she was helpless to save him. Wondering if these were warnings, she remembered that Winston Churchill had described how when, in 1914, he was asked to become First Lord of the Admiralty he had opened the Bible at random and found comfort and reassurance from the verses on which his eyes fell. One night Barbara prayed for a long time then she opened her Bible with closed eyes and put her fingers on a verse. It read: 'And there went a proclamation throughout the host about the going down of the sun, saying every man to his city, every man to his own country.' She knew then she was doing the right thing, that God would take care of them all and they would arrive safely.

On 14 November, the day of their sailing, Montreal was struck by the third blizzard of the winter, and it was bitterly cold. All the kind people who came to see her off told her that they would have no idea at which port in Britain they would arrive as everything was veiled in secrecy. The ship on which they were travelling was *The Duchess of Richmond*, the sister of the one that had brought them from England. Barbara wired Hugh, 'Look at the Gordon Lennox family tree' and hoped he would be clever enough to understand what she was implying, the head of the family being the Duke of Richmond.

When they went aboard they found the ship filled with the First Empire Training Unit, sunburnt, stalwart young men who had been on an intensive training course and who were to go directly into action as soon as they reached England. There were no other children and no women, with the exception of two wives of diplomats returning from the Far East. Aft there were two big Army transports and an aeroplane, and Barbara learnt that the hold was filled with munitions from the new Canadian factories.

She had not long been aboard when she learnt that the crew on the voyage over had heard, and seen in the distance, the heroic fight of the *Jervis Bay*. They were therefore very concerned for the safety of their own ship and its passengers. The ship's doctor made it quite clear that Barbara and Nanny were not to undress and were to be ready every moment of the night to put the children into their snowsuits to which their gloves, socks and pixie caps were pinned to prevent anything from being forgotten. Barbara had Ian in the cabin with her, Glen was with Nanny and Raine had a cabin on her own. It was very different from the crowded discomfort of the voyage from England. As to be expected, there was incessant boat drill, and Raine was so slow in getting on her clothes and warm boots that Barbara thought despairingly that if they were hit by a torpedo from a submarine she would certainly be left behind.

Many times she looked at the small lifeboat which would be theirs in an emergency and at the large, icy-cold sea with glaciers in the distance as they went further north. She asked herself if she was crazy ever to have attempted the journey. She trailed two lifebelts wherever they went and Nanny carried two as well. Raine was incessantly nagged for forgetting hers.

One night Barbara heard a terrific bang and thought, 'Now we are for it.' She sprang out of bed, picked up Ian's snowsuit, then suddenly realized it was very quiet and there were no bells or alarms. She opened her cabin door and looked into the corridor. Everything was as usual, and she realized it must have been a door slamming overhead that had frightened her. Yet it was then that a feeling of sheer terror took possession of her. She and the children were trapped and they had to go on and forward whatever happened. 'Anyone who has been in danger will know that the agony of fear is terrifying.'

Then suddenly Barbara knew with absolute certainty that someone was with her, and it was not Ronald but Glen Kidston. Though he had been killed in a flying accident he had been a sailor and he was there as surely as if she could hear and see him. 'He was beside me as real and unchanged in his relationship towards me as he had been when I had last seen him. I was no longer afraid, my fear vanished and I knew with an unashamed conviction that he had come to take us in to port. I fell asleep but Glen was still there in the morning and for the rest of the voyage. Only when we sighted the coast of England, with Liverpool burning from the bombs the night before, did he go as swiftly as he had come. I have never been close to him since.'

Three days before the ship was due to arrive, Ian was taken ill with the beginnings of pneumonia. There had been no M.&.B. on board, the wonder drug that was to be a standby for every pain and ache for the next five years. The ship's doctor was very discouraging and told Barbara it might be a long time before she could get in touch with her husband, even if he discovered the port of arrival was Liverpool. Then, says Barbara, 'I was looking out of the end of my cabin. Ian was breathing quickly and strangely, neither of us having had a wink of sleep all night. Raine came rushing in to tell me Uncle Hugh was waiting on the deck, thank God.'

It was a surprise to Barbara on arrival in England to find that Hugh had arranged for them to go to the cottage at Great Barford. 'We are very lucky to have it', Hugh said solemnly to Barbara. 'There is not a house in any part of England that is safe to be had for love nor money.' Barbara thought how cramped they would be, but nothing was more important than being home with Hugh. The children were safe and she knew instinctively that she had done the right thing in bringing them back. But another problem developed as soon as she arrived. Mary Cunningham-Reid, who had promised faithfully before Barbara left for Canada that she would not marry again, had married during Barbara's absence with Hugh as witness. It was the disaster that Barbara had anticipated, and as soon as they were installed in the cottage, Mary arrived to say pathetically, 'Please Barbara, get me out of this!'

Christmas Day came and for the first time in her life Polly had none of her children with her. She wanted to be alone. By the New Year, the first letters from the prisoners of war from Dunkirk were beginning to arrive. Polly was sure that each day brought her nearer to hearing from Ronald or Tony. On 4 January, Tony's twenty-eighth birthday, she opened a letter in a strange handwriting. It was from a Mrs Woodward whose son had been one of Ronald's subalterns and who was now a prisoner at Oflag VII:

On May the 30th at about 8.30 a.m. we were about twenty miles from Cassel making our way two miles east of Watou along a ditch bordering a lane. We were not moving very fast, the mist was rising and the country was getting open. Ronald called me forward. In the distance we saw German tanks going into action against other troops half a mile ahead. We decided to conceal ourselves, but later three tanks converged on us and we had to get up. As Ronald rose he was hit on the forehead by a bullet and killed instantly. I was five yards away from him with fifty men following. We were marched off immediately and I had no opportunity to take his belongings.

When the news was known five hundred letters of sympathy poured in from all kinds of people who had remembered this brilliant young Crusader. The Prime Minister wrote:

> 10 Downing Street,
> Whitehall,
> 6th January, 1941

Dear Mrs Cartland,
It is with very great sorrow that I have heard that you have received news that Ronald was killed in action in May last. Pray accept my deepest sympathy in the loss of so brilliant and splendid a son, whose exceptional abilities would have carried him far had he not proudly given his life for his country.

> Yours sincerely,
> Winston Churchill

From Anthony Eden, who had become Secretary of State for Foreign Affairs:

Ronald had everything before him. We were all so sure that he had a great part to play in the world after the war, for he had the true qualities of leadership, vision, courage and faith. Of all the younger men I knew, his was the fairest future.

The night she received the news, alone in her bedroom with her memories, Polly wrote in her diary, 'Oh, my darling Ronald, after all this waiting, and it is Tony's birthday. I do so wonder where he is.' Barbara, however, remembered her strange dream, and knew that just as Ronald had always told her, she had actually known when he was killed, although she had not realized it. As the official report of Ronald's death confirmed, he had been shot in the forehead, just as she had seen in her dream, and she knew he had communicated with her on his death as they had always promised each other.

Barbara also had another vivid dream about Ronald that was contradictory and puzzling. She was walking along a road when he suddenly appeared round a corner, looking as he always did, handsome with his eyes sparkling, and she ran towards him excitedly. 'You are alive! You are alive!' she cried. 'I knew they were wrong when they said you were dead!' She slipped her arm through his and they walked along together. 'You will laugh when you read all the wonderful things people have said about you since you were dead, even those who had nothing nice to say when you were alive', Barbara said. 'Mummy has stuck them all in a scrapbook and I cannot wait for you to see them.' She was with him for what seemed quite a long time and when she awoke she could not for the moment believe it had been a dream and was not the truth. Later she wrote a poem that expressed exactly what had happened:

> I dreamt last night of you,
> It was so real, so true, I knew
> You lived - although they said
> That you were dead.
>
> I dreamed you kissed me, then
> We laughed just as we did when
> You were here - before they said
> That you were dead.
>
> I know you are alive
> I cannot see you but you are beside
> Me still, as you were before they said -
> So stupidly - that you were dead.

Just one month later, Polly was to learn that Tony was dead, too. He had been killed in action one day before Ronald and through the American Embassy she heard he was buried at Zuidschote, north of Ypres. Once again the details had come from a prisoner of war.

> . . . Left to hold the rearguard trench he was surrounded and part of the Company were killed. The German officer asked the survivors to surrender. Tony's reply was, 'I will surrender only unto God.' He then seized a Bren gun and opened rapid fire. He was wounded and three times asked to surrender. He replied, 'I will fight the last man to the last

round.' Finally he was killed by a shot from an automatic rifle.

On the Calvary at Tewskesbury Abbey in memory of Bertie, to which both Ronald's and Tony's names were eventually to be added, Tony's words are recorded for all time, 'I will surrender only unto God.'

Good must triumph over evil. It usually does in life and in any case it's bad for young people to believe it doesn't.

Barbara Cartland

As soon as Barbara had squeezed the family into their Bedfordshire cottage she wanted to do some war work, not only because she was extremely anxious to help the war effort in any way she could, but also because if she was not doing war work, Nanny would have to go into a munition factory. The problem was immediately solved by the Hon. Pearl Lawson Johnson, who was County Organizer for the Bedfordshire W.V.S. She asked Barbara to join the organization to undertake the distribution of books to the various outlying searchlight posts, Army camps and aerodromes. This meant first collecting the books from the villages. People only threw away the most unsuitable material. Barbara found herself looking in despair at a load of dull, stodgy, Victorian novels, Baedeker guide books to Germany and heavily bound volumes of sermons. The situation was to become much improved in the spring of 1941 when the Pilgrims Trust of America sent travelling libraries to the W.V.S., ten for each county. It was a magnificent present in large boxes with about sixty books in each, all new and up to date.

In the meantime County Welfare offices were being set up in every county to help with the comforts of all three services. In short the welfare services were a 'soldier's friend'. The officer in command was usually a retired officer of senior rank.

Colonel Walby Cohen was appointed County Welfare Officer in Bedfordshire and he asked Barbara to help him. The welfare officers were all unpaid, but those who were civilians could be given an honorary commission in the Army. Barbara agreed and was made a Voluntary Junior Commander in the A.T.S. which was actually the rank of Captain. The main officer was in Bedford only a few miles away from her home. Troops were pouring into the country, and there were many secret R.A.F. camps which were so hush-hush nobody was supposed to mention them. In two years Barbara had over ten thousand R.A.F. to look after besides a number of Army units in charge of prisoners of war, and surprisingly some WRENs who had been billeted at Woburn Abbey, the magnificent home of the Dukes of Bedford.

Immediately a unit arrived in the county it was visited by a welfare officer and its needs reported to the head office. As there was practically nothing to give them of any sort, Barbara realized that she must first of all make some money to be able to buy what was required. She therefore approached the B.B.C. Symphony Orchestra, under Sir Adrian Boult, which had been evacuated to Bedford, and they generously said they would give a number of concerts and the money collected could go straight to her special fund.

The one person who suffered from all this was poor Hugh. He was not at all musical, and he only knew 'God Save the King' because he had to stand up for it. Escorting Barbara to the concerts meant he had to sit for hours listening to high-brow music which he never had appreciated, but the result was very important because it enabled Barbara to help those who really needed it.

One of the most hush-hush stations in the county was Chicksands. Barbara was in fact the only person, outside selected R.A.F. officers, who was allowed to enter the station, a beautiful old priory which had stood on the site for eight hundred years. The R.A.F. had put up in the grounds a recreation hut for the WAAFs, and when Barbara inspected it she found it contained exactly two deckchairs which were faded and rather dilapidated.

It was not surprising, she was told confidentially, that the girls were fed up with being there. It was inevitable that when they went on leave they often did not come back. With the money she had raised through the B.B.C. concerts, Barbara started to buy second-hand furniture all over the county. Sofas, chairs and tables were all obtained as cheaply as she could buy them. At least they made the huts at Chicksands and in the other camps more comfortable.

At Chicksands she also had the idea of having meetings with the women when they were off duty. She learnt afterwards that the powers-that-be were rather nervous as to what these would be like. The word 'welfare' always sounds gloomy and pontifical. Apparently some of the senior officers crept down outside the hut when Barbara had her first meeting, which she had organized in her usual original manner, insisting that there should be no officers present. What those listening heard as they approached the hut were shrieks of laughter, and a report was made that everything was quite 'O.K.'

What Barbara had arranged was that she spoke for a quarter of an hour and then asked for questions, which provided an opportunity for originality. 'Are women as trustworthy as men?', 'Should a man and girl live together before marriage?' and 'Do men like lipstick?'. These were just some of the things they discussed and on which Barbara gave her opinion during these weekly talks.

Once the authorities began to trust Barbara, it was easy for her to suggest she did up the operational huts, which were absolutely hideous and cheerless. As she had by this time raised about £1500 for her fund she could afford to spend money. As might be expected she had the operational building painted glowing Nile blue, she bought hessian, which was off coupons, and dyed it a bright coral for the curtains, and purchased coconut matting in the same colour for the floor. McCorquodale's factory in Glasgow supplied her with brilliantly printed railway posters, which were framed and hung, and she finished off painting the operational tables green with a red line. The cost was approximately £70.

After work was restarted in the hut a census was taken on the reactions of those using it. Without exception, both men and women liked it and, what was more important, better and more accurate results were obtained. The R.A.F. officer reported that morale was improved and the M.O. went as far as to say that the general health was better.

In another station, used by 60 Group Fighter Command, the whole head-quarters was covered with camouflage nets. In the winter when snow lay on the nets it was like going down a mine. Barbara was just persuading the officers in charge to brighten everything up when the British Colour Board arrived and repainted the Fighter Command room in battle-ship grey, which at the time was not at all funny! As soon as they had gone Barbara rushed in with her bright Nile blue paint and coral curtains and managed to get a local artist to do some murals on the walls, which definitely improved the whole scene much to the delight of the airmen.

Her real triumph however came later when the 60 Group found themselves in hideous, depressing buildings which had been a tile factory.

Fortunately, by this time Barbara was working with Wing Commander Farrar who was full of ideas. He produced his friend, John Gilroy, who was the famous artist of the 'My Goodness, My Guinness' series, besides having some very fine pictures in the Royal Academy. He transformed the great, high recreational building into a Spanish village. The walls were painted with amusing characters in his own inimitable style in warm, vivid colours. There were bulls and donkeys, señoritas and tourists, each a brilliant little caricature in itself.

Apart from this, Barbara had begun to realize that what depressed the servicewomen more than anything else, especially in Bedfordshire where there was no military action and very few bombs, was not their uniforms, which were on the whole very smart, but the underclothes they had to wear with them. The servicewomen were allowed twelve coupons a year, which was just enough to buy handkerchiefs. They detested their thick, serviceable bloomers and the other underclothes that went with them.

It was Wing Commander Farrar who found there was a hole in the handicrafts allowance which allowed the buying of material for occupational therapy. Barbara realized this was the lifeline and, driving up to London, bought very cheaply at Peter Jones rayon, georgette, crêpe de chine and in fact any materials which would make a woman feel seductively feminine when they were worn next to the skin.

The services personnel came into the small welfare office and bought the material by the yard. They had to measure out the fabric on the floor with a tape measure and Barbara had to put a few pence more on to every yard as surprisingly everyone cheated. The result was that by the end of the war she had bought over ten thousand pounds-worth of material for the women of Cardington, Chicksands, Tempsford, Leighton Buzzard, and dozens of other R.A.F. stations, Army camps, and searchlight posts in Bedfordshire.

After the war she met a senior Air Force officer who had been at Cardington during the war years and he said: 'I well remember the difference you made to the morale on the stations, just by providing the right sort of underwear, which made our girls feel good, or is that the wrong word?'

Inevitably the situation led to a spate of weddings, and the girls all went crying to Barbara that they could not possibly be married in anything but white. 'I have got to have a white wedding!' each one insisted. 'I would not feel married otherwise.' Barbara realized this was something with which she had to beard the senior officers in London. It was inevitable, because what she was doing was so spectacular, that many of them already regarded her with suspicion. When she had first been appointed as an officer she had bought her uniform in a hurry in Bedford. It was not well made and she soon asked Worth, who had all her measurements because she had bought so many dresses from them before the War, to make her a uniform in London. Needless to say the word got round and when she appeared in it a rather sour female of senior rank remarked, 'I quite expected it to be edged with lace!'

Barbara had no answer to this, but on another occasion, an officer who obviously thought she was not conventional enough said, again sourly, 'I understand, McCorquodale, that you call all the generals "Darling".' 'Only the men', Barbara retorted. Actually she found, with, of course, some very delightful exceptions, that the women Brigadiers and Generals were, in her own words, 'a pain in the neck'. She very much sympathized with the Earl of Carlisle who said to her plaintively, 'You have no idea, Barbara, what it is like being married to a General.'

She therefore did not look forward to meeting the heads of the A.T.S. and asking for help over the white wedding gowns. They dismissed her plea immediately as being frivolous in war-time and told her firmly that, of course, the Board of Trade would not release precious coupons for anything so unnecessary. As she looked at them, severely uniformed with unpowdered faces, she suddenly had an idea. 'Would it be possible', she suggested, 'to get wedding dresses without coupons? What about second-hand ones?' 'Mrs McCorquodale must have a very trusting belief in human nature', an aged peeress said acidly, 'if she thinks anyone would part with a wedding dress without coupons!'

Barbara returned to Bedfordshire crushed, but determined to show them they were wrong. She advertized in *The Lady* and bought two lovely dresses, one for £7 and another for £8. She sent them to the War Office with her compliments and suggested the A.T.S. brides might borrow them for their wedding day and return them afterwards. To her surprise the War Office jumped at the idea. They were delighted to arrange for the wedding dresses to be borrowed from them as long as they were bought by Barbara, and all they had to do was to distribute them. By the end of the war Barbara had bought over a thousand white wedding gowns, not only for the A.T.S. but also for the WAAFs and the WRENs. It was, she always felt when she received photographs of starry-eyed brides in the conventional white wedding gown, one of the best things she ever did.

Bombs were meanwhile falling on London if not on Bedfordshire, and one completely demolished Earl Beatty's house next door to the flat Barbara and Hugh had occupied in Grosvenor Square. It cracked the walls of Barbara's bedroom, smashed the windows, and killed and injured several people.

Barbara's work in Bedfordshire was not just frilly and feminine. She looked after girls who were pregnant, discussed their problems with women who wanted a divorce and coped with soldiers who arrived home on leave to find their wives ill with no one to look after the children. Every day more and more cases came pouring into the welfare office and as Barbara was at one time the only female welfare officer in Bedfordshire there was no end to the demand on her time.

War-time marriages always created problems. The girls would soon say they wanted a divorce. The Squadron Leader in charge would send for Barbara who would ask them how long they had been married. 'A week, then he was posted overseas' would be the reply. 'And now you want a divorce? Why?' Barbara would say. 'I am disappointed. Marriage isn't what I expected.' Barbara would try and explain to a very inexperienced and ignorant young woman that married life is not what anyone expects after reading novels and seeing films. 'It is a difficult and specialized job. You learn to read and write, you learn to be a WAAF, but no-one ever bothers to learn about love. What you have to do is learn, make mistakes then try again and of course persevere.' In many cases she was able to persuade the girl to give her marriage another chance and she would write to her afterwards and thank her for saving them from the divorce court.

Pregnancies were always a problem, but Barbara said after six years of welfare work, it was a lot of nonsense when 'the immorality of service-women' was talked about. A number of illegitimate children were born, but she thought it absolutely amazing how few unwanted babies there were. As the Salvation Army explained to her, it was not the bad girls who got into trouble, it was the stupid, ignorant little fools who always paid for being foolish.

Barbara has always believed that if you want something you must go to the people at the top, and she has never been shy in her approach. When she had tried every other source to get a Y.W.C.A. hut for an R.A.F. station she decided to write to Mrs Churchill and ask her help. The Prime Minister's wife invited her to London to their flat overlooking St James's Park to discuss the matter. Barbara was slightly embarrassed to see Mrs Churchill because when the Churchills' eldest daughter, Diana's marriage broke down, her husband, John Bailey - son of Sir Abe Bailey, the richest man in the world - had asked Barbara to marry him. He was madly in love and although Barbara had refused him, she always felt slightly shy when she encountered Diana or any of the Churchill family for the simple reason that it is traditional that wives, even though they have finished with their husbands, are never pleased or pleasant if they know they have been so quickly supplanted in his affections.

When Mrs Churchill came into the flower-filled, sunlit room, I was instantly aware how friendly she was towards me and how vibrant she was. She looked so feminine and attractive in a slim, black frock, her grey hair in curls, but there was a strength of purpose behind her femininity.

I told her about the needs of the WAAFs working on the station and she replied, 'Poor girls. I know what it is like. My daughter, Sarah, has told me so much about the hardships of these girls. There is an executive meeting of the Y.W.C.A. early tomorrow morning. I will go and see what I can do for you.'

It was not long after this that Barbara saw a new building being installed and once again set about decorating it in her favourite Nile blue and coral. Due to the generosity of several large firms who helped with the expenses, two of these large recreational huts were erected on Bedfordshire stations.

Suddenly out of the sky the Americans arrived. The Flying Fortresses came swooping in and the 8th Bomber U.S.A.A.F. were stationed just five miles outside Bedford. Barbara, who was told to look after them until their own American Red Cross arrived, found that one of the most difficult things to cope with was their home-sickness. Most Americans, including the officers, had never been abroad before and they found it desperately depressing to have nowhere to go where they would feel cosy and welcome. River Cottage, Barbara's home in Great Barford, was always full of them. They would arrive shyly, then settle down and tell her their problems and talk about their families, and ended up seeming very much happier. What Hugh found embarrassing, although Barbara became used to it, was that when one of their number was killed on one of the daylight flights to the Continent, his friend would come to the cottage, sit down in the first comfortable chair saying, 'My Buddy went down today!', and burst into tears. It was all very un-English but somehow Barbara was able to help, and she believes that these men really looked at the small thatched cottage as a substitute for their own homes thousands of miles away.

Not content with incessantly raising money for things she needed for the girls, towards the end of the war, Barbara began to arrange a huge exhibition of handicrafts. Every camp in the county was anxious to exhibit and it developed into an enormous effort which once again did a great deal for morale. All the services of Bedfordshire took part. The land girls and agricultural workers ran a tombola, the British Red Cross a gift stall, the St John Ambulance Brigade a first-aid post and several of the hostels had stalls or side shows. The B.B.C. Symphony Orchestra presented a rare copy of Chopin's works to be sold, signed by every member of the orchestra including Sir Adrian Boult and Clarence Raybould.

When everything was ready the exhibition was opened by the beautiful Princess Marina, Duchess of Kent. Instead of the Princess being presented with the usual bouquet, Barbara arranged for the WRENs to give a model ship to her children, the A.T.S. a lorry and the WAAFs an aeroplane.

When she was going round the exhibition, Princess Marina was very interested in the stall arranged by the prisoners of war. The Italians had made the most exquisite little miniatures of shoes, clogs and other things. As they had no material allotted to them, they had made them out of bread which had hardened and which they had then painted. The Italians were so good at anything like that and hated working on the land in the enormous fields of brussels sprouts. The German prisoners were different and Hugh always said that he had never known such good beaters as the Germans when they had partridge shoots - they walked across the fields in precise Prussian fashion!

Princess Marina was so entranced with the little shoes that the prisoners asked her to accept them as a gift. She was just about to do so when her lady-in-waiting, a rather stiff-necked peeress, whom Barbara had known before the war and had never liked, rushed forward to protest saying it was quite impossible to accept a present from anyone who was a prisoner. Regretfully, Princess Marina handed back the shoes and it was difficult to know when she left the stall who was the more disappointed, the Italians or the Princess.

The services were allowed to sell anything they had made and were to give the County Welfare one penny out of every shilling for expenses. This fund provided £602 clear profit which, of course, Barbara was able to put to good use as soon as it was in hand.

Sometime before this she had found what she had thought of as a wonderful cabaret turn to cheer up the stations where people were often depressed and bored. She found a Queen sitting in a small village, apparently no one having any idea she was there. She was Queen Marie of Yugoslavia, daughter of the gloriously beautiful Queen Marie of Romania, whom Barbara had met before the war and whom she considered the most romantic person she had ever seen. She was also the sister of the notorious King Carol. Queen Marie had been living simply and dully in a small cottage in a tiny village with only two Yugoslavian servants and a rather tiresome lady-in-waiting to look after her. She kept up no pomp and ceremony and was really delighted when Barbara asked her if she would help by going round some of the camps and talking to the men and women working in them.

Queen Marie, whose husband, King Alexander I, had been assassinated at Marseilles on a goodwill mission to France, had brought her two youngest sons to England and they had been sent to public school. During her first interview with Queen Marie, Barbara told her of the lack of comfort in different stations nearby and of the desolate recreation rooms where in some cases there was not even an armchair for the pilots to sit in. After that the Queen was quite willing to let Barbara take her anywhere she thought she could do some good. Barbara whisked her off to one R.A.F. station after another and the girls particularly were delighted to see her. 'Is she really a Queen?' they would ask. 'I wish she was wearing a crown.'

Besides going to the stations and convalescent camps, Queen Marie went with the two young princes to the McCorquodale factory at Wolverton where many of the government contracts were printed. She was fascinated to see the pension forms, the leave books, telegram forms, casualty returns, postal orders, money orders, postal drafts, letter cards, airmail letters, registered envelopes, entertainment tax tickets, railway forms and many other books and forms which were in daily use in the services.

At this time flying bombs were proving a dangerous hazard. The first one fell on England on 13 June 1944. Five days later one hit the Guard's Chapel at Wellington Barracks during Sunday morning service. Many people were killed, including a number of Barbara's friends. The following December, Hugh and Barbara were both in the nursery as Ian and Glen were going to bed. Ian was being dried in front of the fire after his bath and Glen was saying his prayers on Barbara's knee. Suddenly they heard a bomb approaching. Barbara looked at Hugh over Glen's bowed head and as their eyes met they heard the engine cut out. Almost immediately, while they held their breath, there was a crash and the lights flickered. The flying bomb had landed in the village, but fell on open ground and did no damage. The bomb carried a large number of propaganda leaflets intended to frighten the British people.

Apart from his work in the firm, Hugh was out several nights a week in the Home Guard. This consisted primarily of elderly men, who found it exhausting to work all day and to be on guard all night; but they felt that they were doing something important, as indeed they were, and that was all that mattered. Often when they arrived back at two o'clock in the morning, Barbara, who had never liked cooking, would go downstairs and make scrambled eggs for Hugh and several other members who lived in the village. Eggs were severely rationed in London, but they were fortunate simply because they kept chickens in the small garden at River Cottage.

Despite all this activity, Barbara still struggled to bring out a novel every so often. She felt in some way it was a relief from the fear that always lurked behind everything she did and the constant worry and difficulties that were inevitably part of the war. At this stage, when the British public were being asked by the Prime Minister to make even greater sacrifices, love was about the only thing that was left unrationed.

——20——

Courage has always been the foundation stone of our national character, and national character is, as we all know, made up by individual convictions.

Barbara Cartland

In July 1941, Barbara rang Polly very worried. 'I have just heard', she told her mother, 'that a friend of Ronald's, who is also an author, is considering writing his biography. I cannot believe, as he is a foreigner and knows little about politics, that he will do him justice.'

Polly did not hesitate. 'You must write it!'

'But I couldn't! I am sure it is too big for me!'

'Nonsense', Polly said, 'I could not bear it to be anyone but you, darling. Start at once.'

There was no more discussion, and that is exactly what Barbara did. Although she always dictates her novels, and managed somehow to do this even all through the war, Ronald's book, she felt, needed to be written. She bought some note-books, took up a pencil and in that funny spidery writing of hers began:

In 1910 a small boy aged three sat at a minute table in a big toy cupboard scribbling on the backs of old Primrose League tickets. Every now and then he would rise solemnly and, coming to the front of the cupboard, would make a speech to the assembled throng in the nursery, consisting of Nanny and his elder sister who paid little attention to him. Clapping himself enthusiastically at the end of a short peroration he would return to 'his desk' and continue to write. . . .

Whenever Barbara had a minute to spare during her days filled with her welfare work she rushed to her desk in the cottage and wrote.

Amazingly it was the easiest book I have ever written; the words seemed to flow out, as if they were dictated to me. I was helped of course tremendously by the fact that my mother had kept every letter Ronald had ever written to her and that she had stuck every newspaper reference to him and his speeches into press-cutting books. I wrote and wrote and the book was finished in a month.

When the manuscript had been typed she gave copies of it to Leo Amery, Secretary of State for India and Burma, who had always been a great friend of hers, and to Ronald's oldest political friend, J. P. L. Thomas, the Member for Hereford. She wanted to be sure that the Parliamentary facts were correct. So many of Ronald's colleagues had written glowing tributes when he had died, including the Prime Minister, so it was natural that Barbara hoped that he would write the foreword to her book. Hesitating to make a direct approach she asked Brendan Bracken, then Minister of Information, to sound out Mr Churchill about writing a foreword. A week or so later she received through the post a letter from the Prime Minister's office containing his preface:

Ronald Cartland was a man of noble spirit, who followed his convictions without thought of personal advancement. At a time when our political life had become feckless and dull, he spoke fearlessly for Britain. His words and acts were instinct with the sense of our country's traditions and duty. His courage and bearing inspired those who met him or heard of him.

Fortunately this country has not lacked men prepared to spend their lives in its service. Ronald Cartland was one of these. On May 30th 1940, when he was killed fighting with the rearguard of the British Expeditionary Force during its retreat to Dunkirk, the Army and the House of Commons suffered a grievous loss. Those who read this book will realize that this is true. They will also derive from it a renewed assurance that the way of life for which he fought will certainly prevail and persist because of the striving and sacrifices of such men as he.

It was a luminous tribute not only from a great Prime Minister to one of his youngest Members of Parliament but also of a sixty-seven-year-old intellectual to a young disciple thirty-four years his junior.

Barbara says: 'Ronald had loved Mr Churchill. How angry he had been when an elderly Member of the House had said, "Take my advice, Ronald, keep away from Winston, he's no good to a young man." Ronald's reply had been ice: "Thank you, I must be allowed to choose my own friends."'

The book, entitled *My Brother Ronald*, was published the next spring but not without its own drama. The corrected proofs were lost in the post *en route* from Bedford to Glasgow, and the publisher was frantic. With her intolerance of bureaucracy Barbara telephoned the postmaster, only to be told that she could not speak to the great man personally, but must fill in a form. It was already too late that day to go to Bedford but during the evening she telephoned various friends and told them about the incident. In the morning she was amazed when the postmaster telephoned her as he had seen the story in the newspapers. 'You should have insisted on speaking to me', he reproved her unctuously. The corrected proofs finally turned up in the publisher's office where a messenger boy had put the registered parcel in a waste paper bin!

My Brother Ronald was an unqualified success, and for Barbara it remains the most important book she has ever written. It proved without question that she could have taken her place as a serious biographer had she not chosen to write romantic fiction and that her grasp of the political scene was sound. Void of sentimentality it caught the essence of her brother's character. Left of the Right in his political views, he was a man ahead of his time. This is what she captured in every page as her readers were quick to appreciate.

> Courage was the keynote to his character, a courage clear and unflinching, a courage which never faltered, never prevaricated whatever sacrifice was demanded of him . . . But the courage of his convictions meant more than life itself - it was his life - a crusade of moral bravery. To those who knew him the fire of truth, vision, and strength of purpose burned more brightly; at times it shone almost too brilliantly; stupid people who got a glimpse of it were afraid because it was something they did not understand.
>
> The Christian life as he saw it was a living, working philosophy, controlled and guided by the Great Creative Force of which he was always acutely conscious. Other people were seeking a formula for living; he knew that for him personally - self-control, high endeavour and the sense of initiative which comes from freedom, with faith in the

destiny of oneself and one's race, remain the immemorial prescription for a happy life.'

The book was well received by every critic. Raymond Mortimer, one of the most discriminating critics of the day, described Ronald's life as 'a crusade of moral bravery'. The *Observer* wrote: 'To further the ideals of Disraeli's Young England he employed the personal technique of a Lassalle and whatever the future may have held in store the contemporary political scene is the drabber for his passing.' And the *Sunday Times* declared, 'This unpretentious (though perhaps slightly over intimate) record should be widely read and pondered.'

And it was. Barbara was to receive letters from all kinds of strangers. From men serving in battleships, from soldiers overseas, from factories and farms. They all wrote in a similar vein. 'The book inspired me' . . . 'For the first time I understood politics' . . . 'I know now what I want of the future . . .' Mothers wrote too. Moving, tender letters: 'This is the first book I have been able to read since my son was killed - it has helped me more than I can say. . .'

The Reverend Mervyn Stockwood, the Bishop of Southwark, was to write, much later, 'Ronald Cartland was the hero to many of my generation, even those, like myself, who had different political affiliations. In 1942 I read his biography by his sister, Barbara. It made a deep impression upon me and now forty years later I still look to it for inspiration.'

Writing Ronald's biography inspired Barbara in 1943 to write her thirty-seventh novel, *Sleeping Swords*, the story of political developments in Great Britain since the beginning of the century. In her research for Ronald's biography she had become so mentally immersed in politics that her mind naturally flowed towards using the Parliamentary scene as a background. Its young hero Michael is a cleverly veiled portrait of Ronald and the love interest is supplied by Jennie, a pretty socialist candidate. The plot weaves through political intrigues and ends with Michael, full of enthusiasm, courage and hope for the future, being killed.

I think I read every book and pamphlet published during this period. They were sad fare, and one was often ashamed. It was not a cheerful picture and yet there was in contrast the spirit of Britain rising strong and undefeated, her people moving slowly but surely towards reforms - the improved conditions in industry, the benefits of compensation and pensions, the betterment of medicine, hospital services, and housing.

Barbara dedicated the novel 'To Ronald, killed near Cassel, May 30, 1940'.

> On the 'Dunkirk beaches' of England's story,
> She finds her soul and her greatest glory,
> For the men who love her are always the same
> Ready to die in freedom's name.
>
> The vision that once our fathers knew
> Has been born again. Can we make it true?
> So that out of the muddle and sins of the past
> England may find her peace at last?

Confident within herself that she had written her best novel to date Barbara took *Sleeping Swords* to her publishers. Alas they were not so enthusiastic and greeted her with the words 'It is not the usual Barbara Cartland novel' . . . 'It is good but . . .' She was desolate. Here was clear proof that what the publishers wanted was Cartland romance and they were not really interested in her altering her style and type of story. She was furious. She then took the book to Robert Hale who agreed to publish it under the name of Barbara McCorquodale with the built-in security of the name Barbara Cartland under it in brackets. Though he was willing to take the risk, Robert Hale was not so generous with the advance, which was considerably less than she would have received had the book been under the name of Barbara Cartland.

When *Sleeping Swords* appeared the reviews almost without exception were extremely good, but because of the paper shortage there was no question of it being reprinted after the initial edition was sold out. Barbara wrote to J.V. Kitton, the distinguished librarian of the House of Commons, and asked if a copy might be included in the library. In acknowledging the gift he wrote back: 'Very many thanks indeed for your gift of Sleeping Swords. This library has a general rule banning fiction, but I think it only proper to make a unique exception in the case of this book, which cannot fail to be of great interest to Members who knew and appreciated your brother's ideas and hopes.'

Ronald's influence on Barbara was to remain with her for all time. Undoubtedly his death was the most traumatic experience of her life, and though she came to terms with herself the shock remains as painful today as it was then. I cannot believe that some of her crusading energy does not come from Polly's blood, but undoubtedly Ronald inspired much of her instinctive reaction whenever she sees signs of injustice. Though over the years Barbara has been offered three safe seats from the Conservative Party to become a Member of Parliament she never felt that she could give it the full-blooded devotion that Ronald would have done.

In Barbara's life her family has always come first, and always will, and she makes no secret that the weekends, when her two sons are at Camfield Place, are the highlight of her week. Arguments flip across the dinner table and there is little need to speculate as to who gets the last word! Like Ronald, Barbara can arouse anger as well as admiration, even from those who admire and love her. In the Cartland family they speak of 'blood rows' but like a thunderstorm they pass over quickly.

Barbara explains herself in her own words:

. . . What has really happened now is that I have developed on my own so much that instead of being the soft, sweet Ethel M. Dell heroine I have obviously become much more positive, because I have had to. I've had to take on myself and Ronald, do you understand?

When I decided that I couldn't be a Member of Parliament I became a County Councillor. They came to see me in 1955 and said, 'Will you be a County Councillor for Hertfordshire for the Hatfield Division?' I refused and explained that I hadn't got the time because of the family. They went away but came back again and said, 'We can't find anybody.'

I always had this feeling that I ought to carry on Ronald's ideals. In this case they never thought I'd win because the Comet had just come to the De Havilland factory in Hertfordshire and two thousand people had been moved in from London, mostly from well-held Socialist strongholds.

I agreed to stand and then I thought if I am going to do this I will do it properly and run it like a Parliamentary campaign. I was in the headlines every week. People used to write to me and say: 'We've never heard of our Councillor until you came.' During my canvassing I had two people knocking at doors either side of the road and I walked down the centre. If the person opening the door said 'No, they were not interested' I didn't bother, but if there was the slightest curiosity I went over and shook their hands and had a quick word. In that way I called at eighteen thousand houses myself. As I was a County Councillor for nine years I did it three times and the last year the houses who received me had trebled.

I was always well dressed and wore a pretty hat, but flat shoes of course. It was hard on the feet I can assure you. When I won everyone was absolutely stunned. The County Council said 'Oh God, she is coming here now'. They didn't know what to expect.

They were right. For one thing I visited all the homes for old people.

I had never seen anything so appalling, so terrible! I said something must be done. I decided to visit a home for old men one Saturday and asked Raine (then the Countess of Dartmouth) if she would come with me because at that time she was a Councillor for Westminster and a very live wire. Six of the committee were there to meet us so I knew they were frightened. There was a clean cloth on the table and rather nasty-looking sliced bread and jam. I asked the Warden if this was their tea. He said 'Yes' and then I asked 'And what do they have after that?' There was an awful pause and he said, 'Well, they don't have another meal but of course they have had a lot of food during the week.' As if they were camels! I still didn't say anything. When I got home I rang up County Hall and said, 'Do you realize that these old people do not have any food from four o'clock until eight o'clock the following morning? Which is absolutely abominable because the taxpayers pay for it.'

Then I got on to the Red Cross, the Townswomen's Guild and the W.V.S. and said , 'Why aren't you visiting these old men? They had excellent explanations but in the end I got all the visitors in and arranged that the old men had a proper supper.

I visited every other home in the county. In some I suggested that a little Jeyes Fluid might be a good thing. In others the old people had nowhere to put their belongings except in a suitcase under the bed which was tied up with string. In one the ceiling was crumbling over the stove where their food was cooked. Just think of all those germs! Everything I did was reported in the Press. Afterwards, when I was opening an exhibition of old people's work the County Officer said to my astonishment, 'I want to thank you for all you have done. I hated you at first because I thought you were destroying all I was trying to achieve, but because of your exposure of what was happening, the County Council have given me much more money to spend, so I am very grateful.' I nearly cried!

Raine was absolutely marvellous because as I couldn't leave my husband, who was not well, she visited 250 homes all over England. She found some good and others frightful.

I had fought a hard battle and when our reports were finished Duncan Sandys, then Minister of Housing and Local Government, set up a Government Enquiry into the housing and conditions of old people. When it was debated in the House of Commons, he sent me a letter saying, 'According to the Gospel of St Barbara.'

Undoubtedly the experiences Barbara had had when she accompanied Ronald on his many visits to the Distressed Areas and Birmingham had quickened her attention, in that she was able not only to recognize what was wrong but to take the initiative to get it put right. Like Ronald she stood for ideals, not only theoretically but in practice.

During the year of 1943 Barbara edited a symposium of Ronald's speeches and asked the Earl of Selborne, with whom as Viscount Wolmer Ronald had worked for the Distressed Areas, to write the preface. 'The intimate relationship between a Member and his constituents is revealed and demonstrated in the reading', he wrote. 'He is talking to people whom he knows as friends; he is talking to people whom he loves. He is thinking aloud for them, and bridging for them the gulf between principle and practice.' Surely this is the criterion for any politician worth his salt and as valid today as when these words were written forty years ago.

The booklet was to produce many letters to Barbara and Polly from all kinds of people. Quite apart from Members of Parliament, candidates and local councillors, they came from ordinary working men and women, from the factories and the offices. They only had one message - how Ronald's words had inspired them. Barbara donated the proceeds of the symposium to Mrs Churchill's special appeal for Russia. In acknowledging it the Prime Minister's wife wrote:

My dear Mrs McCorquodale,

I am much touched that the proceeds of the sale of your Brother's book should be devoted by you to my Red Cross 'Aid to Russia' Fund. I am most grateful; thank you so very much. I hope to read it this weekend.

I wish that during his brief life I had seen more of your Brother. He made a great impression on me, as he did on my Husband, and we shall always be glad that he was a friend of our son-in-law, Duncan Sandys.

Yours sincerely,
Clementine S. Churchill

Barbara's third literary effort that year was a frothy topical comedy, *French Dressing*, written in collaboration with Bruce Woodhouse. The play opened in Glasgow, and when she arrived for the dress rehearsal she found not only an under-rehearsed cast in a state of frenzy but a hideous set. She spent the morning rearranging the furniture and rushing round in a taxi buying large pictures from back-street antique dealers to cover the bilious pink walls of what was meant to be a gentleman's country house. Even the leading lady's dress was too big for her and borrowing a needle and thread Barbara trimmed it down to size. All her last-minute efforts could not save the play, although the criticisms were not as bad as she and Bruce Woodhouse had expected. The play toured Liverpool, Leeds, Nottingham, Bradford and Wimbledon but failed to make the West End. Barbara chalked it up as a new experience in a crowded year. Sometimes she remembers when she first met Tallulah Bankhead in the twenties and she had said, 'Dah-ling, I hear you write plays - write me a really Goddam wicked one!'

By now her twenty-fourth novel, *The Leaping Flame*, and her autobiography, *The Isthmus Years*, were published in addition to a full year of welfare work in which she drove thousands of miles in her car. It had been a year of hard work and inspiration. Her autobiography was written as a social history of the years between the two wars and represented the generation of the period. Of the many letters she received, this is the one which she cherishes most simply because it came from a man whose opinion she respected. Captain J. F. Sullivan, M.A., Ph.D., L.L.D., D.H.L., was in Britain from the U.S.A. to write the official history of the war. He wrote:

> As an ordinary rule I don't read a book in one sitting, but I must say that is exactly what I did with your latest volume. I may be a bit bleary-eyed this morning but I feel very satisfied with myself because I enjoyed every minute and line of *The Isthmus Years*.
>
> Would you like to know what I think of it? If I were rating it, I would put it on a par with McCarthy's *History of Our Own Time*, or with Vol. 1 of Prince von Bulow's *Memoirs*. You write as one who lived not only through but in the period, and the result is gratifying. I have reviewed many books in my day, but yours is superb not only from a viewpoint of good literature, but also as a live document that is more than a skeleton; it is flesh and blood.
>
> One thing in particular struck me very forcibly. There isn't a bitter word in the whole fabric and you would be an exception if you hadn't been hurt somewhere along the line. It is difficult to be dispassionate but you have achieved it.

—21—

*Most brilliant men were inspired
by brilliant women.*

Barbara Cartland

Everyone who tuned into television on 29 July 1981, the day of the most romantic Royal wedding of the century, will remember the six o'clock news programme that night. While the B.B.C. showed a replay of scenes from the wedding, on I.T.V. there in her flower-filled drawing room we saw Barbara in the immensely smart black uniform of the St John Ambulance Brigade.

There was much speculation in the popular Press as to why Barbara, as the mother of Princess Diana's stepmother, Countess Spencer, was not present at St Paul's Cathedral. The plain truth is that when her son-in-law, who had only been allocated fifty seats for St Paul's, therefore gave her tickets for herself and Glen, she immediately suggested that her own seat be given to her elder son, Ian. Later, in fact at the last moment, another seat was found for Ian's wife, Anna.

I feel that weddings are for young people and it was much more important that my children should be actually there in St Paul's than me. After all Prince Charles will be their King one day.

I decided that I would hold my own party for the one hundred members of the Hertfordshire St John Ambulance Brigade who were on duty that day. I invited them to come back to my house after they had finished and celebrate with me.

There were 1,002 members of the St John lining the route. They did a marvellous job of coping with 3,200 accidents, over 1,200 from the fireworks the night before. Everyone was not only unpaid, as the St John Ambulance Brigade is entirely voluntary, but they paid their own fares to London, their own food and each Division produced their own bandages and other equipment. I only wish I had been younger so I could have joined them on the route, but I am too old to stay up all night.

In Hertfordshire the St John members still speak to this day about Barbara and the delicious buffet food she had waiting for them as they trekked back tired and hungry, to toast the health of the Royal couple in champagne. Next day Barbara received the following cable, which I found in her scrapbook, from Geoffrey Meek who was public relations director for the St John Ambulance Brigade in England:

THANKS FOR THE PUBLICITY IN EVENING STANDARD, ITV ETC RE-GARDING ST JOHN AMBULANCE ROLE AT WEDDING VERY MUCH APPRECIATED PARTICULARLY YOUR KIND HOSPITALITY TO THE BRI-GADE. FRIGHTFULLY BUSY BUT HAVE TIME TO GIVE YOU MY LOVE GEOFF.

It had been thirty-eight years since Barbara had first become involved with the St John Ambulance Brigade through her friendship with Lady Louis Mountbatten.

It was in February 1943 that Edwina Mountbatten went to stay at Great Barford when Barbara wanted someone glamorous to visit the R.A.F. station at Cardington. She felt they needed an 'event' because the personnel not only did a splendid job there but, because of the high security nature of their work, organized entertainment was scarce, although they did have their own amateur dramatic society.

Of all the society beauties in uniform at that time only Edwina Mountbatten had that special mystique and sympathy to appeal to all ranks of men and women. She had the unique gift of being able to communicate with anyone within her orbit whether it was a small beggar child in Calcutta or an aircraftsman from the Gorbals in Glasgow. Her luminous smile broke down barriers of nationality and religion.

As Commandant of the St John Ambulance Brigade 'Lady Louis' was also one of the busiest women in uniform. When Lord Mountbatten left for service overseas at the outbreak of the war she had abandoned the luxury of the penthouse in Park Lane and rented a house in Belgravia with three floors of small rooms linked by the inevitable steep staircase. Each night, after a long day's work at the St John Headquarters, she went out in the heavy raids visiting every St John Aid Post in London. She not only worked in some of these but also did voluntary nursing in the Westminster Hospital.

Her visits to troops in South-East Asia, where she was to die on duty in North Borneo, are now legendary. As wife of the Supremo she wanted to find out for herself what conditions were like and hcw the servicemen and women could be helped. Even more important, through her presence she bridged the gap between their war and that of the people back home. Often travelling in appalling primitive conditions she visited service hospitals in India, Burma, China and Ceylon and even medical units in the forward areas. Barbara knew that with Edwina's special blend of charm, wit and compassion she was the best speaker she could have. Because of their long years of friendship and the knowledge that it must be an important request for Barbara to ask her, Edwina agreed to visit Cardington.

She arrived from Coventry, where she had been inspecting and speaking the day before. She was quite happy to stay in our tiny cottage, sleeping in my husband's dressing room with its sloping roof which hit you sharply on the head when you sat up in bed if you were not careful. I don't think Edwina even noticed where she ate and slept as she had been in so many strange and weird places during the war.

It must have been a merry sight as these two charmers set off in their impeccable uniforms - the brunette in the black of St John and the blonde in the Army khaki - in Barbara's Talbot car for the R.A.F. station. They arrived to find a large hall packed from floor to ceiling with over two thousand men and women. The WAAFs only had eyes for Edwina Mountbatten's bean-slim figure and elegant legs in sheer black nylon stockings. Silk, wool, lisle and cotton were the only stockings available in wartime Britain, and the devastating sex-appeal of nylons had not yet crossed from America, but as her travels criss-crossed America, Edwina was able to keep herself supplied.

Edwina was marvellous. She kept the whole hall spell-bound as she told of her visits to Russia, Malta, Canada and America and made it a thrilling and human experience in which we could all share.

Though it was late when they both got back to Great Barford, Edwina was awake at 6.00 a.m. catching up on her correspondence and reports on her inspection of the divisions in the southern half of the county. Before she left the house shortly afterwards, in her direct manner she asked Barbara to help with the Brigade in Bedfordshire as they were desperately short of executive officers. Though Barbara had more welfare work than she could cope with, a family to bring up and books to write she could not refuse Edwina. Besides, the Brigade's motto, 'For Service to Mankind', was something she had understood from the days when Polly instilled it into her head that she must earn her place on this earth.

On joining the Brigade her first job was to raise the social status of the St John Ambulance Brigade in the county and to recruit new cadets as there were too few divisions.

> I recruited 2,500 cadets and then found I had no officers! I made mistakes - everyone does who experiments. I 'put my foot in it' with the adult divisions and went ahead too fast. I was impatient, but Captain Knight, the County Commissioner, was patient and encouraging and with him behind me I could take things in my stride.

To make the Brigade an attractive proposition for young people Barbara decided that they needed as a stimulant a marching song not just to relax the nerves through the intake of oxygen but to give the children a sense of identification and pride in belonging to the Brigade. When the B.B.C. moved to Bedford from bombed and blitzed Bristol, Archie Camden, the world famous bassoonist, and his family had taken a cottage at Great Barford. Joyce Camden was already in the W.V.S. but agreed to help Barbara in her recruiting drive for young cadets. She had a considerable amount of experience in running music festivals and a children's orchestra as well as composing music for her husband. While Barbara wrote the words she agreed to set them to music, and the song was dedicated to Lady Louis Mountbatten.

Years later, in 1953, Barbara was made a Commander of the Order of St John of Jerusalem, and was invested by the late Duke of Gloucester at Buckingham Palace, and in 1972 she was made a Dame of Grace for her thirty years' service in the Brigade. Two years later she was among the few women in one hundred years of St John history to be admitted to the Chapter General. Today she is Deputy-President for Hertfordshire and Chairman of the Order.

Sitting on a flower-fringed lawn at the medieval house in Gloucestershire belonging to his mother-in-law, Lady Maureen Fellows, Geoffrey Meek told me about Barbara's consistent contributions to the St John Ambulance Brigade over the years. Quite apart from her hours of service she has contributed a large amount of money in the most unlikely ways:

> When I first met Barbara I approached her with great trepidation because I had heard that she was quite formidable, but after meeting her at St John headquarters when she was a member of Chapter General, I suddenly realized that she is the most human person I had ever met and as a result we became great friends.
>
> Whenever I wanted any help with fund-raising or any other thing for

St John she was always available. I remember when I first joined I asked Barbara whether she would be kind enough to sign a letter for me to various people asking them for money, which is a difficult thing. And she said, 'Of course, I'll write to all my friends', and quite honestly that was the most successful fund-raising effort that St John had put up for some time. She signed about 3,000 letters personally - she topped and tailed them - they bought in an enormous amount of money. I rang her one day and said, 'Barbara what are you going to do about the hundredth anniversary of St John, and would you like to write the history of St John for us?' She told me that she did not have the time to do the research but would write a novel instead and donate the profits to the fund.

There was another difficulty, too, as all Barbara's heroes are dashing, aristocratic, attractive to women, and the Knights of Malta were celibate.'

Barbara could obviously not accept a celibate hero, so she made him a ship's Captain. She wrote *The Dream and the Glory*, about Napoleon's war in the Mediterranean and how he captured Malta. The profits from this book amounted to £37,000 which gave the St John funds a great boost.

This was one of the first books Lord Mountbatten helped to write. I said to him, 'I can't do the rigging on a Napoleonic ship' - so he did it!

One of Barbara's most engaging fund-raisers for St John was the horse she bought and christened Amber Lance. First, there was a competition in the St John Review to select the name and the readers played on 'ambulance', which Barbara thought was very clever. The great day came when the horse ran its first race with the jockey wearing orange and dark blue, which had been Barbara's grandfather's colours. Amber Lance was second and continued very well by being placed in five consecutive races. When it broke a leg and had to be put down it had already won £12,000 prize money for St John. 'Whenever you want something positive, Barbara is there like a bunny. Marvellous. I adore her. There is no argument about what she has done for St John and she deserves her Dameship. I only wish that she was a Dame of the British Empire', Geoffrey Meek told me.

During these wearying years, no-one was more aware than Barbara of the value of Royalty and the aristocracy as a morale-booster among the men and women in uniform. Through her welfare work she realized that as the restrictions got tighter and the war more prolonged, boredom, with its various psychological off-shoots, was as damaging as physical illness to the Servicemen and women.

Queen Elizabeth's eldest brother, Colonel the Hon. Michael Bowes-Lyon, and his wife Betty were neighbours and became close friends. When the authorities were looking for someone to liaise with the American Red Cross, Betty Bowes-Lyon was recommended for the job. She had been totally overworked in a factory and was then on the verge of a nervous breakdown when the position of director of home hospitality was offered her. She was warm-hearted, sincere, easy to talk to, and she appreciated these same qualities in the Americans.

Through her deep affection for her brother, who had been a prisoner of war with the Germans in 1914-18, the Queen made many visits to Bedfordshire. She would inspect the Home Guard which Colonel Bowes-Lyon commanded and visit many of the camps and aerodromes. Barbara was often involved with these arrangements.

> The Queen was fantastic. I took her soon after the G.I.s arrived to visit them in a very crowded, uncomfortable garage. She chatted to everyone. One G.I. said to me afterwards, 'She talked to me about my bicycle. Who'd expect a Queen to know about bicycles.?'

If the G.I.s found the English strange, they often surprised us, too. Barbara went with General Overacker one evening to visit the Flying Fortress. There was an entertainment taking place and the General and Barbara slipped into the first seats they saw in the large hangar. A G.I. came up to them and said, 'Hi General, that's my seat!' 'I'm sorry', General Overacker replied, and he and Barbara moved.

When the King and Queen, with Princess Elizabeth, were to make a tour of the U.S.A. aerodromes in Bedfordshire and the adjoining counties, it was treated as top secret as it was a military visit and the civilian population were to know nothing about it. American officers, however, came over to Great Barford to borrow moulds for ice creams and vases for the luncheon table. Apart from the Royal Family there were to be sixty generals, including General Doolittle. It was a hot summer's day and remembering her own visits to American bases Barbara jokingly said, 'I hope you are giving His Majesty a good luncheon and not vegetable soup and thickly cut beef.'

The officers looked at each other and asked, 'How did you guess?' She explained that British people did not like the American method of serving chunky slices of beef. 'What do you suggest?' they asked. She told them that cold salmon, chicken and 'some of your nice ice cream' would be an ideal meal for that time of year. After they left Barbara turned to her husband and said, 'Will they get a salmon?' 'Quite easily', Hugh assured her. 'They can either buy one in London or send an aeroplane up to the Tay.'

When the American friends arrived back the evening after the visit to return the vases, they were filled with the charms of Princess Elizabeth, who had christened a Flying Fortress, and how all four aerodromes had 'tried to stun the Royal party with the novelty of ice cream!' When Barbara inquired about the rest of the luncheon they replied, 'It went splendidly. We got the chicken all right, but we couldn't manage the salmon. We sent a bomber to every aerodrome but they just hadn't got a can left.'

Towards the end of the war Barbara asked if she could stop wearing uniform - 'I felt like a roast potato in khaki' - and wear her own clothes. She thought that this would be an advantage in her job where the women she interviewed were often pregnant, unhappy, and sick of the sight of uniform. Through her friend, Gwen, Lady Melchett, she bought some suits and dresses that had belonged to the beautiful young Queen Alexandra of Yugoslavia and her mother, Princess Aspasia of Greece. As all their clothes had come from the great couture houses in Paris, they were a godsend to Barbara who had always appreciated well-made clothes. They were also free of coupons!

Encouraged by the success of the services exhibition, in 1945, Barbara envisaged a huge touring exhibition for the St John Brigade. Before Edwina Mountbatten had left for an extensive tour of South-East Asia she and Barbara had discussed just such an idea. It was a mammoth task, the various services all collaborating, with all kinds of friends of St John who wanted to help.

> The services were, of course, wonderful. I told the various stations and units what I had undertaken, and once again the most amazing talent was unearthed. Artists, sign-writers, wood carvers, modellers, sculptors and cartoonists were found disguised in khaki and Air Force blue, and there was even a Czech in the R.A.F. whose job before the war was modelling tin soldiers. Every spare piece of wood, canvas, rubber, and tin was utilized somehow. One unit made a model with a Red Cross ship standing at the quayside, another carved a Southern Railway Red Cross train out of a solid piece of wood. A Salvage Corps had great fun making a model of the blitz.

At last the exhibition was finished and set out in the Town Hall and once more Edwina Mountbatten went to Bedfordshire to open it. Later it was to tour the country and make £35,000 for local divisions after it had been opened at St James's Palace by the Queen.

Earlier in the year, optimistically believing that the war was drawing to a close, Barbara had persuaded her husband to take a London house in preparation for the peace. It was an extraordinary decision, as most people were doing their best to stay clear of the flying bombs that came over day and night. Barbara has never been afraid of her own convictions and reasoned that she wanted to be ready for the peace when her sons could go to a day school in London. She rented a charming house called Chesterfield Lodge in Hay's Hill and asked her friend Eily Donald to decorate it. Owing to the devastation of the surrounding houses it took a fortnight and cost £25 just to clear it of dirt. It taxed even Eily Donald's strength to get everything painted in time so that the furniture that had been in store at Great Barford could be sent back to London.

Just as she was nearing completion I was contacted by house agents who told me that the U.S. Government wanted to rent the house for a very important person. They were so hush-hush that it was not hard to guess who this was, especially as a week before he moved in himself a large antique sword arrived labelled 'General Eisenhower'.

Special telephones had been installed beside the flame coloured velvet bed in my bedroom. The Nile blue walls had been matched from a scarab I had been given in Luxor many years ago. In my green drawing room and pine-panelled dining room many important decisions were made. The dining room was built out at the back and as the light came from a skylight it was certainly a vulnerable target.

Edwina told me how one night when she dined there with General Eisenhower, Winston Churchill, and Chief of Staff, General Sir Hastings Ismay, bombs began to fall outside. Everyone at the table ignored the noise and continued talking and laughing as if nothing was happening. The General's black servants brought in the soup with unsteady hands and after the first course appeared in tin hats.

The servants' sitting room was turned into a 'tailor's shop' - at least that is what the Americans called it, and when they said that the General would want the room for his tailor I could not think what they meant until I discovered that the tailor was what we called a valet.

Barbara had reconnoitred the neighbourhood around Hay's Hill to find a suitable air-raid shelter for General Eisenhower. She found one in the old wine cellar of a house in Berkeley Square, which had been built by Lord Clive of India. The shelter was operated by the

Oxford Group* and furnished with a bed, blankets, electric heaters and a kitchen. The General remarked drily he thought it rather strange he had to seek protection from avowed pacifists!

The fifteenth of August 1945 was VJ Day in Britain. The Japanese had surrendered and the World War was over. After the tumult of celebrations had died down a battered, heart-saddened world took stock of the price. Barbara had lost two brothers and a brother-in-law at Dunkirk, her first cousin had been sunk in H.M.S. *Perth*, and so many of those golden boys of the twenties and thirties who had asked for her hand in marriage now lay buried in foreign soil. She was thirty-eight years old when the war began and now she was forty-four. Six years of heart-rending shocks had passed with Ronald's death the most poignant of all. Life without him seemed inconceivable, but she knew within herself that like millions of other women, there was a new future to be faced with her children.

In a yearning to be in direct contact with Ronald, Barbara was taken by one of the leaders of the Spiritualistic Movement in London to all the most important mediums there. Some of them went into trances and others were 'direct voice' mediums. She asked them all one simple question to help her to decide if they were really in touch with Ronald. Ronald had often quoted a verse by Robert Browning in his speeches. She had chosen from it the title of the symposium of his speeches:

> The Common Problem, yours, mine, everyone's
> Is not to fancy what were fair in life,
> Provided it could be, - but, finding first
> What may be, then find how to make it fair
> Up to our means - a very different thing.

When several of the mediums told Barbara that Ronald was there beside them she said, 'Will you ask him what he thinks of the Common Problem?' Not one had the correct answer. They gave the same fatuous replies: 'He says he is often with you . . . he says he is very busy . . . he says he is very happy where he is.'

Remembering Ronald's closeness to me when I wrote his biography, and the way our brains were attuned to each other's all those years, it was inconceivable that he would not understand my question. I could

---

* A movement founded by Dr Frank N. Buchman, the American evangelist who came to England in 1921. In 1938 the group took on the title Moral Rearmament and moved in to Berkeley Square.

not believe that the sender of such dull, drab, commonplace messages as those was Ronald. This is not to say that mediums are deliberately trying to deceive those who seek to communicate, but when people are unhappy and emotionally unbalanced it is easy to believe what they want to believe.

By now Barbara was half way through her life. She had lived through immense sorrow, which is perhaps necessary for the development of the human spirit. What she did not realize was that the next forty years were to be gloriously happy and successful. It had all been written in the stars, as she was to find out when visiting India over twenty years later. An Indian astrologer in Madras who did not know Barbara's identity and could not speak English, was sent to see her by the Maharani of Mysore with whom Lord Mountbatten had arranged that she, Ian and Glen should stay. Her predictions, written in small, flowery hand-writing were to be remarkably accurate.

She will have a wonderful era in the years to come and is destined to be contented and happy. It is to be emphasized that she has no worries until she joins the Lotus Feet of the Lord.

She has an irrepressible desire for travel and she will benefit from such frequent and wide journeys. She will be linked by persons of importance and authority. The dignitaries and high echelons of society and Governments will welcome her warmly and render all possible help. She has strong and lasting links with members of the Royal Families.

She is a noble woman of charitable disposition and great piety. Always alert and extremely intelligent, she has great and remarkable faith in the decisions of God. She is a great lover of Shastra, religious books and other connected subjects like astrology, palmistry and astronomy.

It must be said with certainty that she will acquire more wealth and that she will not lose any either movable or immovable. The longevity can be well predicted. This noble lady will live a full and contented life up to eighty-five years.

It was all so true, as we shall find out in the second part of this remarkable life. Barbara was merely living according to plan.

Barbara Cartland, Dame of Grace of the Order of St John of Jerusalem. She has served the Brigade tirelessly for forty years. Her novel, The Dream and the Glory, *about Napoleon's war in the Mediterranean, raised £37,000 for St John's funds*

Three generations: Mary (Polly) Cartland, aged eighty-two, Barbara Cartland and her daughter Raine, Countess Spencer. This photograph was taken at the Foyle's Literary Luncheon to launch Barbara's biography, Polly, My Wonderful Mother

(Above) *Camfield Place in Hertfordshire, only seventeen miles from London, once belonged to Beatrix Potter's grandfather. Here Beatrix Potter wrote* The Tale of Peter Rabbit. *(Below) Barbara plus chauffeur and her famous white Rolls Royce, registration number BC29, at the front door of Camfield Place*

The Barbara Cartland 'factory' in
operation. Barbara with three of
her secretaries in the office where
twenty thousand letters are
answered every year, and the
manuscripts for all her novels are
prepared for publishers all over the
world

The secretaries' office is papered
with the framed covers of over three
hundred Barbara Cartland
novels. Though the artist varies,
her heroines remain the same:
heart-faced, beguiling and pure

(Above) *Lord Mountbatten on his seventy-ninth birthday snaps his hostess Barbara and Twi-Twi the dog. Barbara's chef had prepared a special cake, decorated with ships and signals. (Below) Barbara flanked by two men she greatly admires – Lord Mountbatten and Sir Arthur Bryant, the historian, whose books have inspired several of her novels*

This family snapshot was taken by Barbara's son-in-law, Earl Spencer, in the newly-opened gift shop at Althorp. From left: Lady Sarah Fellowes, Lady Diana Spencer, Viscount Althorp, Countess Spencer, Barbara and Lady Charlotte Legge

Christmas luncheon at Camfield Place. On the left is the Earl of Dartmouth, Barbara's former son-in-law, her son Ian stands behind her and, on the right, Viscount Lewisham, her eldest grandson. Ian's daughters, Iona and Tara, complete the picture

(Above) *Barbara surrounded by her Romany friends at Barbaraville, a permanent site in Hertfordshire which she fought to secure for the gypsies in a battle that lasted several years, but which resulted in a change in the law.* (Below) *Tea with Barbara Cartland was the first prize in an American competition on the definition of romance. Here the prizewinner from the Black Feet Tribe relishes afternoon tea at Camfield Place*

*bara continues to devote her life
rusading for better health. Here
*signs autographs after opening
ealth Store

*re is no more amusing speaker
*ritain than Barbara. Here she
*smerizing television
viewer, Sandra Harris

The best Health Book
you have ever been
offered !

Barbara as I like to remember her. A froth of pink and spun-gold hair with her dog, Twi-Twi, as she says goodbye in the doorway of Camfield Place (Photo: Norman Parkinson)

22

Women love love. They want to be loved.
They long to be hunted, to be pursued.
They long to surrender.

Barbara Cartland

With the move back to London in 1945 Barbara was able to concentrate once more on her writing. By now she had written thirty novels, and she resumed her journalism with articles entitled: 'Has the War Done us Any Good?', 'Women Still Bear the Heaviest Burden', and 'Let's Stop Nattering'.

We had all of us looked forward to the end of the war. We were apparently over optimistic - less fat, less cheese, and now less bread is our portion. BUT - we must not let ourselves be crushed and defeated by these privations.

Tomorrow get up intending to praise, admire, and extol everything that is nice in your home, in your family, and in everyone with whom you come in contact. Flatter your husband, compliment the children, salute the sunshine (if any), tell the postman you're pleased to see him!

Ian and Glen were away at day school but the biggest change of all was in her daughter Raine. By some miracle she completely skipped the horsy stage which afflicts many English girls and at sixteen was already extremely pretty. It was as if from her own flesh and blood Barbara had created one of her heroines. Though not classically beautiful, Raine had Barbara's heart-shaped face, laughing tawny eyes, handspan waist, abundance of brown curls (even if they were still achieved by the use of rags overnight), and most of all an intriguing air of innocence and vulnerability. And like every Barbara Cartland virgin she knew exactly where she was going and there was a big bright star to guide her.

Scholastically Raine had proved to have an academic brain and passed her school certificate with eight distinctions and four credits. Later she was to receive the Gold Medal at the London Academy of Music and Dramatic Art for elocution. This is not surprising as since she was a small girl

Barbara had encouraged her to make her own speeches, which is probably the reason why today she is such an accomplished public speaker. After a period at the Three Wise Monkeys finishing school in Sussex, where Barbara hoped that she would learn the art of being an accomplished chatelaine, Raine went to Murren in Switzerland, the fashionable thing to do at that time.

Barbara had hopes that she would have decent meals there, as even young people were run down and lacking in vitamins from the war years, and Raine had never been strong. Unfortunately, the school was doing it on the cheap, and Raine reported that she was fed almost exclusively on potatoes which gave her boils. The one advantage of her being there was that she learned to speak French well, and just like a Cartland heroine she met a young man, Gerald Legge, while skiing on the top of a mountain.

Barbara had taken the family to meet Raine at St Moritz, her first holiday since 1937. The holiday was not without drama. As there was too little snow, Glen fell on a rock and broke an artery in his forehead. The hotel doctor was sent for, and produced a huge syringe in front of the child. Glen immediately began screaming in terror - clearly the doctor was going to do the sewing-up without even an anaesthetic. 'The English are so brave', the doctor said. Barbara tried to explain that Glen was frightened of injections and as the boy continued to scream and scream finally the doctor threw some chloroform swabs on Glen's face.

How he didn't die I simply don't know. The doctor was angry with me because I was so upset at the way he was treating Glen and I said, 'We've been brave in the war while you were sitting out of it, but this child does not have to be brave now.'

When the doctor arrived a couple of days later and tore off the dressings from the wound, with its six stitches, Glen again began screaming. This was too much for Barbara who ordered the doctor to leave the room. Luckily through a man feeding birds in a villa below the St Moritz Hotel she was able to contact another Swiss physician, a Dr Otley. She went to see him and explained what had happened. 'I always give anaesthetics but it is unusual in Switzerland', he explained, and he agreed to take on Glen as a patient.

Many years later Barbara was able to repay Dr Otley for his kindness. The Princess Royal was going on a visit to Switzerland to recover from an illness. Barbara's own beloved Sir Louis Knuthsen was also the Princess's physician and through this connection Dr Otley was asked to take care of the Royal patient during her stay in Switzerland.

As Raine was 'coming out' that spring at the Queen Charlotte Ball, Barbara bought up dozens of yards of white tulle, blue ribbon and white silk while she was in Switzerland and brought it back to be made up by Worth as Raine's coming-out dress. Barbara designed all Raine's other ball gowns herself and had them made up by Nathans the theatrical costumiers because Archie Nathan had helped her with all her spectacular pageants.

Raine's tulle dance dresses were a sensation. Two quite irrelevant facts helped to bring this about. Christian Dior had launched his New Look that year and tiny waists and billowing skirts were 'in', in contrast to the years of war austerity. A friend of Barbara's had found in her attic a small Victorian crinoline. All Raine's dresses were based on that crinoline frame, the white, green, and scarlet tulle that Barbara had brought from Switzerland and artificial flowers, which were coupon free.

I *made* Raine the Débutante of the Year. Wherever she went everyone looked at her because she was not only very pretty but had the loveliest dresses. She was photographed hundreds of times wearing them. The white tulle dress that she wore at the Queen Charlotte Ball was inspired by a portrait I had seen of the Empress Eugénie. The dress I designed in green tulle had bunches of pink roses at each shoulder, and another one in poinsettia red tulle had white pom-poms like snowflakes all over it. A blue taffeta dress, which Raine had bought from a girl at school for £3, was hauntingly beautiful worn over the crinoline and with a wreath of poppies, daisies and cornflowers sewn round the neck.

Barbara's daughter not only had three 'coming-out' balls but was also asked to forty other dances given by girl friends from Miss Fyfes school where she had been educated during the war years and which was the most fashionable in England. Barbara gave her a ball in London, the Duke of Sutherland, who was her godfather, one at Sutton Place in Surrey, and Alan Lennox-Boyd, M.P. for the Mid-Division of Bedfordshire, a third at his home. He had become a close friend during the last election when Barbara had 'held' a meeting until he arrived, as she had done for Ronald in Birmingham. It was rather more difficult in Bedfordshire where the meetings were often miles apart and the speakers found themselves talking passionately in a school hall to an audience of twenty or less. Nevertheless, Alan had romped home with a large majority.

Champagne was practically non-existent in the post-war austerity but even Barbara's chimney-sweep supplied six bottles from out of his top hat. After the first drink to start the dance going, there was cider and beer until supper time when champagne was doled out with discrimination by the waiters to those who they thought would appreciate it.

As a prelude to the ball Barbara gave Raine in her own house, she asked twenty-four men to dinner. Twenty-four eligible young bachelors, Raine, Polly and herself. Her friends were horrified at the idea but Barbara had her reasons, as she explained:

> I did it for a purpose. It not only meant that Raine would have a partner for every dance but also that her girl friends would too. I can't bear girls standing around at a dance, and you remember this was just after the war and we had two million surplus women in England so you were very conscious of the fact. As each girl brought her own partner I had made sure that there would be twenty spare men and no girl could be possibly left out.
>
> The Brigade of Guards used to say 'Who is giving a party tonight, let's go and have some champagne.' And off they went. They had a good supper, drank as much champagne as they could and didn't dance with one girl. Absolutely useless. I simply wasn't having that, so my little ruse worked well.
>
> I would never let Raine drive home at night with a young man. In Polly's day it was because a girl might be seduced, but the danger when Raine grew up was from bad or drunken drivers. She was kept just like my heroines pure and cherished.

All the razzamatazz of the débutante scene had clearly not gone to Barbara's head. The down-to-earth newspaper article she wrote after Raine's début comes straight from the heart:

> In fact there are only two schools of thought about the spectacle of débutantes *en masse*. If you are related to one you say: 'How sweet and fresh the girls look!' If you are free of such an encumbrance you ejaculate "Good Lord!" and take a taxi to the Bag of Nails. Let us be frank. Débutantes, unless they are your particular property, are bores.

When, in February 1948, Hugh McCorquodale had to go to America on business, Barbara decided to go with him. Needing a reason to travel as the foreign travel allowance had been suspended, she elected to represent 140 British authors. Barbara thought it would be easy to get British books accepted in America. It turned out to be the hardest thing she had ever tried to do. She had radio interviews and coast-to-coast broadcasts, but even that, she says, didn't sell any books. However, she was able to gather more background material for her own novels:

> I visited Harlem much against the wishes of my husband and our friends, and everyone was delighted to see me there. Even the coloured guests who were banished from the best tables so that I and my friends might sit in their places, smiled at us good humouredly. Because I am dressed as I am, people recognize me from television appearances and come up and greet me.
>
> I have always visited the back streets, the ghastly night clubs, the sleazy joints in every place in the world - Hong Kong, India, Bangkok, Egypt, France or New York - and I have never experienced any unpleasantness or even rudeness. I don't dress down. I go glittering, befurred, bejewelled - even if they *are* fake because these days I leave my real jewellery in the bank.

While they were in New York, Barbara and Hugh received a cable from Raine saying she had become engaged to Gerald Legge. Barbara was not altogether happy as she felt that at eighteen Raine was too young and had not yet had time to look around to make quite certain that he was the right man. Gerald Legge, dashing, charming and very intelligent, was the son of the Hon. Humphrey Legge, Chief Constable of Berkshire and heir presumptive to the seventh Earl of Dartmouth. The Legge family had a long history of serving England in various capacities. The Earldom was created in 1711, but the Baronetcy of Dartmouth goes back to 1682. Raine was to change her name three times without changing her husband. She became first Mrs Gerald Legge, then the Viscountess Lewisham and finally wife of the ninth Earl of Dartmouth.

All Barbara's American friends, on learning that England was still on coupons, rallied round with clothes for Raine's trousseau. When Barbara arrived on board the Queen Mary to return to England she found boxes and boxes of hardly worn clothes, including a deliciously pretty négligé which the bride was to wear on her wedding night.

Just as she had been the Débutante of the Year so Raine now became Bride of the Year. For her wedding at St Margaret's, where Barbara had also been married, Raine wore her tulle 'coming-out' dress once again. It had been altered with the addition of bell-shaped sleeves of tiny tulle frills and by substituting its blue ribbon with white, which was caught up with posies of orange-blossom. An heirloom Brussels lace veil fell from an exquisite diamond tiara that had been lent by Lady Patricia Lennox-Boyd.

The *Queen* magazine enthused: 'The bride looked a perfect Winterhalter portrait.' True enough, but she was also a replica from the cover of a Barbara Cartland novel as drawn by the artist Francis Marshall. As Raine, on the arm of her father, swept into the church in a foam of tulle she was followed by her two half brothers Glen and Ian in family kilts leading a retinue of sixteen bridesmaids also in white tulle with bouquets of pink sweet peas. This surely must have been one of Barbara's happiest moments. Everything she had wished for her pink-and-white baby had come true.

Like most weddings it had not been without a family trauma. The day before the wedding Glen had arrived back from school with a pudding face and a severe case of mumps:

> We were all in despair, not only because of Glen but because of Gerald, who had not had mumps, and everyone knows it affects grown-up men very badly. We held a family council and agreed that no one was to know, least of all the bridegroom. I decided that something drastic had to be done. I telephoned Lady Weir, the widow of General Sir George Weir, to whom my brother Tony had been A.D.C. She was a saint, as by the power of prayer she was able to take other people's illness upon herself. I asked her to pray that Gerald would not catch mumps. 'He won't,' she answered confidently, 'and I'll pray for Glen too!'
>
> Next morning Raine said to me 'Oh Mummy, Glen is so much better - do let him come to the church.' So he was able to walk up the aisle in his frilled shirt and kilt and then slipped away from the reception and was taken home to bed.

Barbara feels today that it was entirely due to Lady Weir's prayers that the bridegroom did not get mumps, and neither did anyone else. Lady Weir was to play an intriguing role in Polly's life as she inspired Polly, a staunch Anglican, to convert to Roman Catholicism.

The list of wedding guests had grown longer and longer, until it reached over nine hundred and the wedding reception had to be switched from Barbara's house to Londonderry House, where the famous staircase was a seething crowd as everyone queued to see the wedding gifts which were on display. Barbara gave her daughter a five-strand pearl bracelet with an aquamarine clasp, a diamond and aquamarine clip and a white fox cape. Earl and Countess Mountbatten, who had gone to the reception straight from the House of Lords, gave a silver cigarette box made in India, and Lady Delamere's present was a dark blue ermine coat. The Earl and Countess of Dartmouth gave not only a set of diamond bows but also a canteen of old family silver, silver entrée dishes, and a complete dinner service. No bride that year had a more valuable collection of presents with which to begin her married life.

The happy bride and bridegroom chose Paris for their honeymoon, just as Barbara herself had done when she first married Sachie and later Hugh. One would wish to think that as in all Barbara Cartland romances this young couple would have lived happily ever after. But in real life it often does not happen that way, and this love story was to come to a sorrowful end in a dreary London divorce court twenty-eight years later. Raine, by now the Countess of Dartmouth, had fallen in love with the ninth Earl Spencer and gone to live at Althorp House.

The glamour of period gowns and the heady romance of her daughter's wedding may have subconsciously been the reason why Barbara responded to a request from a woman's magazine that she write them a period novel. Up till then the thirty-five books she had completed were just light-hearted modern love stories.

She set this new novel, which was prophetically called *Hazard of Hearts*, in the Regency period, which was to become her favourite. She began serious research for the period so that every single detail was correct, not only in clothes and manners, but such trivia as the food that was eaten. Her research led her into a whole new world, and today she is one of the most knowledgeable people in England on the social customs of the Georgian period. Since then Barbara has written over three hundred period novels set not only in England but in various countries round the world. She prefers to write in the past because she enjoys history. It is more glamorous, and a virgin was more credible than today.

Between the years 1955 and 1958 Barbara became so intrigued with historical research that she published seven biographies, ranging from Queen Christina of Sweden to King Carol of Romania, Empress Elizabeth of Austria, Empress Josephine, Diane de Poitiers, Prince Metternich and King Charles II of England. In all these books her facts were unassailable, although she related history from a human angle. She made history interesting and understandable as well as highly entertaining.

23

I heard your footsteps coming up the stairs
Or were you moving just ahead?
I keep on wondering who you are and where
You lie unknown.

Barbara Cartland

For some years Hugh had been wanting to leave London. Essentially a sporting man, he loved his Scotland with its shooting and fishing, and though he had adapted to Barbara's social life in London, at heart he was the essence of a country gentleman. Hertfordshire, in the green belt surrounding London, was an attractive choice as parts of the countryside are completely unspoilt and there is still some excellent shooting. Originally Hugh and Barbara wanted to buy Woolmers, a house that belonged to the Earl and Countess of Strathmore, but at the last moment they were 'gazumped' and so the sale fell through. Barbara was broken-hearted because the house was pure Georgian, her favourite period, and had been built by the Duke of Bridgewater.

In March 1950, while shooting in Yorkshire, Hugh was told by a friend that Lord Queenborough had died, which meant that his house, Camfield Place, would soon be put on the market. Barbara immediately telephoned the agent in London and said that she would be down the next day to view the estate before it was advertised for sale.

We arrived at the village of Essendon near Hatfield in pouring rain, and the house looked gloomy and awful. Lord Queenborough had covered the walls with family pictures, which had been removed with the furniture, and now all those faded patches were like ghostly reminders of the past. Everything was painted 'margarine' which is *not* my favourite colour. Also it was very large.

Hugh said that I was mad to even look at it, and he didn't bother to go round the estate, but I knew immediately that I could make the house liveable. I only have to close my eyes when I am dictating a novel and I can see every detail of the house I am describing. It was the same with Camfield Place. Already I had a strange sense of belonging there. I had the feeling that the house was right for us.

All through the weekend Hugh and I argued about buying the estate, but on Monday morning he put in an offer for the house with 400 acres of good farmland and fourteen cottages.

The family moved into Camfield Place on a Monday morning at the beginning of May 1950, much to Hugh's trepidation. The price had been astonishingly low even for those days, but he could only foresee problems in making such a large house viable. Private owners in those days were restricted to spending only £1,000 on structural alterations and £100 on decoration, and the law was harsh on offenders. Lord Peel was actually sent to prison for exceeding the sum.

Looking round on that May morning at the bad state of repair of the house, it seemed a hopeless task. But with her irrepressible optimism Barbara went round giving orders and spreading joy as she organized the unpacking of the crates.

Camfield Place was built in 1867 by Edmund Potter, the grandfather of that beguiling children's author, Beatrix Potter. When he bought the estate he had pulled down the beautiful gabled Tudor house with its latticed windows which had stood there since Elizabethan times, and, as befitted a prosperous calico printing manufacturer, he built himself an imposing mansion. The original Elizabethan dovecote still stands in the farmyard like a sentinel from the past.

'Capability' Brown, the celebrated gardener, who created some of the most beautiful parklands in England, including the grounds of Blenheim Palace, had landscaped the park in the eighteenth century. Lord Queenborough had later created two artificial lakes as a foreground to the sweeping view over the Lea Valley which lay beyond. 'Capability' Brown's brilliant planting of groups of majestic trees has created an effect of breathtaking beauty. Today the lakes are fringed with hundreds of rhododendrons and azaleas, added by Lord Queenborough, and in early summer they are ablaze with colour, shading from Cartland pink to Royal amethyst.

Edging the sweeping lawn in front of the house are the thousands of daffodils which Barbara has planted, which in the spring look like a long yellow ribbon threading through the green grass. In the extensive shrubbery there still stands the mighty oak tree which was planted to commemorate the spot where Queen Elizabeth I shot her first stag. Each year Barbara has some of its leaves and acorns dipped in gold and threaded on elegant gold chains, or set in onyx-like Perspex paper-weights, for use as personal gifts. People write from all over the world to tell of the luck their acorns have brought them - love, babies, contracts really do appear like magic. Barbara wears two herself and Ian carries an acorn key-ring in his pocket.

The Elizabethan walled garden with its mellow bricks lives in the minds of tens of thousands of children, for it was the original 'Mr McGregor's Garden' from *The Tale of Peter Rabbit*. The locked door in the wall which 'the fat little rabbit couldn't squeeze underneath' is exactly the same today as when Beatrix Potter first saw it, and has never been repainted. There is still the same goldfish pool where the white cat sat twitching her tail and the potting-shed, where Peter Rabbit hid from Mr McGregor in a watering-can. Flopsy, Mopsy, Cottontail and Peter probably lived under the roots of the big fir trees in the Home Wood, where undoubtedly all their relations still live today.

Rows of brussels sprouts stand like guardsmen in front of Mr McGregor's shed today, a tempting dish to set before Mrs Tittlemouse. The place is alive with foxes, Berking deer, pheasants, squirrels, moles, and of course it is impossible to get rid of the Peter Rabbits, who eat every flower except geraniums. Barbara is obliged to fill her flower-beds around the house with hundreds of them in coral pink.

In *The Journal of Beatrix Potter from 1881 to 1897*, transcribed from her secret code by Leslie Linder, we read of Camfield Place:

. . .the place I love best in the world and the sweet balmy air where I have been so happy as a child. I shall never want a record to remind me of this perfect whole, where all things are part, the notes of the stable clock and all the pervading smells of new mown hay, the distant sounds of farmyard, the feeling of plenty, well assured, indolent wealth. . .

Further east, beyond the sweep of grassland and scattered oaks the blue distance opens out, rising to the horizon over Panshanger Woods. If you get on any rising ground in this neighbourhood you would fancy Hertfordshire was one great oak wood.

Can you not see in your mind's eye as plainly as I who am here, the windy north front on its terrace, with the oaks moaning and swaying on winter nights close to the bedroom windows?

The biography of Beatrix Potter tells how she sat beside her grandmother on a big green sofa in the drawing room before dinner and wrote in her note-book in the tiny code, which took six years to decipher, how the twelve big candles which lit the room went out one by one 'as if snuffed by an unseen hand'.

. . . There are two mirrors facing each other on the stairs. Miles of looking glasses and little figures in white muslin. I never dare look in them for fear of another head beside my own peeping round the corner. . . .

How Beatrix would enjoy Camfield Place now, blazing with colour. Today that same staircase is regally splendid with a scarlet carpet, large gilt mirrors and a tall ormulu clock. It gleams with light and life from a huge candelabra which Barbara and Glen recently bought in Venice.

Soon after the family moved into Camfield Place Barbara asked the local rector, the Reverend Canon H. Lovell, to bless the house and so exorcize unwelcome ghosts or unhappy spirits. It does, however, have two friendly ones which appear from time to time. One is a former housemaid who died many years ago. Her shadowy figure has been seen on several occasions as she stands at the bottom of the staircase waiting for Barbara to go upstairs and change for dinner. The other is Jimmy the cocker spaniel who was put to sleep twenty years ago because he had cancer of the throat. He has roamed the rooms of Camfield Place ever since, and Barbara has seen him many times. The first time when she was carrying a large vase of flowers and put out her foot to push him out of the way. When her foot touched nothing but air she realized that it was the ghost of the dog she had had put to sleep. He positively refused to allow the live cocker spaniel Murray to eat in the dining room. Whenever his food was placed before Murray he would back away from it with a shriek and snarl as if another dog was attacking him.

We have grown used to our ghost dog. I know he stays with us because he was so happy and we loved him. I still see him from time to time. About a month ago he was waiting for me at the top of the stairs as I came up to bed, and I saw him clearly before I realized it was not Duke, my present black labrador.

The next few years were to be a period of 'pure contentment and tranquillity' in Barbara's life, as she brought Camfield Place to life with her own brand of magic. All that power-house of energy which had been used in her war-work in Bedfordshire was now transferred to turning this sprawling house into her own fantasy world. Right from the beginning Barbara imposed her own style on this Victorian mansion by splashing it everywhere with her favourite Nile blue, deep coral and gilt. The handsome wrought-iron gates must be the most romantic in England, the lodges on either side of them with Nile blue doors and window-frames.

At the time she furnished the house Barbara did not have unlimited money - far from it. She scoured antique shops every week-end, and wherever her travels took her, and she seldom came home empty-handed. Collecting antique beds became an absorbing game. Apart from her own deep coral draped, gilt four-poster which originally came from Spain and was her marriage bed, in York she and her son Glen discovered an ornately carved French bed, made in about 1650, which still had the original gilt on its carved canopy, a festoon of flowers around the headpiece and a sunburst of angels blowing trumpets around the Virgin Mary. A third bedhead was originally carved as a sideboard in 1820 for Mary, Duchess of Sutherland. Twelve feet wide, richly carved with large urns on either side, it is a romantic link with Dunrobin Castle and the Sutherland family.

Barbara is proudest of having collected some of the Granville family pictures for her sons: no mean task when one realizes that her husband was the third son of a fourth son, so not many came his way. But it was sheer luck when, buying Christmas presents in Hitchin, Barbara saw a portrait of a man on the stairs.

'Who is that?' she asked.

'A farmer brought it in today', the owner of the antique shop replied. 'I gave him £10 for it. You can have it for £12.10s.'

It was Bevil, the Elizabethan Granville, and inscribed with his name.

When Barbara was arranging the deliciously pretty colour plates for her recently published cookery book, *The Romance of Food*, all the food was prepared in her own kitchen by Linda Collister, who often cooks for the Queen and the Queen Mother, assisted by Barbara's own chef Nigel Gordon. The food was cooked strictly according to her instructions and arranged as picture cookery on the plates, down to the last petal, in the *nouvelle cuisine* style of presentation. In order to create a romantic and new appearance for this charming book, Barbara merely went round the house and selected pieces from her much-loved collection of Dresden and Staffordshire china which she has gathered together over the years. Many of the pieces were bought by her sons for a few shillings, as Glen especially has a great knowledge of antiques after years of shopping with Barbara.

Barbara's day begins at 6.50 a.m., when she is awoken by the buzzer in her bedroom. This means the housekeeper is downstairs waiting to take out Duke, the black labrador given to her by Lord Mountbatten. As part of her health-giving breakfast that includes natural yoghourt and honey she downs the seventy odd vitamin and food supplement tablets that she consumes every day. When she is travelling they are made up into little sachets, one for every day that she is away from home. After breakfast she reads all the main newspapers of the day. She believes that even the flashy tabloids are part of life, and their human stories often give her ideas that she can use in her various writing activities. She reads very fast - she calls it 'block reading' - and has an amazingly retentive memory.

By nine o'clock, made up and wearing a pink négligé, Barbara is ready for her secretary to bring up her first batch of mail. In one year alone she answers personally anything up to 15,000 letters on health that come winging in from all over the world, and the same number from her fans. A secretary sits by her bed as she goes through the letters and dictates the replies. These will be checked and signed at the end of the day. She is an expert on etiquette and every letter is scrutinized and does not go out unless it is perfectly typed and correctly addressed. Not one slip is allowed to pass her perfectionist eyes!

During the morning she may well work at dictating a chapter of a non-fiction book on which she is working, as the afternoons are sacrosanct for her novels. By noon, dressed in one of her pastel suits in winter, or floaty dresses in summer, she is ready to take the dogs for a short walk round the grounds. Barbara always goes alone because it is during this half hour that she gets into the mood of the novel she is working on, and manipulates her characters.

It is interesting that Agatha Christie, also a prolific writer, used to plot her crime novels while walking in her garden every morning. She always carried a pen and pad and made notes. Barbara works quite differently and is able to carry the plot and all the characters in her head from day to day.

After a light luncheon which again she always eats alone, she retires to the library for the most important two and a half hours of the day, when she dictates her novels. Nothing is left to chance. Before 12.45 p.m. Mrs Audrey Elliott, who has been Barbara's literary secretary for eleven years, has checked every detail in the library. She has arranged the glass doors of the bookcases, which contain over five thousand books, so that they will not reflect in Barbara's eyes as she lies on a sofa with Twi-Twi her white pekingese close at hand. He has snored his way through hundreds of romances, and this is the only noise permitted in the room.

With a hot water bottle at her feet under a white fur rug Barbara settles down and begins dictating. Behind her sits Mrs Elliott who is not allowed to sneeze or cough, with several sharpened pencils and her notebook, backed up by a tape-recorder. The whole operation could possibly be done without Mrs Elliott's presence, but Barbara likes to have someone present - as if she becomes the story teller from *Scheherazade*. To complete the six to eight thousand words - one chapter - which Barbara Cartland sets herself as a target each day means total concentration.

No one else is allowed to be in the room when Barbara is dictating, but I have heard several of the tapes. What is completely compulsive listening is not only how she rarely hesitates, but how she changes her voice to capture each character - a young girl's voice for the heroine, and a deeper one for the hero. Though there is a pad and pencil by her side, she rarely stops for a minute in her telling of the story which is unfolding in front of her eyes as she lies there. It is the most remarkable feat of concentration for anyone, and in a woman in her eighties it is nothing short of a miracle!

The formula may change from century to century - though she prefers to stay in the nineteenth century - and from country to country, but the output never fails. Any such mundane illness as a cold or a headache is never allowed to interfere with dictation, and she has told me that invariably after a good day of seven thousand words she feels fresher than when she began.

When I want a book, I say to my subconscious, 'I want a new plot'. And then I leave it, and suddenly it all falls into place. Suddenly something, perhaps just a flash of colour, or some flowers, or somebody saying something, and the whole plot is there. The subconscious will always do that, it has been proved scientifically. Your subconscious does the work for you, and we can't use our subconscious enough!

The 'hymenal heroines', as they are called in America, meet the heroes early in the manuscript. You automatically know that the Duke/Marquess or even the lowlier Baronet is going to ask her to marry him in the last pages and find 'the glory and ecstacy of divine love', but it is the twists and turns of the plot during the interim 160 pages that show Barbara's consummate skill as a story teller. Embroidered with her painstaking social and historical research, here you have the essence of a Barbara Cartland novel. Words are rarely wasted on description, and the plot unfolds at an exciting pace until the last rapturous embrace. This is what her readers want, and they are never disappointed. Clearly Barbara has never forgotten the lesson she learned from the novelist Ian Hay many years ago when he told her, 'When you write, do so as if you are going to an office. If you wait for the Muse it never comes.'

By 3.30 on the dot Barbara wakes from her story-telling trance with the same words every day: 'How many words have I done?' Mrs Elliott has been keeping a check by numbering the pages of her notebook. Satisfied, Barbara bounces back into every day life. A brisk walk with the dogs again and she is ready for tea and her afternoon guests.

The next two hours of every day are filled with seeing somebody - television crews, journalists, discussing details of a new cover with her artist, meeting the various publishers who arrive regularly from France, Germany, Spain, all places east and west - to discuss her new books. Although her son Ian runs the business side of Barbara Cartland Promotions, Barbara herself enjoys meeting the people who are actively involved in selling her books round the world.

On normal days, since she has stopped doing public work, Barbara's day halts for a while at 5.30 when her secretaries go home and the last guest has gone. On working days she retires to bed and dines alone, correcting proofs and articles and reading the twenty or thirty history books she uses for the background of each novel. She enjoys watching the news on television, then begins the night's reading. She must be the most prolific user of the London Library, from whom she borrows any books she needs that are not in her own library. Long into the night, in between telephone calls to and from America and her friends, she works. To use the word 'workaholic' about Barbara sounds vulgar. It is more correct to say that work is a way of life for her. She cannot conceive not working, and writing is the skill she knows best.

Once a week Barbara drives in her white and pale blue Mercedes or her white Rolls Royce to London to see her dressmakers and hat-maker and for other personal business. Lunchtime always sees her ensconced at her favourite table in the restaurant at Claridges. She is not only a Claridges 'institution' but also a tourist's delight as she is recognized by her frivolous and beautiful hats and her vivacious talk. She rarely has lunch with more than one guest at a time, but, ringing with laughter, hers is always the gayest table that day.

The weekends too at Camfield Place have fallen into their own kind of rhythm, with Saturdays devoted to her sons. In 1976 Barbara made herself into a company with her sons and this has worked out very well. All the business of the week is discussed in the most hilarious 'board meetings' round Barbara's bed or at the dinner table. Barbara turns the books out, Glen, a stockbroker by profession who took a history degree at Oxford, listens to the week's output. He is quick to point out to his mother if he thinks the story is 'sagging'. Ian, who not only manages his mother's huge empire but is also chairman of Debretts, will produce a bunch of contracts to be signed. It is a blissfully efficient literary machine, each one contributing in a very definite way. But as Ian McCorquodale says: 'It all comes from Mum. Even if she is my mother, I must say that she is a most amazing woman. And the main thing of all is her total professionalism and the fun whenever you are with her.'

Sundays at Camfield Place are given over to entertaining. During the winter there are house-parties and sparkling luncheons and on Saturday evenings, dinner parties. Because Barbara herself is always superbly dressed, and often wears the clothes we see her wearing on television, her women guests vie to outshine each other. With Barbara at the head of a table of twelve guests these luncheons and dinner parties are always awash with laughter. She never monopolizes the conversation but has that rare gift, much as the Queen Mother does, of bringing out the best in her guests so that they become prettier, wittier, and at their most charming round her party table.

Just as Emerald Cunard in the twenties had such a flair for mixing her guests, Barbara does the same today. They may include visiting Royalty, well-known journalists, actors or actresses - anybody she has met who will contribute to the success of the party. There is no place for bores at Camfield Place.

'You are what you eat' should be inscribed in every kitchen in the land.

Barbara Cartland

Barbara's message about healthier living is simple. She makes no extravagant claims for health foods but simply stresses loud and clear what they are and why they are good for you as a supplement to today's artificial living. Since everything we eat now has been tampered with - sprayed fruits, caponized chickens, hormone-fed meat and milk that has been meddled with - she advocates that we need to take natural vitamin supplements.

She herself is living proof that her theory works, and is the best possible advertisement for the health foods she promotes with such conviction and vigour. She is backed with all the right attributes - an almost indecent amount of energy, staying power, great style and an infectious personality. On the physical side her looks are phenomenal for a woman of her age. As my husband said in astonishment when he first took a telephone call from her: 'I thought it was her granddaughter speaking. Her voice is so young.'

It is perfectly in character that when Barbara turned to health as her personal platform she would go straight to the medical, scientific source.

Our food is absolutely ruined by the soil being poisoned, the sea being polluted, the vegetables and fruit being sprayed. All these chemicals combine to kill vitamins. If we haven't got enough vitamins in our bodies we die, it is a slow, miserable illness and death caused by taking poisons. So the only answer is to take natural vitamins separately. It seems crazy but it works. As soon as people take vitamins they feel better. Factory foods are usually deficient in natural vitamins, minerals and enzymes so the only thing we can do is to supplement our daily diet.

Barbara's interest in food supplements goes right back to the thirties when after working with Lady Rhys Williams in the Distressed Areas she got in touch with the famous Mrs Layel from the herbalist, Culpeper, and studied herbal medicine. Mrs Layel opened her eyes to the dangers of modern drugs, many of which have side effects not envisaged when they are first prescribed. It was from Mrs Layel, too, that Barbara first heard of ginseng, the root which the Chinese have for generations prescribed for vitality and eternal youth. At that time she had no idea how important it was to become to her personally and to the National Health Movement.

The following year Barbara went to a sanatorium in Baden-Baden where she studied the methods of the eminent Dr Dengler who pioneered the internal treatment of patients suffering from sclerosis and other complaints of the liver, with olive oil. At the time Dr Frank N. Buchman of the Oxford Group Movement was also a patient and Barbara was interested in his religious ideas, which had captivated thousands of people on both sides of the Atlantic, including Queen Marie of Romania, King Paul, the ex-King of Greece, and King Alfonso of Spain. She asked him to speak to a gathering of thirty patients:

I wanted to feel the vivid spark which he ignited in them, but I felt nothing. As the meeting broke up my friend Eily Donald, who was with me, said: 'Wouldn't it be awful if when we get to Heaven we find that God is Frank Buchman?'

While in Baden-Baden, Barbara did an interesting experiment with Eily Donald who had been a professional medium. She was a clairvoyant and had frequently dreamed of the winners of famous horse-races like the Grand National. To amuse themselves they did automatic writing. Eily had a contact called Bertie, and Barbara said to him: 'If you are genuine, prove it by letting us win at roulette.'

'All right', he replied. 'Go this evening to the Casino and play at six o'clock at the table near the window and I will tell you what number will win. But you are only to put on two marks and may not accumulate.'

They did as he told them. Eily stood near the roulette wheel and Barbara had the money ready. Eily was sure she would not know what the number was until the ball was rolling. She said a number, Barbara put on the two marks, and the money was lost. Barbara knew that the Casino in Baden-Baden had a clock. She looked up at it. It was not exactly six o'clock. They tried again.

Eily gave the right numbers ten times, then suddenly she said, 'It has gone - I can't do any more.'

They were paid thirty-five marks to one on each number and Eily covered her fare from England and some of her expenses in the clinic. Barbara has never heard of anyone doing the same thing and winning ten times in a row at roulette.

Dr Pierre Lansel, M.P., was the first practitioner to give injections of vitamin B and C, and Barbara also followed his experiments with the use of hormones for rejuvenation and his use of the Neihus treatment for cell therapy which had such diverse followers as Somerset Maugham, Noel Coward, the Duke of Windsor, Chancellor Konrad Adenhauer and Pope Pius XII.

Fringe medicine was beginning to infiltrate conventional thinking, and whenever she heard of something different Barbara tried it. She became so absorbed by yoga that she began to read everything she could about Tibet and reincarnation. Her yoga teacher was then the only white yogi in the world, and she wrote for his magazine for nearly two years. Today Barbara uses yoga breathing before she speaks in public and recommends it to anyone suffering from what is called 'nerves'. If you breathe in for eight seconds, hold for sixteen and let your breath out very gently over eight seconds, the harsh lines will disappear from your face and your voice will become more musical. Barbara says that if you are doing any public speaking this makes your voice carry better and allows it to be heard at a greater distance.

It was during her stay in Canada at the beginning of the war that Barbara saw at first hand the developments that had been made in nutrition overseas. At that time the British medical profession was cautious of any kind of biochemical medicine and its members were mainly concerned with diagnosis and treatments *after* the patient had become ill. Barbara became fascinated with preventative medicine and in 1946 she brought back to England from America the first B-complex multi-vitamin capsule which had been synthetically manufactured by Ledele. This is what Barbara used until ten years later when the first natural vitamin firm opened in England.

The war had left a tired and listless nation through shortages of food and sleepless nights. Barbara herself felt very limp after years of active war work, and she was deeply concerned for the British women who had not only managed their own homes during the war but had done an exhausting and often debilitating job in factories all over the country.

In America evergreen Gaylord Hauser had already become an accepted health food guru and Adele Davis had begun her crusade of educating people in the role that vitamins play in everyday diet. Fired with their enthusiasm Barbara wanted to change the eating pattern of 'chips with everything' that permeated thousands of British homes. She became a one-woman crusade for healthier eating and therefore healthier living. The benefits of vitamins were confirmed to her in a very personal way:

In the summer of 1951 I had a hysterectomy from which I was taking an abnormally long time to recover, and no one could find out why. Unknown to me, when I was in the nursing home I had been put on morphia to which I am allergic, and then to help me to sleep I was given sodium amytal. For someone like me who had never ever taken an aspirin the result was disastrous and I became dangerously ill. When my haemoglobin count was down to ninety instead of the prescribed 150 despite a blood transfusion I was convinced that I was dying.

I was so desperate that I told Hugh to get me out of the nursing home and take me back to Camfield Place. My fingers had begun to turn blue and I was bathed in sweat - pouring. All I wanted was to get back in my own bed.

Under the care of her own sensible local doctor, who listened to Barbara, she was put on a course of vitamin injections. She recovered, to finish her third book that year *A Ghost in Monte Carlo* in time for Christmas. This personal experience had been so traumatic and revealing that she was determined to devote a part of her life towards spreading the gospel of vitamins wherever her voice could be heard. It was her way of making repayment for the sparing of her own life.

The crusade began in a small way, talking woman to woman, on the radio, at meetings of the Women's Institute, Townswomen's Guild, and so on. No matter what else she was asked to speak about, vitamins and health always crept in. To prove her point everyone in her own household was put on vitamins and she even began giving them to the livestock on her farm. From the local brewery she bought large tubs of brewer's yeast - a valuable source of vitamin B1 - and fed her fifty-two farrowing sows with it. The result was that for four years she held the record production for Great Britain with an average of eleven piglets a litter. When she told this story to her enraptured audiences it never failed to bring a titter of laughter as she cautioned: 'If you nag your husband, slap your children, and hate your neighbours, you are short of vitamin B1. The easiest way to take it is as brewer's yeast tablets. But one word of warning: I gave it to my sows and they all had abnormally large litters.'

The results were, in fact, so spectacular that Sir Harry Haig, of Ovaltine fame, copied her pig farm and her feeding. Barbara's dairy herd, each named after one of her heroines, were also given vitamins, and the prize-winning bull had vitamin E injections.

In 1960 Barbara was able to extend her vitamin 'platform' when she met James Lee Richardson who asked her to write a monthly article and answer readers' letters in *Here's Health* magazine. No one could possible have seen that this would result in Barbara answering 10-15,000 letters a year, as she does today, about health problems - letters that now come from all over the world. Barbara had originally agreed to do this writing on the condition that she could say what she wished, and would accept no payment. She has never varied from this rule.

Today Barbara puts aside time every day to attend to her own personal health crusade. Apart from heart-rending requests for help in such serious illnesses as cancer there are the homely requests which she answers in her own way: 'My child always gets sick in the car ... My husband is frightened of having a prostate gland ... I have a birthmark on my cheek ... My doctor says I must give up salt ... If tea and coffee have caffeine in them what am I to drink? ... I am having trouble with my eyes as they sting and are gritty ... What shall I do about my mother-in-law who is nearly fifty and very hysterical at times?'

Over the years of course she has made a few enemies among the stodgy medical profession. When a Dr Colin Brewer wrote an insensitive, ill-informed, and impertinent article about her in *World Medicine* several well-known medical figures rushed to Barbara's defence, including Maurice Hanssen, President of the European Health Food Manufacturers' Association, who riposted: 'Far from being a self-appointed and completely unqualified dietary advisor she certainly has more training and knowledge of nutrition than the average doctor.'

When I was talking to Dr Leonard Mervyn, technical director of Booker Health Foods, he told me:

> I think where Miss Cartland is an expert is first she will try everything and she will give an opinion. She has excellent ideas that she can't put into practice, simply because she does not have the facilities, but she comes to people like me, and being a practical person I can produce the product.
>
> I first met Miss Cartland about six years ago and she asked me to produce a pill or tablet that would overcome stress - the sort of stress we all undergo during everyday lives. We had a long chat and the result was GEB 6 - ginseng, vitamin E and vitamin B6. These three ingredients have been shown by many clinical trials and studies to be anti-stress agents. After I had got this combination together I asked her to try it out among her own friends as well as our laboratory testing. It was an enormous success and is now sold world wide. This is her great contribution towards helping people. She is often the innovator and leaves it to the scientists like me to interpret her ideas. I think she is a remarkable person because the ordinary members of the public listen to her and they benefit from her knowledge - and she really is an expert.

Barbara's individualistic way of sharing her vitamin experience has wide repercussions. She is never too busy to send a package of something new on the market to anyone she knows who needs it. When she was at an evening reception at Number 10 Downing Street for her friend of many years, Mrs Indira Gandhi, Mrs Thatcher happened to mention the subject of jet lag and its effect on people who are constantly travelling by air. Within days a small pink package arrived on the Prime Minister's desk from Barbara, who knew that the way to travel without strain is to take Indian ginseng.

Regular packages of vitamins and natural cosmetics are sent by her to India where Barbara has many friends. Whenever she travels, and that is about three or four times a year, her luggage always contains pretty packages of vitamins and food supplements which she gives to her hosts much as anyone else takes flowers. It is all part of Barbara's positive crusade for bringing biochemical medicine, in which she passionately believes, to the fore.

One of British television's most awe-inspiring (for the participants) 'chat programmes' was that run by the chatterbox Robert Robinson. On one occasion he was brave enough to have the late, dear, dotty Patrick Campbell - in private life Lord Glenavy - and that tantalizing tease

Malcolm Muggeridge on the same programme as Barbara.

> The programme, of course, was all an attack on me, questioning whether people who read books should be given love and romance or the facts of life. I fought for what I believed was right, knowing that my books are enjoyed by people of every age who are not disillusioned or spoilt by cynicism.
>
> I then said that my mother, who was eighty-eight, loathed television where people walked away into a fog and there was no happy ending. She liked things to end happily.
>
> Patrick Campbell then remarked to me: 'She is a very foolish old woman.' I drew in my breath. For a moment I wondered if I should throw the glass of water in front of me in his face. Instead I bent forward and replied: 'What did you say about my mother?'
>
> Again he repeated: 'She is a very foolish old woman.
>
> 'I think that is very rude', I replied, and hoped that my voice was as icy as I felt.

In reporting this event, the *Daily Mirror* wrote: 'Inside Page congratulates Miss Cartland on her admirable restraint. She should have slapped old Campbell's face.' Another newspaper commented: 'By all the laws Miss Cartland should have been counted out long before Robinson applied the closure but in the end it was Muggeridge and Campbell who were gasping and spluttering for breath and Miss Cartland, immensely composed, who serenely held the middle of the stage.' The programme had in fact run long over its time and finished with Malcolm Muggeridge admitting defeat by covering his bent head with his hands.

In the warm-up before the programme began Barbara had told Patrick Campbell that she could cure his famous stammer if he would take the vitamins that she would recommend. 'You would d..d..do me out of my j..j..job', he explained, as his endearing stutter was part of his television charm, of course.

The next day she sent both of her prickly adversaries a package of Bio-Strath which was her current discovery. In a letter of thanks Lord Glenavy wrote:

Dear and Beautiful Barbara,

Thank you very much, very sincerely for being so lovely and generous, and not only in the matter of the Bio-Strath.

And please, please apologize fiercely and passionately to your mother, for me.

I look forward to seeing you again very soon, both of us Bio-Strathed up to the eyes!

Yours ever,
Paddy Campbell

Among the hundreds of letters in Barbara's scrapbooks which touched me was this note Arthur Askey had written from St Thomas' Hospital. It was to be one of the last letters he dictated to his sister before he died:

. . . Needless to say I am still in the throes of despair and still cannot fully appreciate what has happened to me. I had been pondering about retiring but now the decision has been made for me. What a lousy exit!

My only consolation is that nice people like you will give me an occasional thought. I have made many friends during the years and hope to keep them till the end of the road.

God Bless and again many thanks.

Your old Playmate,
Rene (for Arthur Askey)

Nor are sportsmen exempt from Barbara's notice when she feels that vitamins could help them. In a letter written in May 1981 on the writing paper of the Yorkshire County Cricket Club, Geoffrey Boycott wrote:

Dear Barbara,

It was very kind of you to send me the Indian ginseng and the stress pills. I am trying them out and drinking the ginseng tea. To be honest I have not had that awful tea for four years, drinking ginseng all the time. I feel very well and it all started from reading quotes you had made to the medical press. Honey I've been taking in my tea - and decaffinated coffee - for many, many years.

Perhaps one day we may meet. I'd love to call on you for tea as you are a great lady and have done memorable things for many people re health and vitality.

With fondest wishes,
Yours
Geoff Boycott

Since she cured Hugh of his bronchitis in the early days of their marriage Barbara has been a keen user of honey in her own home, and wherever it is possible it is substituted for sugar. White sugar, she is convinced, is a killer and should be forbidden in every household:

Honey is the Elixir of Life. We are only just beginning to find out what the ancients knew without newspapers, radio or television to instruct them, that it is the natural medicines with which to combat ill health.

The more I looked into the history of honey the more convinced I became that it is one of the wonder foods of all time. Although ninety per cent of honey is sugar in its purest form there is a four per cent that scientists have never been able to break down. They knew that honey contains vitamins and minerals which are absolutely necessary to life but there are also other products which give it its magical quality. The curative powers of honey are endless and even Mohammed referred to honey as the 'Medicine of the East'.

In 1970 Barbara was invited to write a book about honey which proved to be a best seller. Brought up to date and reprinted in 1982, *The Magic of Honey* has sold over five million copies over the world. Barbara points out that not only did the athletes of Ancient Greece train on honey, but the Russians in recent years, when preparing for the Olympic Games, had a diet of steak and honey. Barbara says that when the Japanese read that honey was an aphrodisiac they bought up the world supplies of honey. 'We were then desperately short of honey, but that year resulted in the production of an enormous number of Japanese.'

One ardent woman reader of *The Magic of Honey* simply wrote: 'Dear Barbara: I gave my husband honey. It works!'

Of all Barbara's revolutionary health claims, I for one found her warnings against taking one of my favourite drinks pretty startling: 'Never, never drink grapefruit juice or orange juice. Not only have toxic poisons infiltrated the skin through spraying but citrus juice is too strong for the average stomach. It pits the softness of the flesh and does irreparable damage.'

Challenged on this provocative statement she can produce an immense amount of medical evidence against strong citrus juices collected by J.I. Rodale.

'If this warning is unheeded', she adds, 'look at the complexions of most American women, who can't start the day without their juice and their coffee!!'

What stirs within my restless heart?
What magic trembles and awakes?
Like ripples from a wind-stirred harp
In this remote, enchanted place.

Barbara Cartland

No two people could have been less alike than Barbara and Hugh, and yet theirs was a truly romantic marriage. In their dissimilarity their personalities complemented each other's. A quiet and gentle man, Hugh was protective and proud of Barbara's public achievements as well as her gift for writing. When they married in 1936 the doctors had warned Barbara that she would probably have no more than five years with Hugh. He had been badly wounded at the battle of Passchendaele and the effects were expected to cut short his life. But, although his injuries always affected him, Hugh did survive, was awarded the M.C. for gallantry and went on to live until 1963.

Christmas that year brought appalling weather over the whole of England. Though he had slowed down a little over the years Hugh continued to go to his office each day, travelling by car on the slippery roads in the bitter cold winds. Although Barbara had been able to cure Hugh's bronchitis through the years, by giving him two spoonfuls of comb honey night and morning, the winter brought back a slight resurgence of it.

On Christmas Eve there was the same hilariously happy old-fashioned family gathering as in previous years. At Christmas dinner they waited on themselves so that the staff could also have their party. Ever since the boys - Ian and Glen - were old enough to come down to Christmas dinner Barbara had insisted that the men each made a speech, beginning with the youngest. After dinner they all sat round the fire first to recite home-made poems and then to sing the songs of every generation, starting with Polly and the Boer War, the favourite being 'Goodbye Dolly I Must Leave You', which had of course been sung by her young men as 'Goodbye Polly'.

On 28 December Barbara and Hugh had celebrated their twenty-seventh wedding anniversary quietly together. In the scrapbook for 1963 is the card that was attached to Hugh's present of jewellery on which he had written, 'To Thank You for 27 Wonderful Years Darling.'

It had indeed been twenty-seven wonderful years, a marriage of great contentment and love. Barbara would have made a success of any career that she had taken up simply because of that extraordinary inner driving power that motivates her. In Hugh she had found the right background. He was filled with admiration for the way she ran their home and took care of the family. Whatever Barbara had become engrossed in over the years she had always put her own family and home first - just as Polly had. During his business trips away Barbara and Hugh were never out of touch and they both telephoned and wrote to each other every day. His love letters are gentle like the man himself, as this extract shows:

Station Hotel,
Inverness

My Own Darling Wife,

Thank you darling for your lovely letter. I did not read it until I was tucked up in bed and it made me very happy. I do love you so much my darling. . .

All my love to you my sweetest one. I love and adore you. Take great care of your precious self and don't forget me. I shall always be thinking of you and I missed you so much last night.

God Bless you my darling wife. I love you.

Your always adoring husband,
Hugh

On Boxing Day Barbara was worried for Hugh, who was clearly not well. She telephoned Mrs Gibson, a healer living in Scotland, and asked her to help. Mrs Gibson had come into Barbara's life many years before in a fascinating way. The link came through Joyce Camden back in the war days in Bedfordshire. A friend of Joyce's was Gwen Catley, who had a marvellous singing voice. While she was performing in Scotland one night she heard that her only child, a son, had been taken to hospital in London to be operated on for cancer of the rectum, a difficult, dangerous and painful operation. As Gwen Catley was rushing from the concert hall to catch the train back to London a Scotswoman handed her a bunch of flowers. The singer was distraught and in thanking her said: 'I can't stop to talk now', but she did tell her about her son. The woman, who was Mrs Gibson, said in her broad Scots voice, 'Don't worry, everything will be all right.'

When Gwen Catley arrived at the hospital the little boy had already gone to the operating theatre. She sat down and waited, desperately anxious. Soon afterwards the surgeon came out to tell her in an amazed voice: 'It's alright, Miss Catley. Everything is alright. There is nothing wrong with your son.'

Gwen Catley was naturally upset and admonished the surgeon saying: 'How dare you operate on my child unnecessarily?'

'You don't understand', he replied. 'It's a miracle. The malignancy was there on the X-rays and now it has gone!'

On her return to Glasgow to continue her concert programme Mrs Gibson again appeared with flowers at Miss Catley's dressing room. She looked very tired but said: 'Everything was all right, wasn't it?'

'How do you know?' Gwen Catley asked.

'We were working on him all night.'

It was through this that Mrs Gibson has come into Barbara's life and has helped her through many crises over the years. When Barbara's son-in-law, Earl Spencer, was apparently dying from a cerebral haemorrhage in a London hospital, she asked Mrs Gibson for help.

I am sure it was Mrs Gibson who kept him alive. Whenever I go away on a trip I always ask Mrs Gibson for 'cover' so that I don't fall out of the aeroplane and end up kidnapped in the Sahara! She's absolutely marvellous. She is now seventy-seven years of age, lives in Scotland and never takes money for her work.

When she telephoned Mrs Gibson that night, alarmed at the deterioration in Hugh's health, Mrs Gibson promised to telephone back. Barbara was horrified and angry when the Scotswoman spoke to her a short time later: 'I must be honest, dear, and tell you there is nothing I can do; his time has come. I have covered him in blue and he will pass peacefully.'

Barbara could not believe what she had heard. She slammed the telephone down. That evening as he was getting out of bed Hugh collapsed. The scar tissues from the wounds he had received in 1917 had at last touched his heart.

Shock, pain, and anguish. But no tears. Barbara behaved just as she had always done when she hears bad news. She was stunned into numbness. It was, strangely enough, the first time in her life that she had ever seen anyone dead. Her father and two brothers had all died in the war and so many of those young men who had loved her had met violent accidental deaths.

As Barbara said farewell to Hugh she thought he looked happy and his expression was of a man who had fulfilled his life's ambitions. In his black leather wallet were several worn snapshots that he had always carried with him. They showed Barbara when he had first fallen in love with her. She tucked them into his pyjama jacket before he was lifted into the coffin.

As I stood beside him as he lay in a blue bed wearing blue pyjamas I could not believe when he had loved me so much that he had left me alone. I had always known that Hugh's life hung on a thread and I was deeply grateful for having him with me so long. He did not suffer, and for him it was the peaceful, quick death he would have wanted. But that didn't assuage the loss and the terrible sense of shock.

All through those twenty-seven years of marriage Barbara and Hugh had often talked about the possibility of after-life and had differed in their viewpoint. Barbara has a passionate belief that this earthly life is a mere passage in time and part of the mysticism of the universe. How often had she asked Hugh, did he really believe that Ronald's struggle to help other people through his hope, belief, ambition, ideals and energy had been wasted? She had never been able to convince him that Ronald was still alive.

'I have been nearer death than anyone else,' Hugh sighed, 'and there were no angels. I have no conviction of anything outside this world. When you are dead, you are dead! That is the end!'

A week after Hugh died, Barbara's maid, Rose Purcell, told her she had smelt the wonderful scent of carnations outside the room where Hugh had died. Next day when Barbara got up at eight o'clock to have breakfast with her son Glen before he left for London, she passed through the *entre-salle* outside her bedroom, connecting her husband's dressing-room and bathroom with the room in which he had died.

It was astonishing. As I came outside my bedroom door suddenly I was aware of the most marvellous, over-powering scent of carnations. They were not the English kind but the true, exotic fragrance of Malmaison. The first thing we always did when we arrived in Paris for our 'second honeymoon' year after year, was to drive to the Madeleine and say a prayer for our marriage. When we came out Hugh bought from the flower stalls a huge bouquet of red carnations for our bedroom and he wore one in his buttonhole every evening. I knew then that this was Hugh telling me there was life after death.

The fragrance came and went for three weeks, sometimes more intense than at other times, but was always imperceptibly there. No one could explain it as there were no carnations in the house and it was certainly not perfume coming from a bathroom. Barbara knew Hugh was telling her that he had been wrong. In his own quiet and thoughtful way he was trying to convey to her the truth. She had been right - there was survival.

Of all the things Barbara has told me about Hugh perhaps the most poignant was that when she once asked him: 'If a fairy could wave a magic wand and give you anything you wanted, what would you wish for?' Without any hesitation he had answered: 'I have everything I have ever wanted.' In a world where marriages crumble and hate supersedes love, even between husbands and wives, it was touching to hear Barbara say: 'He was the most contented man I have ever known.'

In the immense well of loneliness that opened up on the realization that she would face the years without Hugh, Barbara turned to poetry. This poem of love was called simply, 'To Hugh'.

> I love the silver of the mist at dawn,
>> I love the shadows underneath the trees,
> I love the softness of the velvet lawn
>> The fragrance of syringa on the breeze.
>
> I am so lonely without you here,
>> You who loved everything the garden grew.
> The birds, the flowers are very dear,
>> But it is empty beauty without you.

As always Barbara immersed herself in work and more work. In April 1964 she published her seventy-fifth novel called *The Fire of Love*. It is the story of a girl called Carina and a little boy called Dipa, son of a Javanese dancer, whose father lives in Gloucestershire. All the Barbara Cartland ingredients were there - mystery, passion, colour, and escapist reading.

Once again Barbara proved that romance and glamour were what women needed most, and that rule number one for a successful romantic novel is that the heroine and hero must always be good people. The subordinate characters can be as bad or lecherous as can be but the heroine must preserve her innocence. Virtue is a drama in itself.

By now Barbara had an established and solid market of British women breathlessly waiting for her next book to come out. More than anyone else she understood their need to fulfil their fantasies. Whatever the popular Press said about pornography, wife-swapping and male pin-ups, deep within themselves women were still seeking something that would bring love and beauty into their own drab house-bound lives. This is the need

Barbara fulfilled. It is as old as time and the reason why the romantic novel will never be replaced. Sales may fluctuate but basically romance is here to stay.

Barbara had never before been in such demand as a speaker and now with the necessity of recharging her life after Hugh's death she accepted all kinds of engagements. Since the publication of her ninety-eighth book *The Many Facets of Love* in 1963 Barbara had been made into an oracle on love and blissfully she never let her audiences down. Witty, pretty and sublimely un-selfconscious she dived into any controversial subject.

Englishmen make the best lovers in the world. They're taught at school never to show their emotions. And they never flirt. But they make magnificent lovers once they're married. This is why so many foreign girls want to marry Englishmen and come from all over the world to find one.

When addressing a group of two hundred salesmen she looked round the room before pronouncing:

It takes eighty grammes of protein to make a virile, exciting lover. What we've had for lunch today is about seventeen grammes.

If every woman fed her husband two pounds of good red meat every day he would be satisfied and there wouldn't be any need for all those dirty books. A man will not go chasing other women if he's properly looked after in his own home. The act of love is far more important than the contract you are drawing up on that new project in your factory. It is far more important than the board meeting you are going to attend tomorrow.

A man should always remember that a woman is an idealist about love. Women may well tell you that they are not, that they are hard boiled, that they take love as it comes, but that is not true. With the first stirrings of adolescence, she believes in a knight in shining armour who will rescue her from all the terrors of evil and will dedicate his life and love to her.

Two hundred satiated and bemused salesmen went home to their wives that night devoted to Barbara for understanding the man's cause. They gave her a standing ovation as she swept around the room, shaking each of them by the hand. They had never had such an entertaining speaker before.

The year ended with Barbara all set to successfully complete one of her most original crusades to date. After a fight of three bitter years she was to open the first Romany gypsy camp in the world at Hatfield.

When you wish upon a star, wish hard enough and believe and your wish will come true.

Barbara Cartland

In Hatfield today is a small camp of romany gypsies living in their caravans in Barbaraville. They are there because for three relentless years Barbara fought for their rights. She thought it extremely unjust that this small minority group, with roots deep in traditional English country lore, should be persecuted by being moved every twenty-four hours so that no gypsy child could go to school. 'One cannot have, in a democracy', she said, 'education for everyone but the gypsies.'

Today through her efforts, the support of the Earl of Onslow, who, Barbara says, was a 'tower of strength', and of the second Earl of Birkenhead, son of the famous 'F.E.', there are, apart from Barbaraville, ten other gypsy camps in Hertfordshire, and there is also a gypsy officer at County Hall.

The Earl of Onslow's involvement came about when he rang Barbara up when the first newspaper report appeared and said, 'I'm always grateful to the gypsies in the New Forest who were my friends and who taught me so much of their lore when I was a boy. I will help you in any way I can.'

Lord Onslow told her that when he was a little boy in the New Forest the gypsies told him how to make a dog know you to be his master. Take a piece of liver, they said, and carry it all day in your armpit. Then, when evening comes, give it to the dog, who has not been fed, and when he has eaten it he will follow you for the rest of his life. Lord Onslow had often tried this method and said it was infallible. The Romany gypsies are dear to Barbara's heart because of their high moral code. In France even today if a Romany woman so much as flirts with anyone who is not her husband the family shave her head.

The crusade for the gypsies all began when a midwife complained to Barbara, who is president of the Hertfordshire Branch of the Royal College of Midwives, that a gypsy woman who was pregnant in a caravan near Hatfield had to go to St Albans Hospital to have her baby. Her caravan was moved every twenty-four hours, and there was a little girl of eight in the same family who was unable to go to school. When Barbara heard this, in her capacity as a County Councillor she raised the question at the next council meeting and learnt that nothing was being done.

Within a week she had visited the gypsies on Colney Heath, a traditional gypsy camping place since the reign of Henry VIII. There she found among many others the Davis and Buckland families whose ancestors had been born, camped and died on this small clearing on the heath for generations. When she arrived they were sitting outside their caravans listening to the schools' broadcast.

Once the gypsies, who are shrewd judges of character, realized that Barbara was honest in her intentions, and not just an interfering official, they poured out their hearts to her. They explained that they were anxious to keep on the right side of the law but they were fined, not only for camping for more than twenty-four hours in one spot, but also for having any of their belongings deposited near their caravans.

They had just been summonsed for having a dustbin, two milk churns filled with water, and a perambulator containing a baby outside their caravan, and when the case came up Barbara went to the police court and defended Luke Davis, the head of the family. The magistrate dismissed the charge of litter but fined him for camping. When Davis asked where he could go without breaking the law, there was no answer. Incensed by such injustice Barbara immediately consulted the Chief Constable of Hertfordshire who confirmed that in law gypsies could go nowhere and must move every twenty-four hours, which meant it was impossible for any gypsy child ever to go to school.

In August 1961 the gypsies on Colney Heath were evicted by the Rural Council which had taken over the original heath from its owner, the Earl of Caledon, whose family had befriended the gypsies for centuries. Fifty caravans were ordered to leave by the police, and moved off quietly, the women in tears. 'What will become of us?' they asked Barbara, the only outsider present to witness this emotional upheaval.

During the preceding summer months the Press had reported the gypsies' case fairly and sympathetically but they had no other friends. Religious or welfare organizations made no effort to contact them in their plight - indeed the Vicar at Colney Heath had even turned off the water in the churchyard because the gypsies used the tap for drinking water for the children.

The Earl of Onslow helped Barbara to form a fund to establish gypsy camps. The Earl of Birkenhead also persuaded many of his friends to become patrons. When the Marquess of Salisbury offered two acres of land for a camp near Hatfield it was rejected by the local planning committee. A site was eventually chosen by the Hertfordshire County Council and Hatfield Rural District Council but it was bitterly opposed by the Hatfield Development Corporation, and the Minister ordered a public enquiry. In the meantime Barbara had written to Sir Keith Joseph, then Minister of Housing and Local Government, who promised to investigate the whole problem. Lord Onslow appeared on several television programmes and questions were raised in Parliament. Sir Keith finally decreed that all local councils in Great Britain must provide camps for their own gypsies. Barbara had won!

But it was not until 22 February 1963 that the official enquiry was heard at Hatfield. The Development Corporation was determined to win and brought down from London the legal 'heavies' - an eminent Q.C. and his junior. Against them - Barbara and Leslie Asquith the acting clerk to the Rural Council. When she was allowed to speak Barbara made an impassioned plea:

> . . . Everyone agrees it is unjust and unfair that people should be denied education when they ask for it, but they don't want gypsies. From John O'Groats to Land's End, you will find that everyone has a wonderful reason why a piece of land is the one place where gypsies cannot have a camp. But we must educate the children and how can you educate children who must move on every twenty-four hours?

Barbara acknowledges today that it was Mr Asquith who made the most impressive remark when he said: 'Hertfordshire gypsies are becoming a racial problem. We must remember that this is Hatfield, Hertfordshire, not Little Arkansas.'

By the end of the hearing everyone except Barbara was getting a little edgy. Even the Q.C. became testy when she asked if she might speak again. 'She has already spoken', he insisted, but the poor man had not reckoned on Barbara, who insisted on her rights. There was a hushed silence as she sweetly said: 'I only wanted to say thank you to the Inspector. He has had many hours of listening to what we have had to say. I feel we all owe him a vote of thanks whichever side we are on.'

Barbara wrote five thousand letters - a good rough figure she uses for all her charity appeals - to set up a trust to raise funds to make the site habitable. Here the churches did help with His Eminence the Archbishop of Westminster and the Archbishop of York leading the way, and many other bishops also contributing. Donations poured in from Barbara's friends, as well as members of the public, including many old-aged pensioners who had read of her fight for the gypsies in the Press. One of the larger contributions came from John Stais, the owner of the White Tower, one of London's smartest restaurants. His explanation was simple and heartfelt. 'I am a Cypriot. When I came to England with no money people were very kind to me. I want to do something for those who are not so fortunate as myself.'

It was one of the most satisfying days of Barbara's years of service as a County Councillor when she visited Barbaraville for the first time in 1964. Waiting to greet her were the eight families, all of whom are still there today. With a gypsy baby in one arm and a white parasol in the other Barbara was told by Mrs Betty Buckland, 'Mrs McCorquodale, dear, we've done it all for you. It makes us pleased to know that you are pleased.' Priscilla Davis chimed in: 'We wanted to do everything to please you, ma'am.' Luke Davis quietly pointed to the water gushing from a newly installed tap and told her, 'Look at that tap. It means everything to us. Never will we refuse anyone who comes here for water.' Israel Buckland joined the group as Luke told how they had collected scrap-wood for fences, seeded the lawns and brought in twenty tons of hoggin, six tons of shingle and 120 gallons of tar. When a tar barrel blew up Israel was taken to hospital and kept in bed for a week but their enthusiasm and energy never flagged. The women took Barbara to see their flower gardens where they explained that they did not know the names of the flowers. 'Pansies and geraniums, and there you've got some French marigolds', she explained. Children clambered to hold her hand, to touch her parasol, to be near her.

Nor were the gypsies' problems completely over even now. When the children began going to school they were ostracized by the local children. One of the loudest protestors in another county, Kent, was the local Baptist minister whose two children went to the same school. He said in public: 'It came as a tremendous shock when we heard that gypsy children were to be taught at school. They smell I'm afraid and they have an educational standard of retarded children.' When Barbara heard about this she was so angry, so outraged, that people still behaved like this, that she wrote a letter to the West Kent Education Committee. 'Edenbridge is deliberately reviving the bitter, age-old racial prejudice against gypsies which is neither just nor Christian.'

In 1967 Barbaraville at last got its own bathing facilities, some of the money coming from an exhibition of the drawings of the gypsy children which Barbara arranged in London at the Royal Hotel in Bloomsbury. 'There's going to be quite a rush when everything is connected up', Mrs Betty Buckland commented. 'Everyone will be throwing away their galvanized baths - because don't forget that just because we haven't had a proper bath with running water, it doesn't mean we never bath at all.'

Today Barbaraville flourishes, the children have all been assimilated into the local schools in Hertfordshire without any problems, over seventy babies have been christened in the local church. The trust still supervises the site from its own funds and the gypsies are required to pay a nominal rent each week. There is much happiness and contentedness as the eight families have their own telephone line, electricity, television sets, washing machines and water and sanitary facilities. Each year the gardens are planted with flowers and the lawns mown, and no one will ever forget the fight that Barbara had for their rights.

In the whole of Hertfordshire there are now something between 240 and 250 gypsy families according to Robert Dale, the county's gypsy officer. 'Barbaraville especially is a well conducted, homely and happy place which is now accepted and well respected in the community. Barbara Cartland put a great deal of muscle into it and did a lot of hard work.'

With her involvement with the Romany gypsies over three years it was natural that Barbara should use the gypsy theme in a novel. For her romance, *Bewitched*, she studied over forty books on gypsies.

Everywhere that Barbara looked in those days of the 'swinging sixties', there were things that upset and distressed her. While the sixties had brought with them such brilliant trend setters as the Beatles, Mary Quant and David Hockney, the period also had its dark side with the introduction of pornography, drugs and misguided flower power. Barbara had been appalled when she saw the avalanche of sex magazines that were pouring into her local bookstalls from America. She did not merely believe that the magazines' sexy nudes were wrong in themselves, but was upset to think that they were corrupting teenage girls and boys. This was confirmed to her when she attended a juvenile court and watched horrified as a fifteen-year-old girl was sent off to approved school. 'It's the books and magazines she's been reading that have brought her to this', the girl's mother sobbed.

In one of her typical get-to-the-heart-of-the-matter actions Barbara bought up all the magazines she could find and took them to the Conservative meeting at Lemsford, a small village in her division. Making sure that the local Press were present she publicly burned the magazines in a stove. It was a flamboyant gesture undoubtedly, but as Barbara well knew it was guaranteed to get a Press coverage and draw attention to the problem.

She asked all the mothers present to join her in a campaign to 'clean up the bookstalls, sweep away the pictures of perverted nudity, of little girls dolled up like prostitutes, and stop this deplorable and unnatural sexual trend'. Barbara's eyes blazed with fire as she sat down, and every woman present clapped their approval. It was then agreed that because of her well-known public image and success in crusading Barbara should write personally to the Home Secretary, R.A. Butler. . . 'We feel that this sort of literature will incite further crimes against young girls and will certainly undermine the morals of our young men. We would be most grateful if you would take action to prevent this literature from being distributed.'

A month later Barbara received a letter from the Home Office in which it was mentioned that 'the importation of obscene books and magazines from abroad is prohibited by the Customs Consolidation Act in 1876'. This, of course, did not placate Barbara who was quick to point out that an Act that had been convened in 1876 surely could not be expected to apply to this day and age. Though this was one of her few personal crusades that did not succeed, and Barbara's critics tried to cite it as an excuse for personal publicity, she was, in fact, merely acting as a catalyst, as she had done all her life, and bringing injustices before the public eye.

*The Light of God comes to us unexpectedly, and
suddenly the whole world is radiant and beautiful. This
happened to me in Greece, and I can still see vividly in
my mind the glory of a view which suddenly became
Divine.*

Barbara Cartland

With Hugh's death Barbara began to create a new pattern of living. The
heartache was intense but the lonely moments were always kept for when
she was alone in bed. Glen had moved from London to live with her that
first year, travelling up and down each day, just as his father had done. He
returned each night to Barbara vibrating with energy and the repose of a
superbly run household. Because she has an unquenchable curiosity about
life, as well as being an incurable romantic, there is no resisting the
freshness of Barbara's creative conversation. Dull happenings become
incredibly funny when spiced with her wit. Though Ian and Glen resemble
their father in looks, both have inherited Barbara's quick tongue.

Travel has always been a passion in Barbara's life. She always wears
when she is travelling a small diamond cross given to her by Hugh and a
tiny piece of cloth which had touched the body of Saint Thérèse and which
was given her by the nuns at the Convent of Lisieux. These relics of faith
have now travelled with her well over 500,000 miles.

In 1965 Barbara took her two sons to the South of France which held so
many memories for her. She never goes there without visiting Nôtre-Dame
de Laget, a mellow sixteenth-century church situated beyond La Turbie
high above Monaco. Nôtre-Dame de Laget is the patron saint of accidents,
and all the way round the small church itself are pictures painted or drawn
in gratitude by those who owe their lives to the saint. Barbara lit a candle in
front of the saint's statue.

That evening mother and sons dined at Nice, and on the way back to
Cap Estel where they were staying, they stopped on the Corniche to look
at a battleship all lit up, anchored in the harbour near Cap Ferrat.
Suddenly round the corner, travelling crazily fast, came a French car. It
scraped the side of Barbara's car, buckling and damaging the body. Had it

been two inches closer certainly Barbara and one or both of her sons would have been killed. Barbara was sure this escape was due to Nôtre-Dame de Laget.

The following year they all three went to India which had enchanted Barbara since she had first visited it in 1958.

Having read so much about Madame Helen Blavatsky I hoped when I visited the Theosophical Society, which stands on a large estate on the Adyar River, that I should feel the presence of the Great Beings - the Masters - who she believed, had completed their human evolution but continued to guide and develop us. It was possible, she said, to get in touch with them.

There was only, however, a feeling of peace and tranquillity as we stood in the shade of the largest banyan tree in India. Three thousand people have sat there, a universal brotherhood of humanity, without distinction of race, creed, sex, caste or colour. Perhaps this is what the Masters intended?

India has always quickened paranormal experiences for Barbara, and it was in Mysore that she stepped back in time to the eighteenth century. It was just as J.W. Dunne had described in *An Experiment with Time*, to which both she and Ronald had been so attracted. Barbara and her sons had been given an introduction by Lord Mountbatten to G. Rajagopalachari, always known as Rajaji, who was acting Viceroy and Governor General. As his guests, they were staying in a magnificent white-pillared mansion built by the British which was now used for special guests. There were something like twenty-five servants to wait on Barbara, Ian and Glen, and their meals were prepared by the chef who had cooked for the Queen on her recent visit:

As she lay in a four-poster in her vast bedroom one night, Barbara had the distinct feeling that she was not alone. Suddenly she became aware that a British officer - a middle-aged, florid-faced man, hot and cross - had entered the room. She watched as he threw himself down in a chair and ordered a native servant to pull off his boots. He cursed the man because he was so slow and began drinking a whisky and soda. He then commanded the servant to fetch him a woman from the bazaar. The vision faded. Barbara had returned to the twentieth century.

In Bombay they were taken to the red-light district where the young girl prostitutes stand like dolls in the doorways of small cell-rooms luring their customers. The pathos and tragedy of the whole scene tempted Ian to take a photograph. The Indian guide immediately asked him not to as Muslim women resent being photographed. 'Just one quick shot is all I need', Ian pleaded. As he pointed to take it the camera jammed. When the film was finally developed across the negative was a blood-like streak.

It was not until they were in the ruins of Ankar Wat in Cambodia two years later that Barbara was to hear of a similar experience. A woman tried to take a photograph of the mysterious temple, now being consumed by nature, with the trunks of trees and twisted branches among the ruins. The tourist was told not to do it but she persisted. Her camera jammed for no apparent reason and would not work again for twenty-four hours.

In Agra Barbara had one of her most vivid esoteric experiences. Ian and she had motored from the pink city of Jaipur to Agra. It had been a long, tiring journey in the heat and they arrived at their hotel late in the afternoon. Barbara was shown into a newly decorated bedroom but when she saw that it did not have any air-conditioning, she asked the German proprietor if she could change her room to one that did have, as she had been promised when they first booked months before. She was shown to two inferior bedrooms that might have been Army barracks.

Suddenly because I had lost one of Nehru's speeches I particularly wanted to read I started to have a scene with Ian. I raged. I screamed at him and kept reiterating: 'I want to go home! I hate India! I want to go home!'

Ian was astonished. 'But you love India, Mummy!' he protested.

Even while I spoke I knew that I was not myself, but someone called Annie, who was married to a British soldier at the beginning of the century when they wore white veils hanging behind their topees to protect their necks. I can still see her quite clearly. She came from Glasgow in Scotland. She had red hair and freckles and she was desperately homesick, she wanted to go home. I understood, too, in some manner that I can't explain, that Annie was dead and that she was buried somewhere in the country she hated.

I am certain that people's emotions, passions, violent actions, imprint themselves on the atmosphere. That may be why people are so afraid and restless in houses where dramatic events have taken place.

In Khatmandu Barbara met the Living Goddess, a precocious child who had been chosen from many others at the age of six years for this illustrious position. She remains a Goddess until she reaches puberty and during that period stays strictly within the family house, with a courtyard as her playground. The Living Goddess is also the Goddess of Destruction and is supposed to have the power to destroy the King of Nepal's enemies and all that threatens him.

Barbara and Ian were allowed to call on her and speak to her when she appeared at a third-floor window. The child was then nine and heavily made-up with kohl-rimmed eyes and heavy slanting lines drawn from the corner of her eyes up to her temples. She had flowers upon her head.

> She glanced sulkily for some time and the guide told us in a hoarse whisper that if she is unhappy everyone believes that a great calamity will befall the King. Then she said something to her mother who repeated it to the guide. He translated it to us.
> 'She admires the lady's hat very much.'

Barbara was wearing a small hat of white flowers. Although she tried through the interpreter to ask the Living Goddess questions about herself, all the little girl and her mother could talk about was her hat.

At the foot of the Himalayas Barbara was to meet a Holy Man who was 132 years old. Though born in the south of India he had travelled round the world and stayed in England for five years. Despite his great age he had his own teeth, was not deaf and had a long beard. He told Barbara with twinkling eyes that he was getting a little frail. He also spoke of self-discipline, of avoiding violence and anger and lust. Barbara asked him to tell her of some of his spiritual experiences. In perfect English he replied enigmatically: 'If I eat a delicious fruit I know what the taste is. But there are no words in which I can describe it to you. To know what it is like you must taste it for yourself.'

It was at Jhajuraho, where Barbara visited the temples that had been built between 900 and 1100 A.D. under the great Chanela Kings, that she met another Holy Man who lived just outside the village. Through her guide she asked him what he thought of the future and he replied: 'Only by love will there ever be any understanding between nation and nation and man and man.'

So deep is the impression that India has left on Barbara during her five visits there, that she wrote a poem in celebration.

> Heaped fruit, vegetables and grain,
>   Mustard, masala, musk and ghee.
> Dust rising in clouds to fall again
>   On silk and silver, gold and tea.
> Crowds drifting, jostling, wandering where?
>   With Brahmin bulls, sacred and old.

Veiled women giggling stop and stare,
   Or listen to the storyteller's ode.
This is India under a burning sun,
   The glory of the dawn o'er plain and peak.
Swift opal twilight when the day is done,
   And nights of whispered magic as men speak
Of gods and love, rebellion, battles won.
   Here hides the truth for which I seek.

But it was in Bali that Barbara sought out the most prestigious fortune teller who, much to her surprise, turned out to be a thin young man sitting on a comfortable cool verandah. He had once worked for the government but had given up this post to concentrate on work with the spirits. He spoke English quite well.

He didn't tell me anything of great importance except that I would travel all over the world seeking. 'So far you have only touched the branches of the tree, you have not yet reached the roots.'
   It was twelve o'clock by the time he had finished and he told us that he could not charge us anything because the Gods who directed him stopped their work at eleven-thirty. It was the first time that I had ever heard that Gods kept office hours!

The next year, when Barbara, Ian and Glen were motoring from Taxco to Mexico City, they saw some interesting local Indian paintings for sale. They were vibrant and colourful, so Barbara bought four from the impassive Indians. She brought them back to England, had them framed, and hung three in a bathroom at Camfield and gave the fourth to Ian for his flat in London. They were to provide one of the very few unpleasant experiences of the paranormal Barbara ever had:

I was suddenly aware that in the happy atmosphere of my home there was something disruptive which I could feel quite vividly. I realized that the paintings had been painted with hatred - perhaps of the white man. I was conscious of enmity and I knew I could never keep them. I had all four of them in their frames burnt in the garden and after that the peace and happiness of the house which had come when it was blessed, remained undisturbed.

Wherever she travels Barbara is recognized and fêted, even in the most unexpected places. When she arrived in Manila during one of her

lightning trips one February she was delighted to find all the bookshop
windows full of Valentine cards saying: 'Welcome to Manila, Barbara
Cartland'. Some of the cards were so big that they filled the whole window.

Well, I had no idea I was so important in Manila but it was because of
my virgins. Only east of Suez everyone appreciates and understands a
virgin bride. This is why I am determined, despite pleas from some of
my publishers, that all my heroines will remain virgins and never go to
bed without a ring on their finger. That's the way they like it in Manila,
and I had a lovely time with all the librarians thanking me for the good
influence I've had on their girls.

—28—

*How often we try to change those we love instead of
loving them more because they are as they are. That is
real and true love.*

Barbara Cartland

All her strong, gallant life Polly had been afraid to die. When death finally
came to her she was ninety-eight and a half, and she just fell asleep in front
of the television. She had been furious when, aged ninety-five and having
broken her leg, Barbara had forbidden her to drive her car any more.
Although she had never taken a driving test and was totally ignorant of the
highway code, yet in over sixty years she had never had an accident.

Barbara had planned to go to Peru with Glen, and on the last day she
saw Polly she had jokingly admonished her: 'Promise me you won't die
while I'm away, Mummy, because it will be such a bore changing
aeroplanes!'

Polly replied in her typical way: 'No, of course not. I would hate to be a
bother and spoil your holiday.'

Barbara and Glen were flying back from Barbados when Polly slipped away, and on their arrival back Ian telephoned them from Scotland to break the news. It had been a wonderful death, says Barbara - a marvellous death for her. When Anne, who looked after her, had gone in to fill her hot water bottle at nine o'clock she was dead. There was no pain, no suffering. Like many old people she was afraid of dying and although she used to say to Barbara, 'I'm longing to go to God', really she had fought like a tiger to go on living.

Polly had been converted to Roman Catholicism under the influence of Lady Weir, wife of General Sir George Weir to whom Tony had been A.D.C., and herself a convert. With her innate consideration Polly had written to all her children to ask them if they minded if she became a Roman Catholic. Barbara replied typically: 'I don't care if you become a Hottentot as long as it makes you happy.' When Polly was quite old she became President of the Sword and Spirit for six counties and was regularly visited by the priests. After she retired from this position she confided to Barbara: 'I am rather hurt, you know. I never see a priest now. Malvern has a new one who never calls on me.' Barbara was annoyed. Any slight to the aged who have given so much to life - and especially to Polly - was more than she could bear. She wrote to the Archbishop of Birmingham and told him she thought it was extremely unkind that his priests no longer called to see her mother, who was now often not well enough to go to the church.

What do you think he did? He went himself and called at Poolbrook. He never told her he was coming but just walked in and said: 'I want to see Polly.'

Of course when the local priests heard about it they were stunned. The Archbishop sat by her bed and talked to her and was absolutely sweet to her. I said to him afterwards: 'That was the most marvellous thing you could have done.' After that, of course, the priests never stopped calling on her and took the Mass to her when she couldn't get to Church.

On that Sunday morning in 1976 when mother and son arrived back from Barbados and heard that Polly was dead Barbara immediately telephoned the Archbishop and asked if he was going to bury her. 'Of course', he replied. Polly departed in a blaze of glory. Barbara had told the Archbishop that she did not like black, so the five priests wore white robes and the church was filled with spring flowers.

It was just what Mummy would have enjoyed, a lovely sunny day and apart from the wreaths lots of poor people had brought little bunches of flowers. They were the people whose lives had been helped by Polly. She had chosen her plot and bought it overlooking the Malvern Hills which she loved so much. She had even bought a marble angel for her grave and had chosen the hymns she wished to be sung.

I have always felt that it is un-Christian to mourn. We cry for ourselves, not for them, and if we believe in after-life, then they are happy and at peace. Personally, I believe that neither life nor love can die and although our bodies wither and decay, the life-force within us goes on . . . What is important, what matters is that there is no death.

On Polly's gravestone Barbara had inscribed: 'With courage never submit or yield'. That was how Polly had lived all her life. First she had lost her adored husband Bertie, then her two fine sons, Ronald and Tony, but as she said after Dunkirk: 'If crying would bring them back I would cry my eyes out, but I must just go on living to help other people.'

The year 1976 was a full one for Barbara. In February she visited Antigua, Martinique and Barbados and in April, Greece. The following month she was off to America on a promotion tour where she did five television shows and nine live broadcasts in eight days. That year she had an amazing twenty-two novels published and the year before sales had reached well over 50 million.

It was also the year of a personal drama within her own family as her daughter Raine had fallen in love with Earl Spencer, and, after twenty-eight years of marriage, had left the Earl of Dartmouth and her four children. This was the kind of situation which Barbara would never allow in one of her novels and here she had to face it in reality. She was desperately upset, but Raine said simply, 'It is just like one of your books, Mummy. I am wildly in love and there is nothing anyone can do about it!'

Two months after her divorce came through Raine married Earl Spencer at Caxton Hall on 14 July in a ceremony which took ten minutes, the antithesis of her romantic wedding at St Margaret's with that trail of sixteen bridesmaids. Now there were only two witnesses, one being her brother Glen. Two months later the wedding was celebrated with an evening party held at Althorp. Several hundred friends gathered there in grand style. In a renaissance green silk gown the new Countess Spencer greeted her guests wearing the fabulous Spencer heirloom emeralds and diamonds.

It was a glittering occasion with the women's jewels and the Spencer gold plate gleaming under the chandeliers. The guests were a wide selection of friends through the years. The Duke and Duchess of

Gloucester were there, and Princess Diana, as she would become, then aged sixteen in pale pink, and her sisters hovered in the background as the new mistress of Althorp proved what a superb hostess she could be. Among the guests, says Barbara, the most attractive man was Mervyn Stockwood, Bishop of Southwark, dancing away merrily in his purple silk cassock. Barbara was dazzling in white and diamonds.

Like her mother, Lady Spencer has the engaging habit of enjoying giving presents, and the guests left with small mementoes of a new chapter in the life of Althorp - gold pillboxes for the ladies, and packs of playing cards for the men.

One of Barbara's most fascinating books was published that year - *Barbara Cartland's Book of Useless Information*, some of the proceeds of which were ear-marked for the United World Colleges. As she wrote at the time:

Every English woman is a hoarder. She has attics filled with old trunks, straw boaters, battered fancy dresses, picture hats, ice-skates, wicker baskets, a dressmaker's model, and a hundred other things 'too good to destroy'.

My mind is also a lumber room. In the fifty years I have researched for my books, strange pieces of quite useless information haunt me: a mosquito has forty-seven teeth - Beau Brummel employed three hairdressers to arrange his hair - Robert and Elizabeth Browning never saw each other naked.

These quite irrelevant facts are useless to my wide-eyed innocent virgin heroines, or my dark, cynical, raffish heroes, so the only way I can exorcize these ghosts is to publish them. Once I have written a book I never think of it again. So here is my brain-litter, useless, irrelevant, unemployable, but fun!

And fun it certainly is! With a foreword by Lord Mountbatten, who was deeply involved in the setting up of the United World Colleges and became the International President, the book is compulsive bedside reading. Who else but Barbara would ferret out such titillating facts as 'the ordinary mosquito has forty-seven teeth ... Princess Pauline Borghese when she lived in Paris in the house which is now the British Embassy in Rue Faubourg St Honoré, was always carried to and from her bath by Paul, her negro servant. She had five gallons of milk added to the warm water ... Elinor Glyn's husband hired the Brighton Public Paths for two days on their honeymoon so that Elinor could swim up and down naked, her long red hair trailing in the water behind her ... Soon after Prince Aly Khan was fourteen his father, the Aga Khan, sent him to Cairo to an old Arab doctor, a Hakim, who taught him the art of making love. For centuries a special technique had been known to the physicians of the East, which in Arabic is called *Imsak*. It means 'holding', or 'retaining'. The ancient Taoists considered it an extension of the man's vital force. Aly learnt to control himself indefinitely. . . A Parisian doctor for some astrological reason would only make love to his wife on rainy nights. His exasperated wife finally arranged for the servants to pour water on the roof with a watering can, so it rained every night! . . . Napoleon Bonaparte, who disapproved of twin beds, alleged that nothing should separate a husband and wife after they had exchanged 'their soul and their perspiration'! . . . Aristotle believed that when a north wind was blowing more girls were conceived; in warm weather more boys.

The year 1976, despite its sadness had been a year filled with blessings, surprises and the sweet smell of success - stupendous success.

—29—

Men in top jobs never have dirty shoes or long hair.
You need short hair to be a success.

Barbara Cartland

The extraordinary statistic about Barbara Cartland is that when the market for her novels 'took off' in the mid 1970s, and her publishers kept saying that they must have more of her virgins, she was able to increase her output so that between the age of seventy and eighty-three she has averaged twenty books a year - which means two hundred books in all during that period.

At an age when other women are thinking of taking life easier she has worked even harder than at any other period of her writing career. Even more fantastic is that the quality and style have never diminished, and in their class her novels are not only romantic, but extremely exciting.

When I was discussing the Barbara Cartland empire with her son Ian

McCorquodale, he said that occasionally he reads a batch of six or seven novels at a time to keep in touch, as he handles the business side of the family firm Cartland Promotions. 'I can't put them down. I keep saying how is Mum going to get out of this one? And she always does.'

The blooming of the Barbara Cartland empire was all part of the revolt, in the late sixties and early seventies, when all the countries in the Western world were suddenly sick of the 'permissive society'. With the lifting of censorship in the early sixties the market was flooded with pornographic material. Then publishers began to realize that women are not necessarily 'turned on' by pornography and that they were thoroughly sickened by what they saw in cheap magazines and books. The logical reaction was to swing to the opposite end of the scale, which was a Barbara Cartland novel with her spirited virgin heroines.

Romance had never really been a major line for any publishing house before, and it was merely considered as peripheral publishing. Then a smart English publishing house, Mills & Boon, recognized that women throughout the world were yearning for romance, and the romantic novel in inexpensive paperback form was the answer to fulfilling so many dreams and fantasies.

In other words, if you did not have a live, handsome man in your life, then the next best thing was to fall into his arms between the covers of a book.

Mills & Boon were looking for a North American market which is how they came to be linked up with Harlequin, an enterprising Canadian house. It was a way of introducing Mills & Boon's stable of English writers to millions of American readers. Romance had become big business. The sales of Mills & Boon and Harlequin are today probably unequalled by those of any other publisher in the world.

Avon publishers in America were the first company to recognize the huge potential of Barbara Cartland, and in 1967 they bought two titles. There was no promotion, no fanfare, the books just slid on to the bookstalls along with the other romances, but at least Barbara now had the tip of her elegant toe in the huge American market. Pyramid publishers were the next to bring out her books. They paid very little for them and gave a low rate of royalty but the trickle had begun.

It was in 1972 that Bantam approached Barbara. Oscar Dystel, the dynamic president, did a survey with his salesmen, those wily men who travel the country with their fingers on the pulse of the reading public. He asked them what their projection sales would be for Barbara Cartland novels. When their forecasts came back to him he said: 'I don't believe you. You can't possibly sell as many as that. Look at it again and be more realistic. I sell books not dreams.' So the salesmen did their homework again and came back with a different set of figures - double what they had predicted before. Oscar Dystel had only one comment to make this time: 'We must have this woman.'

Bantam then made an offer and Barbara left Pyramid, who were not too pleased at the time. Although they had not promoted her novels sufficiently they had the instinctive feeling that they had lost a goldmine. Which of course, they had.

To celebrate the first books under the Bantam banner the publishers invited Barbara to New York to promote them. It was then that the miraculous happened. Because of her scintillating personality and careful planning, she was invited on every major television show. Women were wild with excitement when they saw Barbara in her jewels and furs! She was more glamorous, more witty than Zsa Zsa Gabor and Carole Burnett rolled into one. If the wise-guy American interviewers thought they could outwit Barbara they were wrong. With exquisite finesse she twisted them round her pink-tipped fingers just as she had already done many times in England with David Frost and other abrasive interviwers.

From the first, and every time so far, she has been in the Dalton Top Twenty Sales list, which is worked out by computer. On one occasion Barbara was first *and* second - the first author of any nationality to achieve this.

Barbara's arrival at Bantam, pink, poised and formidably organized, is still talked about in publishing circles in New York. Bantam's vice president, Esther Margolis, was slightly bewildered when she had a message from Barbara that she would like to meet everyone who worked on her books. A pink missive was sent round all departments and Bantam's conference room was opened at 4.00 p.m.

Wearing a Cartland pink dress and coat and a pink hat with a flurry of feathers, Barbara stood and talked to everyone she met. 'What department do you work in. . .? Do you read romantic novels. . .? Have you been at Bantam long. . .?' No author had ever been so interested in them before as she handed each person a signed copy of her newest Bantam release. The day before, after a full day's televising, she had insisted on signing three hundred copies.

On hearing that she and one of the Bantam ladies shared the same astrological sign Barbara quipped: 'I'm Cancer too. And that means we have to fight for everything we get. But don't forget, we'll always win in the end.'

To the reporter from the prestigious *Publishers Weekly* who wondered how she could be so fecund, Barbara replied:

I'm very organized. I enjoy writing. I would go batty if I didn't keep busy all the time. I know just what I want to say. I have an idea of the plot and my research is thorough. I read thirty to forty books for every one that I write. Nearly all the people in my books are real except for the hero and heroine. The average reader doesn't know that all this is in it but I know it. My details are always correct. . . We all know the boy meets girl story, but I have never repeated a situation.

She pointed to the storm waterpipes device in *Fragrant Flower* - 'those are unique to Hong Kong. There is nothing like them in any of my other books.'

Bantam were so overjoyed with their new author that as a birthday present they promised to send her caviar, which she likes, every month for a year. The fact that only two jars arrived did not spoil Barbara's appreciation - 'It was a wonderful thought and I can only think that something must have gone wrong. You know how it is. . . '

At the height of the Barbara Cartland boom she was responsible for fifteen per cent of Bantam business. They were printing two new titles a month and the top sellers sold between 400,000 and 450,000 copies for each book. This all works out at something like 8,000,000 sales a year in the United States alone.

No one better than Barbara herself had realized the power of virgins:

Walt Disney used to say that every time they made a porno film he made money, and I'm convinced that every time women look at vulgar, degrading pornography they go out and buy a Barbara Cartland novel. Romance has always sold well, but today there's a backlash against pornography and sexual explicitness. All my heroines are virgins. Of course sex is important, but not just as a mechanical thing. It's got to have a spiritual aspect behind it. I mean, you can't get more naked than naked, can you, and then where do you go from there?

The whole process may be symbolized by the ideal put forward by many cultures, that of the virgin. It is not only an attribute of the body, it is a state of mind.

Up till now Harlequin and Bantam were the only two competitors in the romance market. It was then that Simon and Schuster began their own line 'Silhouette' and several other publishers began to take romance seriously, but now its market is changing.

Today the shelf-life of the average paperback is about three weeks. If a book has not been sold by then it is pulped and 'returned' and most

241

American publishing companies suffer fifty-five to sixty per cent returns in paperbacks. Sales in romantic fiction have fallen for a more insidious reason too: the 'hot historicals' have taken over. As Barbara described them, 'The girl gets raped on every page, and in the end when she marries the hero she still manages to blush. That is very unlikely in real life.'

Over the past few years America has also nurtured its own romantic writers who are writing with historical American backgrounds. Barbara has written three novels based in America, *Lucky in Love*, *Island in the Sun*, and *Love Comes West*, but she prefers to stick to the European scene which she knows so well, or the British Empire in the days of the Raj. Although she knows America superficially she would never write about a place unless she had carefully researched it herself.

Bantam ceased publishing Barbara Cartland in April 1983, when their contract had come to an end, and by which time they had published 188 Barbara Cartland titles. The new exclusivity for her paperbacks in America goes to Berkley Jove who will publish two a month.

I had a wonderful association with Bantam. Ten years, which is probably a long time in publishing history. All the top people I dealt with and loved have retired or gone elsewhere. So it was perhaps fate that I should change.

In the United Kingdom, Barbara is published by a variety of publishers in both hardback and paperback. Hutchinson traditionally published her in hardback, though no longer, and then later directly in paperback through 'Arrow Originals'. At present New English Library, Arrow, Pan, and Corgi all publish her in paperback, simply because her output is too prolific for one firm to handle.

Barbara is not at all depressed now that her phenomenal romantic sales in both America and the United Kingdom are down - with her sublime optimism and insight into human nature, she says it is only a matter of time before the pendulum swings back again. Meanwhile there is a whole new reading audience awaiting her in France, Italy, and Spain. In France in particular, where they know and understand *l'amour*, Barbara's books sell between 250,000 and 300,000 copies a year - strangely the romances with French backgrounds not selling as well as those with English ones. With that particularly Gallic love-hate relationship with Britain, the French love reading about our history, Royalty, aristocracy and the incomparable stately homes of England.

When Barbara went to Turkey some years ago she checked with her agent whether her books were sold there and was told that they were not because they have peculiar copyright laws. Though she travelled 'heavy' as usual she did not take her spectacular 'on show' dresses. On arrival at Istanbul airport she was amazed to be greeted by a battery of the Turkish Press, television, and radio.

'What is all the fuss about?' she asked. 'I'm not known here!' 'You are the most popular novelist in Turkey,' she was told, 'and several publishers are churning your books out. They are also serialized in magazines.'

The wily Turks had found a loophole. They have a copyright rule that is unique in that it says that a book that has been published anywhere else can be published in Turkey after ten years. They simply never signed the Universal Copyright Convention, and it would be a very foolish author indeed who tried to take out a law case in Turkey! Now Barbara is legally published in Turkey and she has captured a whole new younger generation of readers who buy her books because of those passionate, saturnine heroes - and, of course, virginity is very important in the East.

'It is an odd fact', Ian told me, 'that none of her publishers has ever read her romances. They know what a Barbara Cartland is all about. They just take it, put it out and it sells. They even admit it too. It is a great compliment. Mother is quite firm with them all. She does not let them change a comma in her manuscripts, and there is always a row when they don't put enough dots in when the heroine is breathless.'

The immaculate manuscripts, bound at Camfield Place in scarlet and thonged with white laces, have something of her heroines' character. When she is asked about money Barbara has an engaging way of avoiding the subject by saying, 'Oh, I don't know a thing about money. I always get the noughts wrong', and everyone laughs politely. This, of course, is not strictly true. Her head and her heart are splendidly co-ordinated. She has computerized knowledge of where her books are selling and at the drop of a lace handkerchief can tell you, 'Oh, there's two coming out in Brazil, ten in France, they love me in Sri Lanka and now there are all those Spanish ladies who have found me. People write all the time to say: "Let's have more books." '

At about the time of the Bantam deluge, Verna Hillie, a friend and former actress who worked in Hollywood films years ago, was visiting Barbara at Camfield Place. 'Why aren't your books done on television?' she asked. 'Go and do it', was the reply. So Verna went back to Hollywood and sold the rights to all Barbara Cartland novels, past and future, to Ed Friendly, a West Coast producer. The subject of money is strictly taboo in Cartland Promotions but it was rumoured at the time that he paid a six-figure sum which rises to seven figures if he actually shoots any of her novels. So far he has done only one, *The Flame is Love*, which had a viewing figure of 24 million when it was shown on N.B.C. in America. The 300-odd other virgins are lying in cold storage but one senses that it will not be long, with the lifting of the recession, before we see Candida, Serena, Lucinda, Prunella, Gracela, Quenella, and Salena swooning before our eyes in glorious colour into the arms of their dukes.

Not all Barbara's trips to New York have been carefree. In May 1981 she was put under police protection after she had received four death threats from the I.R.A. The last of the callers to a TV station used an I.R.A. codeword, known only to the police. 'Tell her if she wants to stay alive to get out of America fast', the voice said.

Undaunted Barbara carried on with her plans to promote a range of furnishings she had designed, the only difference being that she now had two handsome Pinkerton body-guards with her. That she was photographed with them on the front pages of all the New York papers was coincidental.

'I'm quite used to cranks', Barbara said as she opened an exhibition of her designs in a Fifth Avenue store. 'I often get calls from them but they are usually sex maniacs, not terrorists. I can't imagine why I should be a target for the I.R.A. or anybody else. I don't intend to take them seriously. I haven't decided when I go home but when I do it won't be because of anyone threatening to blow me up.'

In between writing her books, promoting health foods, lecturing the British housewife that chips are death to sex life, and a heap of other exotica, Barbara was delighted when Richard Kirkham, President of Kirk Brummel, a fabrics and wallcoverings company, came along and said: 'Look, you used to draw. Why don't you draw some wallpaper?'

'Wonderful! Something new', Barbara replied. 'I love a challenge.'

The resulting designs made by Barbara would be equally at home in a country house, a castle on the moors or a suburban semi-detached. Right from the beginning Richard Kirkham knew exactly where he stood and recognized that there was no discussion on fashion trends with Barbara. Her mind was already made up.

People are starved today and they certainly don't want nanny grey, beige, brown, and other drab colours. Pink is the wonder colour because it gives people a soft glow and makes them appear both lovable and amenable. That is why I always wear it.

Steely-eyed New York reporters were somewhat fazed when she greeted them: 'How very lovely of you to come today. You know I believe it's up to women to bring a new, bright and gay note into our existence. However depressed we may feel there is a rainbow up there in the sky and all we need is love, love, love, love and beauty. . . .' How better to achieve this, she continued, than by buying her new designs. The chintzes, which are still on sale in America, are romantically named after her novels, *Tree of Love, Say Yes Samantha*, and *The Passion and the Flower*. For them in 1982 Barbara received the accolade of 'Achiever of the Year' from the National Home Furnishing Association of the U.S.A. and went to Colorado Springs to receive it.

One of the prettiest of Barbara's designs of love-knots entwined with roses was inspired by the curtains in the royal suite at Broadlands, home of the late Lord and Lady Mountbatten and presently owned by their grandson, Lord Romsey. It was in this suite that both the Queen and Princess Diana spent the first days and nights of their honeymoon.

A foray into the perfume market was less successful for Barbara. Made by Helena Rubinstein, the three Barbara Cartland scents were packaged in their choice of a Fragonard-style box instead of the brilliant pink one which Barbara wanted. The price was too low, as scent is a luxury product and it was not 'up market' enough. 'Never again', Barbara said, 'will I be overruled by people who use my name. I know best.'

But Barbara was undismayed. It is not merely that she refuses to acknowledge misfortune and turns her back on it. It is almost as though she transforms adversity into a new kind of challenge. Her head is now filled with exciting new merchandise ideas that will filter into the market over the next few years.

When the Royal Philharmonic Orchestra came to Barbara, the acknowledged Queen of Romance, for advice for a proposed album of love themes, she persuaded them the lyrics were as important as the music and that the records should be sung. It was not until she was motoring over the mountains in Guadeloupe with Glen some weeks later that she had an idea. She turned to her son and said: 'Why shouldn't I sing with the Royal Philharmonic Orchestra?' 'You must be raving mad, Mummy', Glen replied.

But Barbara was not dismayed. She already knew exactly how she would tackle the task. Had not Rex Harrison taken London and Broadway by storm in *My Fair Lady* and no one could credit him with a singing voice? Barbara had not sung for forty years but she was going to base her technique on that employed by Jack Smith, the 'whispering baritone' of the twenties. She would whisper her songs and leave the rest to modern technology. Norman Newell, who had just produced a brilliant record with Bette Davis was called in.

'At first I thought they wanted Barbara to read a love story but when they told me they wanted to record her singing an album of love songs, can I be forgiven for wondering whether a lady of her age would be able to sing with a quality that would sell the kind of song she had in mind?' he explained to me.

I was invited to lunch at her home, and after we had eaten we went into what I think was the chauffeur's cottage, because he was the only one who seemed to have a piano. Brian Fahey, who was to be her musical director and arranger, played the piano and Barbara sang. I listened very carefully and wondered what kind of treatment I was able to give to make the voice sound interesting, warm and romantic. I'm not saying that Barbara didn't sound warm and romantic, but sometimes you can get a completely different picture when you are listening to someone singing in a room to what you are going to get when you go into the studio.

Even though I knew we had the backing of the Royal Philharmonic Orchestra the star of the recording was Barbara, and she was the one we had to completely and utterly concentrate on. The first thing we had to do was to sort out the songs. Barbara had a whole list of favourites and every song seemed to mean something in her life. It was part of her own story and this in itself, too, was a very interesting facet of making the album. I wondered how to make the L.P. different and suggested that Barbara write introductions to each song, that we were able to record over Brian Fahey and the Orchestra. I knew that she had a beautiful speaking voice but she was inexperienced and had never made a recording before. I decided to record her with a very small group. You see recording techniques today are on the twenty-four or thirty-six track, which means that you can build up with your violins on one, organ on another and so on, rather like a Lego set. Backed by a pianist, guitarist, bass player and a drummer Barbara sang on possibly six channels of our twenty-four-track recording system.

When she arrived at the studio she was already completely familiar with the whole process that I intended to use. She made the recording and then we did the editing to get the right amount of echo, to make the voice warm in parts, or maybe a little harder in others, because it sold its point in the song. When we had completed this we called in the Royal Philharmonic Orchestra and through headphones the leaders of the different sections listened and played the orchestra accompanying her without seeing her. It was a complete technical achievement. We did a similar experiment with the Mike Sangster choir and finally we put it all together like a jig-saw puzzle.

Barbara was to record at the E.M.I. Studios in Abbey Road, and when she was asked what she would like for lunch she said: 'No, no, no! I'm going to bring the food. How many will there be?' On the day Barbara's chauffeur carried in a huge hamper to a room we had set aside where we had laid a table. She herself had a cup of Bovril but all the rest of the recording staff, the engineers, conductor and musicians had things like smoked salmon and champagne. I was extremely annoyed at the time because in one of the newspapers it reported that Barbara had a delicious lunch and all we had was sandwiches. It was so totally untrue. I will always remember how wonderful it was of her to involve everybody in the recording, everybody in the luncheon and in the social side of the whole event.

I am sure that one day the record will be recognized throughout the world as a definitive recording of a very romantic lady who puts romance into so many people's lives and conveys on this record the way she feels about love and life and the happiness of togetherness.

The *New York Sunday Times* wrote about the second annual Romantic Book Lovers Conference to which five hundred ladies were invited in May 1983: 'It was truly an affair to remember - a time to "think pink", get out the feather boas, long dresses, starched crinolines, and long white gloves and get into the Spirit of Romance.'

Who else to invite as their guest of honour but the Queen of Romance herself - Barbara Cartland? The idea of a 'love train' travelling from Los Angeles to New York picking up 'co-hearts' en route as it puffed along was the bizarre brain-child of Kathryn Falk. It was such a lovely, crazy, ambitious idea that no one thought it could possibly work. But it did and when the train finally slid into Penn Station in New York Barbara-in-pink was there to meet the romanticists.

Television, radio, and newspapers were all there to catch the moment when the women almost danced out of the train singing to the tune of 'Hullo Dolly', 'Hullo Barbara, why hullo Barbara, it's so nice to have you back where you belong.' It was a joyous occasion as the media people crowded with hundreds of passers-by watched Barbara greet each delegate with a kiss and they placed a red tulip in her arms. The meeting of Kathryn Falk and Barbara was quite emotional.

The grand finale of this occasion was the presentation of the award for the best romantic novel of the year at a gala for the five hundred romantic guests at the Roosevelt Hotel. On the arm of her son Ian, Barbara swept in wearing a fantasy in pink chiffon with rivulets of tiny pleated frills and a hundred organza roses. She positively glowed under a *diamanté* tiara as she took her place on the golden 'throne' for the presentation of the Barbara Cartland Silver Cup garlanded with pink ribbons for the best romantic novel of the year. The selection had not been easy, because of Barbara's stipulation that the heroine must not go to bed with her lover until the last page when the wedding ring was firmly on her finger.

For ingenious Kathryn Falk Barbara had brought her own award, a dazzling *diamanté* heart threaded on a Cartland pink ribbon.

It could only have happened in America. The American women are warm and not like the English who hate you if you are a success. In America they drop you if you are a failure and adore you if you are a success. In England they love you if you are a failure and absolutely hate you and grind their teeth if you're a success, saying 'pull her down and bite her and knock her out'! They are jealous!

I am a success snob not a blue blood snob; I've always loved people. When my children went to school I said: 'Be top at something, either games or work. Be captain of tiddlywinks, but don't be at the bottom - I couldn't bear it! You must hitch your wagon to a star!'

30

Love is the sun of a woman's life. Without it she withers, grows old and something tender and beautiful within her dies.

Barbara Cartland

On Monday 27 August 1979 Barbara was lunching with her son when the butler entered the dining room and whispered something to Glen who immediately left the room. He returned a few moments later and said, 'I have some bad news for you, Mummy.' Barbara's immediate thought was that he was going to tell her that someone had run over one of the dogs.

'Dickie has been killed in Ireland', Glen said quietly.

In a lifetime of receiving grievous shocks this was one of the most horrifying that Barbara had to bear. In a friendship that stretched over fifty years Lord Mountbatten had played an increasingly important part in her life. She called him 'my friend, adviser and inspiration - the most glamorous man of this century'.

Soon the news began coming over the radio telling the ghastly details of how Lord Mountbatten and his fourteen-year-old grandson, Nicholas Knatchbull, had been blown up by a bomb planted in their boat at Mullaghmore in County Sligo, just as the family was going out for a sail.

I think he must have had a presentiment that something might happen. I had seen him on the Monday before he was going to his Castle, Classiebawn, at the end of the week. On Thursday John Barratt, his Comptroller, rang me up and said: 'Dickie wants to see you.' 'What about?' I asked, and he said: 'I don't know but he says that he must see you.'

Frankly I was not desperately keen as it was frightfully hot and I did not have a chauffeur that day and it meant taking a taxi to London. I asked John how long Dickie would see me for, as I knew he was desperately busy finalizing everything before his annual holiday in Ireland. 'Oh, about an hour', he replied, 'but you *must* come.'

When I arrived at Dickie's little house in Belgravia he kissed me and said: 'I just wanted to see you - for no particular reason.' I replied. 'I hate Ireland and I wish that you weren't going there.' 'Don't worry', he laughed. 'I've got nineteen security guards!' 'Nineteen!' I exclaimed. 'Last year you had thirty-six - I signed books for them all.' 'They thought so many was unnecessary', Dickie explained.

They sat and talked together and as always laughed. The truth was the Irish Government had cut security guards because they said he was so loved in the village, they would notice strangers lurking about. Had the numbers been as in the previous years doubtless the boat would have been checked before the family embarked on that particular day.

No two people could ignite each other more than Barbara and Dickie. It was as if their magnetic vibrations met and joined. Whereas Barbara and Hugh had been so profoundly different in emotions and instincts, here were two people very much alike. It was an affinity born out of a mutual code of behaviour, and the gift of *joie de vivre*. Both had a tremendous confidence in themselves, a confidence which has so often been misinterpreted as conceit. Both, in their own ways, had proved that they were capable of fulfilling their ambitions. They were both total professionals.

Lord Mountbatten admired Barbara's application to her personal discipline and he was very proud of her achievements.

Dickie loved me to be a success and do well. It was always 'come and tell me everything you are doing'. He wasn't one of those men who were only interested in themselves. He always wanted to put me in a good light. I remember at a Buckingham Palace reception for United World Colleges when he introduced me to Prince Charles and said: 'Do you know Barbara's just made an Album of Love Songs?' 'Yes, I know,' the Prince replied.

Barbara's friendship with the Mountbattens had begun with Mary Cunningham-Reid (now Lady Delamere) and then her sister Edwina. Although she had known Lord Mountbatten throughout the years, it was not until after his retirement as Chief of the United Kingdom Defence Staff that this *amitié amoureuse* had developed in a natural way. They needed each other.

Barbara had received a letter from Edwina just a couple of days before she died in Borneo: 'I promise you, darling, this is my last marathon. I will take my vitamins and grease my face as you have told me to do.' After her death Barbara gave a copy of this letter to Lord Mountbatten and it lies with 150 of Barbara's letters in the archives at Broadlands.

Apart from the telephone calls they had almost every night at 9.00 p.m., Barbara and Dickie observed the old-fashioned courtesy of writing to each other when anything special happened.

Broadlands,
Romsey,
Hampshire
[1970]

Dearest Barbara,

Thank you for your letter of the 10th April and for sending me a copy of the broadcast you did on the 8th April. I have read the broadcast and was very much touched by what you said about Edwina.

I can imagine only too well that it sounded even better when spoken in your warm voice over the radio but even in cold blood it does make splendid reading.

How touched she would have been and how grateful I am to you for what you said.

Much love,
Dickie

After Lord Mountbatten made his spectacular television series recording his life and times Barbara received this letter from him:

Dearest Barbara,

Thank you so much for your letter and cable about the television series. Coming from such a very experienced critic all you say is doubly valued.

I am afraid I only got your letter when I came back from Eisenhower's funeral, as I went practically straight there from Sweden.

Thank you also for the nice things you say about seeing Edwina in the film. I thought she came over wonderfully.

Much love,
Dickie

Of their friendship, Barbara told me:

Of course I was in love with Dickie like a million other women. I loved him very much, and he loved me too, but we were both far too old to be anything but very close, and if you like, romantic friends.

It was awful losing him but one must never be negative in this life. So now I just feel very, very grateful for the wonderful friendship we had for so long.

In a letter written in 1978 just before Christmas, thanking Barbara for all the presents she had given him, he wrote in his minuscule handwriting:

You keep saying 'wonderful' to me but you are even more wonderful yourself. How you can look so smashing every time we meet is a wonder in itself. Our Friendship has meant so much to me in the last few years and with my best wishes for Christmas and the New Year, I send you my love.

Dickie

Towards the end of his life Lord Mountbatten did not like late nights, so Barbara and he used to meet about once a week for luncheon and only occasionally for dinner. They would go to places where they knew they would not be recognized - if possible - or where the Press could not descend on them.

He used to come to stay at Camfield Place, too, on his way back from shooting at Six Mile Bottom and other places, and at other times I would go to Broadlands. The last time I was there we talked until two o'clock in the morning and he told me that it was one of the happiest nights he had ever spent. You see we had both passed through so many years and so many of the same friendships we didn't have to explain anything.

I teased him once about being a walking encyclopaedia - which he was, and he told me that during the war he was walking past a room in the Admiralty and there was a telephone ringing with no-one to answer it. He picked it up and a woman's voice asked 'Is John there?' 'Not at the moment, but can I help?' he replied. 'How long do you boil an egg?' she enquired. 'Three minutes and twenty-two seconds', the Supremo-Supremo replied.

Dickie could turn his mind to anything. He was the first man to invent elastic laces in his shoes so he didn't have to do them up. He wore the first zip fastener on a pair of trousers and persuaded the Prince of Wales to do the same. It was not a success as the first time the Prince went to a cloakroom in a restaurant just outside Biarritz where they were staying, he was closeted there for half an hour as his zip stuck.

The oddest literary partnership of all times must surely be that between Barbara Cartland and Lord Mountbatten. It began in 1971, when he suggested a novel written about the 'Pretty Horsebreakers'. They were the young women who looked after the horses in the livery stables of London.

Some were very respectable vicars' daughters from the country but invariably they were very pretty. They began to be sold with the horses they rode sometimes fetching as much as £2,000. It was the highest form of prostitution known at the time. My heroine was thought to be one. But of course she wasn't. She kept her virtue to the end! *The Pretty Horsebreakers* was the first novel Dickie had read since as a boy he read one by Jeffery Farnol. He told me that the end made him cry.

He was always giving me ideas for books. Some of them were rather improper so I'd say: 'No, Dickie. Not possible. I stand for purity.' He thought he had caught me out once and told everyone that one of my virgins had gone to bed with the hero before the end of the book. It was my fifth book, and in fact she had been raped. He never let me forget that!

Over the years we had a regular partnership. His advice was very useful, especially about naval and court life.

Just before Dickie was assassinated he said, 'I want a novel from you for the United World Colleges.' It has great interest because he thought if it extended with students of every country being educated together it would prevent war. 'Very well', I said. 'You will do the naval parts and I'll do the love.' It was Dickie who thought of most of the plot and told me how the private pirateers preyed on our cargo ships in the West Indies after our war with America ended in 1812. We had done five chapters when he was killed. I finished the novel and John Barratt, who was a former naval officer, helped me and read the proofs before publication.

As Peter Grosvenor of the *Daily Express* wrote: 'It is a corking romance about a dashing sea Captain called "Tiger" Horn who, besides battling with the dratted French and seeing the Yankee privateers off in the Caribbean, falls passionately for lovely Lady Delora . . . only there are some complications.'

The book ends in a typical Barbara Cartland way:

Delora had filled the shrine in his heart that had always been empty.

Now he knew she would be there always and for ever, and he would worship her because she had brought him the true, pure love for which all men seek as they voyage over the difficult, unpredictable and often tempestuous sea of life.

'I worship you', he said against her lips.

Then there was no further need for words.

Barbara and Lord Mountbatten had exercised great ingenuity in the choice of unexpected gifts for each other. Whenever Dickie was off on his travels he would telephone and ask: 'What do you want me to bring you back?' On one occasion Barbara asked for a lucky ivory elephant, but when he returned he claimed that he couldn't find one in the whole of Egypt. Whenever Barbara went on one of her holidays abroad Lord Mountbatten insisted on giving her introductions that would make her stay memorable.

When Barbara and her sons stayed with the Maharajah of Mysore on Dickie's introduction they went first to Madras where the Deputy Governor looked after them, then they went down to Mysore and stayed in the Palace.

Barbara said she had never felt so grand as when they mounted a display of 'pig-sticking' in the middle of the desert, and she sat watching under an umbrella, with a rug for her feet.

The next year when the Maharajah came to England he went to lunch at Camfield Place which was an event in itself, as he very seldom visited people in their houses. Barbara was, however, very strict with him: she told him he could only bring one secretary because, otherwise, if he brought his normal entourage, there would be no room for her other guests.

The best present that Barbara ever had in her life, she claims, was the black labrador that Lord Mountbatten gave her the Christmas before he died. The dog sleeps in a basket in her bedroom every night and never leaves her side. He came from the Queen's kennels at Sandringham and is a nephew of Lord Mountbatten's own dog Kimberley, who was always pictured with him. 'I called him Duke - what else of course?' she laughs.

For Lord Mountbatten's seventy-ninth birthday Barbara's chef, Nigel Gordon, made him a splendid birthday cake which was decorated with battleship and naval signals. There were thirty presents waiting for him in the drawing room, all wrapped up with pink paper and Cartland pink ribbon.

There was one big present and the rest were just little things like chocolates, shirts and handkerchiefs and small things for Broadlands. Once I bought him a tea service in pink. One of my best gifts was a handkerchief with Queen Victoria's descendants on it. I had it framed and it is now hanging in one of the bathrooms at Broadlands. He was delighted because his father was on it.

Barbara also ordered Lord Mountbatten a tape recorder which, with his love of gadgets, she knew he would enjoy. When the manufacturers, Phillips, heard who it was for, they insisted on presenting it to him.

He had the most adorable sense of fun. Life was a joy to him. This was the magnetic power which I've written about in my book, *Barbara Cartland's Book of Celebrities* - life flowed through him.

Dickie was always fascinated by what other people were doing, and that's what made him so marvellous with young people. They all adored him. Prince Charles said he was the most interesting, fascinating and knowledgeable man he had ever known. Dickie was so delighted with the way the Prince had matured. He always said he would make a wonderful King. He was the son he never had, and I only wish that he had lived to see Prince Charles happily married to the lovely girl who has captivated the world and that they have a son.

Even so great a man as Lord Mountbatten in old age could be lonely. After he died Barbara was told by one of his staff that he used often to play a cassette of her love songs while he sat alone at dinner. Of all the many letters that Barbara received after Lord Mountbatten's death, none was more poignant than the one from the cook at Broadlands:

My Dear Miss Cartland,

Thank you so much for your most kind letter. So kind of you to give a thought to me. I was so shattered at the terrible tragedy, as of course you were also. Prince Charles came down to see me in the kitchen and was so kind. He promised me His Lordship would not have died in vain and he would see that good would come out of it. So do hope he is right. Such a sad way to go and he is a loss to everyone.

My very best wishes,
Yours,
Ivy Bird

—31—

Sex and love are the reality of life. They are what makes you a human being, they are what makes you a man.

Barbara Cartland

In a world of fast-diminishing standards of personal behaviour Barbara Cartland is exemplary. Though her life has been filled with seasons of plenty and seasons of heartache, survival has been her keynote. Her graceful manners will remain one of the most enduring memories I have of her - manners so long forgotten in this frenzied world. She has only to hear of someone with a personal sorrow to say: 'What can I do to help them?' You seldom see her name on public charity lists but those pink-signed cheques find their way to the most unexpected places.

No one knows better than the Rt. Rev. Dr Mervyn Stockwood, who wrote me:

Barbara is one of the most generous people I have known. During my twenty years as Bishop of Southwark I had only to tell her of a parson's family that was in financial trouble and immediately a cheque would arrive, on condition that the name of the donor was not to be revealed. But I am not thinking just in terms of money but of an attitude of compassionate understanding.

Barbara is indeed a colourful and expressive personality in more senses than one. In a dreary, bureaucratic and materialistic age her individuality stands out. She is a person - imaginative, loving and creative. Long may she live!

After a year in almost daily contact with Barbara it was obvious that I would learn that she is a much more complex character than her public image allows. Beneath the Cartland-pink, glossy packaging is a passionately caring human being. She is a blend of indomitability and vulnerability. I found her to be generous, lovable, witty, and without any trace of self pity or over-weening bitchiness that one sometimes discovers beneath the surface of women catapulted into being a world celebrity. She has, with great determination and considerable success, tried to live her own fiction.

Wealth and fame have not spoilt her, for the simple reason that whatever she has acquired has been through her own efforts. She has worked hard and daily since those early Charlestoning days and known rigid discipline that is required to keep 'the Factory' going. Despite her eighty-odd years, I doubt that Barbara will ever give up campaigning wherever she senses injustice. It is deeply rooted in her nature. Nor is her style the bland approach. She has never been afraid of upsetting people when she feels she is right. She is awesome in her directness and intolerance of incompetence. When a brash television interviewer asked if he could call her Barbara she replied 'Certainly not!'

I suppose I was born a campaigner. I have to fight injustice. I suppose it can be terribly irritating but when I see something is wrong I go in fighting. I suppose I will always be like this.

Since she freely admits to preferring men to women it is strange that one of Barbara's most convincing and consistent crusades has been against the permissive society and the role that women are forced into today.

Marriage is the best investment that was ever invented for women. It's a security against their old age, against them being deserted after losing their looks and becoming unattractive. To throw away all that when you are young is reckless and very foolish.

There never has been an age when there was more lust and less love in the relationship between men and women - and woman, who is the worst sufferer, can only blame herself. She has thrown away her modesty and with it the mystic power and beauty of womanhood. In its place she has the doubtful privilege of being treated like a second-rate pseudo-man.

Man has always been the provider, the hunter and the gay Lothario. It is the man who has the fun and nobody blames him for it. But women have very rightly all through the ages set themselves on the side of good morals, high ideals, and decent standards. Those are the things that have been their armour, their protection; but today they have thrown all that away, for what? A roll in the hay, the fun of going to bed with a whole lot of men. Well everyone has been able to do that since the beginning of time and we've had rather nasty words for it. Now it's called the 'permissive society' and it's supposed to be free, fun, and young. It's not really fun, it honestly isn't, and it's dangerous to women of every age. Woman's strongest and most invincible weapon is femininity.

It will be a hard struggle to climb back on the pedestal which has been spattered with mud, but it can be done, but only if women can once again substitute dignity for sex, ideals for equality and love for lust.

And when she cites the example of Princess Diana to young women of today one feels that she speaks with conviction and not family loyalty. Her appraisal of women is instinctive, and no one has had a better vantage point than Barbara, who has watched the Princess grow from a shy schoolgirl into the world's most admired young woman, with charm, sympathy, and understanding for everyone she meets.

Princess Diana's own love story could, in fact, have been taken straight from the pages of a Barbara Cartland romance, and since she was brought up reading her novels, and still does, their influence may well be responsible for her phenomenal success. Barbara is convinced that, entirely due to the Princess's attitude, there is an awareness of and return to romance among the young girls of today:

Last year American *Cosmopolitan* magazine ran a questionnaire and asked its young readers if they believed in sex before marriage. They all answered 'only with my steady' or 'with the man I am going to marry'. It was an enormous advance on four years ago when they replied 'any man I like'. In fact, it was unbelievable!

We're bound to have a religious revival soon because no-one could go lower than we've got at the moment.

Her message to the youth of today is clear and bold. She implores that they do not degrade their minds with filth.

Even the word 'sex' is horrid. The only difference between man and an animal is that he has imagination which can lift him up to the Divine.

The nearest thing we have on earth to the love of God is the physical and spiritual love between a man and woman who are one in mind and soul.

We talked one winter's afternoon about so many things that we had only touched on during the year. By now we instinctively knew each other's reaction, and the thoughts flowed between us. Barbara's deep spiritual belief is never far from the surface, since it is part of her creed for everyday living.

A soul is mysterious. Some people even say it does not exist, but I know when I am deeply moved by beauty, when music lifts me up towards the sky, it is my soul which responds. It is my soul, too, which makes me say: 'I believe' with a conviction beyond the confines of my heart. I believe my heart is mine, but my soul belongs to God.

If some of Barbara's views, especially on the subject of men, sound misty and pristine, she speaks with such conviction that even Germaine Greer would be at a loss for a reply.

Equality with men is rubbish. It is a man's world. Either woman must accept this and enjoy the fun and satisfaction of ruling as they have since the beginning of time, from the pillow and being the real power behind the male throne, or they must be pseudo-men, fighting to assert themselves - which every man dislikes and thinks will humiliate him.

We talked about that elusive quality, happiness. Princess Grace of Monaco once discussed the same subject with me. 'I have peace of mind and occasional moments of happiness. Happiness isn't a perpetual state. Life isn't that way', she had said.

Looking back from her eighty-three years, Barbara takes a much more pragmatic view:

Happiness for the average person is virtually always in the past or the future. I say to myself - I can never have this hour again. I mustn't miss one second of being with this particular person, of enjoying this unique minute of my existence, of giving out my vitality, my energy, my enthusiasm.

Refuse to accept that your fate is in the stars. It's in your hands. Make sacrifices for your principles and never tolerate injustice. As Leo Tolstoy wrote: 'There is only one task, and that is to increase the store of love within us.'

Because of her abiding faith and unshakeable belief in reincarnation death holds no fear for Barbara.

I've had a wonderful life with ups and downs, laughter and tears, but so much kindness, so much happiness, and so much love. How could all that be lost, how could the effort, the striving, the sacrifices be wasted? I believe my faith will make it all come true tomorrow! In a hundred, a thousand years, perhaps Eternity - Whenever, however, I will be there!

Who but Barbara could have created Barbara Cartland?

Index